MAKING SENSE
OF SEX

of related interest

The Complete Guide to Asperger's Syndrome
Tony Attwood
Hardback, ISBN 978 1 84310 495 7

Asperger's Syndrome and Sexuality
From Adolescence through Adulthood
Isabelle Hénault
Foreword by Tony Attwood
ISBN 978 1 84310 189 5

Love, Sex and Long-Term Relationships
What People with Asperger Syndrome Really Really Want
Sarah Hendrickx
Foreword by Stephen M. Shore
ISBN 978 1 84310 605 0

Friendships
The Aspie Way
Wendy Lawson
Foreword by Emma Wall
ISBN 978 1 84310 427 8

Freaks, Geeks and Asperger Syndrome
A User Guide to Adolescence
Luke Jackson
Foreword by Tony Attwood
ISBN 978 1 84310 098 0

MAKING SENSE
OF SEX

A Forthright Guide to Puberty, Sex and
Relationships for People with Asperger's Syndrome

SARAH ATTWOOD

Illustrated by Jonathon Powell

Jessica Kingsley Publishers
London and Philadelphia

First published in 2008
by Jessica Kingsley Publishers
116 Pentonville Road
London N1 9JB, UK
and
400 Market Street, Suite 400
Philadelphia, PA 19106, USA

www.jkp.com

Copyright © Sarah Attwood 2008
Illustrations copyright © Jonathon Powell 2008

The Australian Guide to Healthy Eating (food plate) Commonwealth of Australia © 1998 is reproduced with kind permission from the Australian Government Department of Health and Ageing.

The table on p.229 is adapted from the 'Sexual Behaviours Continuum' in *Talking About It: Sexuality Education for Primary Schools, Years P–7* © 2001 revised. Reproduced with kind permission from Family Planning Queensland.

Library of Congress Cataloging in Publication Data
A CIP catalog record for this book is available from the Library of Congress

British Library Cataloguing in Publication Data
A CIP catalogue record for this book is available from the British Library

ISBN 978 1 84310 374 5

Printed and bound in the United States by
Thomson-Shore, 7300 Joy Road, Dexter, MI 48130

To my parents, Donald and Jane Ainscow,
who always said,
'You should write a book!'

Contents

Acknowledgements

I would like to thank all those people – both new friends and old – who have helped and supported me in the process of writing this book.

First, thank you to my endlessly patient and encouraging husband, Tony. I feel so privileged to have had your vast knowledge and wisdom available to me throughout the writing of the book. What a security blanket!

My heartfelt gratitude to those people, all of whom have very busy lives, who have spared the time to read and re-read the whole manuscript. First of all, Kathy Hoopmann and Wendy Lawson, both of whom have read thousands of words and several drafts, and offered so much in the way of insightful suggestions. Thank you, Kathy, for being so forthright and honest: you have helped me see sense on more than one occasion! And Wendy – thank you for your eye for detail, and for sharing your numerous 'aspie' insights. Isabelle Henault, whose knowledge in the area of Asperger's syndrome and sexuality is second to none; your encouragement and wise words have meant a great deal to me. And Kari Dunn-Buron – your characteristic enthusiasm and positive attitude have regularly fortified my own flagging spirit.

Thank you to the people who read specific chapters, and made some invaluable contributions: Robert Hughes, for your guidance on language and your inspiring humour; Kelsey Powell, for your ongoing friendship and support and particular help with the details on sexual health; Julie Peterson, for your last-minute and vital insights into relationships, which finally helped me bring things to a close.

Thanks to all the young people who have read chapters and provided important feedback: Kate Sheahan; Karl and Becky Hoopmann; Jared and Brielle Eiby (and mum, Janet); and all the gang who helped enthusiastically with sexual words: Lottie, Jack and Ryan in England; Katie and friends in New Zealand; Tom, Sally, Emily, Ben, Sam and Rachel in Australia; and Sam, Dustin, Kazyden, Micah, JR, Alec and Sam in the USA.

Thank you to my children, Rosie, Will and Caroline, who each in their own way have offered me support, encouragement, a willing ear and great suggestions along the way. See, I did it!

Thanks to the best technical support ever, Dawn Sheahan. For your patience and willingness to drop everything for yet another of my technically illiterate moments, I cannot thank you enough.

And last, but by no means least, my thanks to Jessica Kingsley, for having the belief in me in the first place. Without your certainty and vision this would never have happened. I am truly grateful.

Author's Note

If you are a stickler for correct grammar, you may notice as you read the book that there is a particular grammatical error that occurs many times throughout the text: that is, the use of a singular noun (e.g. 'the child') followed by the plural pronoun ('they'). While I know that this breaks the rules, I have done it deliberately. This book is for young people, and is not a learned text, and thus the alternatives (e.g. 'the child…he or she'; 'the child…(s)he'; or even 'he' in one paragraph and 'she' in the next) are either too cumbersome or distracting. The singular noun with a plural pronoun tends to be common usage in speech, and I would like this book to reflect that, and be a smooth read for teenagers and young adults. Please accept my apologies.

Introduction

Growing up is normal, natural and inevitable. You can't go on being a child for ever, and I'm sure even if you could, you wouldn't want to. Most people look forwards to being a mature adult who is capable of doing adult things, such as driving a car, going to work, buying a house, enjoying sexual relationships and having children. Of course, not all adults want to do all these things, and you will make many choices and decisions as you grow up.

This book is about sexuality, in particular puberty and adolescence. During adolescence – the time between childhood and adulthood – your body will change, along with your thinking processes and emotions, so that you look and function more like a grown-up. While all these changes are perfectly normal, they can leave you feeling exhausted and bewildered a lot of the time.

In this book we are going to look at many of the changes and challenges of adolescence so that you are well-informed about what is happening to you, preferably before it happens. This is important. For example, if children aren't given plenty of information about puberty, significant changes, such as girls' periods, or boys' wet dreams, can come as quite a shock the very first time they happen. In the past, when children often didn't get told much about the changes at puberty, many of them were confused and scared.

In *Making Sense of Sex*, as well as learning a lot about puberty, you will also read about the things you can do to care for your body and your emotions, so that you stay healthy, and look and feel good. You will learn about friendships and how they change as you grow up; and, of course, we will discuss sex and sexual relationships. The aim is not only to reassure you that what you are going through is perfectly normal, but also to give you the information you need so that you can feel confident and able to make smart choices for yourself.

What's in the book

We begin in Chapter 1, **Your Body**, by discussing your body, in particular the sexual and reproductive organs. As well as helping you to feel comfortable and knowledgeable about your own body, it is essential information if you are to make sense of many of the terms and concepts used in later chapters. Whether you are a girl or a boy, it's especially important that you read about both boys' *and* girls' bodies, since it helps to have an understanding of both as you read the rest of the book

The same goes for Chapter 2, **Puberty**. Although there are separate sections for some of the boys' and girls' changes, it is a good idea for you to read it all. Not only is it very interesting information, it also helps to give you some insight into what is going on with the other sex. This will make you a much more understanding person, and far less likely to say hurtful or inappropriate things to your friends and classmates. This is especially true when it comes to the subject of periods. There is a lot for girls to know about this once-a-month event, but boys who read this section will gain some very useful information, which will help them to be sensitive and considerate boyfriends, husbands and fathers in the future. You may notice that this chapter is more about the physical changes of puberty than it is about the social, emotional or sexual changes. This is because these other topics are dealt with thoroughly in separate chapters.

In Chapter 3, **Caring for Your Body**, we will explore ways you can look after your body, now that it isn't the responsibility of your parents or carers any more. Whilst you may not mind very much whether or not you look fashionable or smell pleasant, other people often do notice these things. You can avoid being teased or even rejected if you look good and take care with your personal hygiene.

As well as making choices about how you look, you will also find as you grow up that you will start to make decisions about what and when you eat, what time you go to bed, and the type and amount of exercise you get involved in. These are what we call 'lifestyle' choices, and all of them have a significant impact on how you feel and function as you go through adolescence. In Chapter 4, **Making Healthy Choices**, we will explore these issues, along with the risks associated with smoking, drinking alcohol and taking drugs, so that you are well-informed and can make smart choices for yourself.

Adolescence can be a very emotional time. Your mood goes up and down, and a lot of the time you can feel very unsure of yourself and worried about your future. This is normal, but it's not fun for you, and your bad moods aren't fun for your family or friends, either. In Chapter 5, **Understanding Emotions**, we look at ways to help you feel good about yourself, and cope with these strong emotions, so that you don't lose your friends or feel like punching too many holes in the wall!

Childhood friendships are very different to those you will have as an adult, and adolescence is the time that your friendships go through this change. In Chapter 6, **Friendships**, we look at some of the features that are important in a friendship now that you are growing up, and explore the skills you will need to learn if you want to be successful at making friends. It is only when you have good friendships that you are ready to move on to sexual relationships. We also look at the very important issues of peer pressure and bullying, since these may well be affecting you, and can have such significant consequences for so many young people.

Although sexual relationships might not be part of your life right now, they may be one day. In Chapters 7, 8 and 9 we look in detail at sex, sexual relationships and sexual health. This is useful information that is worth having ahead of time, since it gives you the opportunity to work out what is important to you. When you have good understanding you are able to make better decisions and are more likely to have relationships that are healthy and successful.

One day you might consider having children of your own. Even if you don't, you are sure to know people who do, and it's good to understand the process of pregnancy and birth. In Chapter 10, **Fertilization, Pregnancy and Birth**, we explore these fascinating topics, and also have a brief look at genetics.

The last chapter (Chapter 11) is about sexual language. All through the book you will read the correct terms for sexual words, but, as you know, there are dozens of other terms for most of these words. Many of them are silly, and some are rude or offensive. It's important that you know how to express yourself correctly so that you don't offend people, and can communicate appropriately and confidently about sexuality.

And it *is* important that you can talk about sexual matters, especially when you have questions, or there are things that may be worrying you. Talk to people you trust, such as your parents or other close relatives, and find out what you need to know. With the right information and plenty of support, you will get through the tough parts of adolescence and find plenty to enjoy about growing up and becoming independent. This book, together with the significant people in your life, will answer many of your questions, offer you some guidance and support, and help you to make sense of sex.

A Note to Parents, Carers and Those whose Lives Embrace Young People with Asperger's Syndrome

Young people with Asperger's syndrome (AS) develop sexually and go through puberty just the same as everyone else – so why does there need to be a book especially for them? Simply because there are some specific issues and difficulties that may arise due to their having AS that are not addressed by regular puberty books. While there are some excellent books available (see the list at the end of this book), many lack the detail that may be appreciated by a fact-loving young person with AS. In addition, the social and emotional difficulties that characterize the syndrome are not taken into consideration by the typical puberty book, and assumptions are generally made that the young reader is socially aware and competent.

In this book I have aimed to give all the usual information that can be found in any puberty book, though I have explored many of the issues in greater depth. In addition, I have included some topics that are particularly pertinent for young people with AS, namely friendships, understanding emotions and dealing with peer pressure, teasing and bullying. I have also gone into some detail about the rules and guidelines that surround sexual behaviour and language. Not only is every chapter packed full of facts, it also includes the logic that lies behind much of the advice; for example, good personal hygiene is not just a whim of fussy adults – it is essential for a range of very good reasons, which are fully explained. I have worked on the assumption that knowledge and logic, presented in a straightforward manner, are the ways to hold the interest of, and get through to, a young person with AS.

As a parent or primary carer, you may choose to read this book from cover to cover; in fact, it's probably important that you do, so that you are aware of what is in it, and what you would like to include in your conversations with your son or daughter. Sexuality is a value-laden as well as fact-laden topic. I have presented the facts as neutrally as I can; but that is not enough. The strong cultural, religious and moral values that *must* accompany sexual knowledge need to be imparted by you as your child's primary carer. There may be suggestions in the book you don't agree with, and that's okay. The important thing is that you discuss your beliefs with your child so that they are able to understand your point of view and perhaps make a choice for themselves from a standpoint of knowledge. It is reassuring to know that whilst many young people question their parents' values and even show some disregard for them during their adolescent years, the vast majority return to and embrace these same values once they become adults. It is also worth noting here that there are times when the fresh, questioning approach of our adolescent can alert us to the fact that some of our values may be decidedly old-fashioned and in need of revision!

Your role as a sexuality educator

Education about sexual issues doesn't begin at puberty, of course, and teaching children about sexuality doesn't simply involve a one-off talk about sexual intercourse and how babies are made. It is much broader than that. Sexuality is about who we are, not what we do, and is an intrinsic part of our self-image and self-esteem. Learning about sexuality is an ongoing, life-long process that begins at the moment of birth. As we love and care for our children, they learn about their bodies, about loving touches, and trust. They become aware of themselves as a boy or a girl, and what it means in their family or culture to be male or female. By observing others around them, they learn about affection, honesty and respect, and how to behave appropriately. We are powerful role models for our children; they learn just as much, if not more, from how we behave as from what we say.

But *how* we talk to our children is very important, too. When we are positive about sexuality, we enable them to develop healthy attitudes. When we answer their questions honestly but briefly, giving them just enough information to satisfy their curiosity, children not only acquire the foundation of good sexual knowledge, but also learn that sexuality is a topic that can be broached without fear or shame. Parents and other responsible adults sometimes worry that giving children sexual information will rob them of their innocence. This is only true if the information is inappropriate or delivered in such a way that the child is made to feel ashamed or guilty. A child who has age-appropriate information about sexuality, has been taught the correct terminology and is not ashamed of his or her body will know when something isn't right, and will have the language and confidence to tell a trusted adult. This helps to protect the child from exploitation or abuse, which in turn serves to *maintain* their innocence.

A similar logic may be applied to teenagers' sexual knowledge. The question often arises: will giving young people lots of information about sex simply encourage them to go out and experiment? The answer is *no* – quite the reverse, in fact. Studies carried out in different countries have shown time and again that it is most often those young people who have scant information who become involved in early sexual experiences, often making mistakes they later regret. Those who are well-informed tend to delay their first sexual encounters, and when they do become sexually active they have the confidence to negotiate effectively with a partner, and use protection. To put it simply, whatever the age of our children, sexual ignorance is *not* bliss.

But, as a parent or carer, how do you ensure that your adolescent is well-informed? Although young children cheerfully listen to and believe what you have to say, youngsters going through puberty seem to have something of a temporary personality change. Your once open, amiable child becomes moody and often intensely private. They can be remarkably squeamish at the mere mention of anything sexual, and your word, which once was gospel, it is now quite likely to be regarded with some suspicion. What could you possibly know about sex, especially at your age? If you have always been able to address sexual issues in your household, then you will probably find you can continue to do so, though you may have to be extra-sensitive to your child's new-found modesty. If you haven't ever said much about sexuality, however, there is a risk that your child has already made the decision that this is a 'no go' area. It can be very difficult raising such topics for the first time when your child is halfway through adolescence. The best thing if possible is to introduce the topic before puberty begins, while you still have some credibility!

Many young people become experts at deflecting sexual discussions, telling you with a degree of certainty and scorn that they 'already know all this stuff'. They almost certainly don't, of course, so don't allow them to throw you off track. You may need to use opportunities that arise, such as issues raised on television shows or in the newspapers, to begin a discussion. Raise the topic casually, keep the intensity out of it and be sure to listen to your child's point of view. Share your own experiences, if this seems relevant. The more often you take opportunities to discuss sexual issues, the stronger the message to your child that you are interested and *can* cope. It is very important, though, that you avoid turning this sort of discussion into a lecture – there's nothing more likely to prevent your child raising the topic of sexuality than the prospect of being preached at for half an hour.

In spite of the apparent show of disdain for what you have to say, it would seem that your child *does* want to talk to you. Studies of teenagers' sexual attitudes have revealed that, while many young people choose to turn to their friends for support and the informal sharing of sexual information (which, of course, can mean *mis*-information), most would like to be able to talk to their parents and carers about sexual matters. This can be even more vital for young people with AS. They are often excluded from teenage discussions, and thus may become the object of ridicule owing to their social clumsiness and ignorance of current terminology. There is no doubt, therefore, that the input of parents, carers and trusted adults into their teenager's sexual learning is very important. Communication with teenagers needs to be ongoing, open and honest – especially so in the case of teenagers with AS.

Special issues for young people with Asperger's syndrome

Many of the social and emotional difficulties faced by children with AS intensify as they go through adolescence.

- Mood swings may be particularly intense, and many young people need help to defuse their bad moods and manage their anger, anxiety and sadness.

- Changes to bodies, emotions and friendships happen quite quickly, and can be especially challenging and bewildering for a young person with AS.

- Existing communication difficulties may become more apparent as peers turn to each other and away from families. Young people who don't 'fit in' tend to be excluded, leading to social isolation and lack of self-confidence.

- Sexual feelings are often strong. Young people with AS are unlikely to feel ready to explore relationships, and, unless they are very clear about social and behavioural boundaries, are at risk of displaying inappropriate sexual behaviour.

- The young person's naïvety and gullibility can lead to their being teased and 'set up', or to their becoming the target of sexual predators (including on the internet).

How you can help

In the face of all these challenges, you could be forgiven for thinking that such children may never be able to lead a happy, healthy sexual life; but they most certainly can. They just need the right sort of help.

First, every young person needs someone to whom they can turn in times of crisis, anxiety or doubt. You may be this 'trusted adult' to whom I refer several times throughout the book. Thus, you will need to be there for your child, believe in them, listen without judgement and advocate on their behalf. If you can't be in this position of trust for any reason, it is vital that you ensure your child is clear about whom they *can* turn to when they need support.

It may also be that, as a parent or primary carer, you feel there are some aspects of your child's sexual development that are just too personal for you to be involved with, and that your child may be more likely to open up to someone other than you. Again, if this is the case, make sure that you and your child enlist the help of someone your child feels confident talking to about personal issues.

Another very important role is that of 'social mentor'. This may be your job as a parent or carer; equally, it may be another family member or even a friend who is around the same age as your child. As long as this person understands the social difficulties faced by someone with AS, and is liked and respected by your child, their role as guide and interpreter to the social world will be invaluable.

Together with the other significant people in your child's life, you can provide both social and emotional support, and sound information about sexuality, all of which will go a long way towards helping your child negotiate the socio-sexual world and form meaningful relationships.

Guide to communicating with your AS teenager about sexuality

- Be prepared to really *listen*, without interruption or judgement.

- If your child wants to talk, but the time isn't quite right, explain why now isn't a good moment, and be sure to make an alternative time.

- Sexuality talks with adolescents always work best if they are *not* face to face. Take the pressure off by talking while you walk side by side, work alongside each other (e.g. preparing a meal), or drive together in the car. In all these situations, the conversation tends to flow more freely because you aren't looking intently at your child.

- Keep well-informed about sexual issues, so that you can be genuinely helpful and speak with some authority to your child. But if you don't know something, admit it, rather than making something up. You and your teenager could do some research together to find out the answer.

- If you are uncomfortable or embarrassed, admit it. Explain why you feel this way. This allows your child to see this as your problem, and one that he or she need not take on personally. And you will find that nothing dissolves embarrassment more quickly than admitting it.

- Be truthful. If you tell half-truths or lies about sexual issues, your child is bound to find out eventually, but will then view you as an unreliable source of information.

- When you do provide information, be sure that it is not only factual, but also logical. When your child knows *why* as well as *what*, they will feel a lot less anxious. This in turn will contribute to a greater self-confidence, enabling your child to be more assertive.

- Take opportunities to talk about feelings, not just facts, and be sure to discuss your values and beliefs.

- Be positive and forthright in your discussions about sexuality with your teenager, taking care not to sidestep the more difficult but nevertheless important topics such as sexual feelings, masturbation and relationships (see Chapter 7, **Sex**, and Chapter 8, **Sexual Relationships**).

- Ensure that your child fully understands the difference between 'public' and 'private' in terms of body parts, places and behaviour (see Chapter 1, **Your Body**). Be very clear about the boundaries for appropriate behaviour and language, and make sure your child is aware of the rules about sex (see Chapter 7, **Sex**, and Chapter 11, **Sexual Language**).

- Ideally, provide your child with information well ahead of time so that none of the changes at puberty cause distress by coming as a shock (see Chapter 2, **Puberty**).

- Have strategies in place to help your child deal with mood swings and intense emotions. Your child will need to be regularly reminded of ways to defuse a bad mood, or relieve anxiety or sadness (see Chapter 5, **Understanding Emotions**). Be vigilant and ready to seek professional advice should your child's anger, anxiety or sadness reach a point that you feel needs intervention.

- Do plenty of 'what if?' scenarios with your child. For example, 'What if you start your period at school?', 'What if you get a drop of blood on your school skirt?', 'What if a boy tweaks your bra strap?', 'What if you get an erection while you are out in the playground?', 'What if your voice cracks and people laugh at you?', 'What if someone calls you "Pizza Face" because of your pimples?'. Together, you and your child can work out possible solutions to these and other similar scenarios.

- Respect your child's concerns. Never belittle them, however trivial they may seem to you, and never, *ever* speak about them publicly.

- Respect your child's privacy, and allow them to be on their own sometimes. This encourages them to be respectful of your privacy and that of other people.

- Enlist the support of a sympathetic young person who is up to date with teenage language, behaviour and fashion, to guide your child through this social minefield. They can help your child work out what to say, do or wear in given situations. Just as importantly, they can also help them recognize what *not* to say, do or wear!

- Social skills groups, drama classes and even simple role-plays with you can be enormously beneficial for your child in helping them to understand social situations and develop effective communication and assertiveness skills.

- Reassure your child that it is normal for friendships to change at puberty, because people mature at different rates, and develop different interests. Encourage them to identify their particular interests, and support them in making new friends by joining groups, clubs and so on where other people share these interests.

- Where your child has befriended someone older or younger, ensure that these friendships are healthy and reciprocal. Make sure that your adolescent isn't taking advantage of a younger child, and especially make sure that they are being sexually appropriate. Where the friendship is with an older person, check that your child is not being exploited in any way.

- Be aware of any infatuation your child may have with another person. Help them to understand that crushes are a normal, temporary phase of adolescence, and are okay just so long as they don't pursue them to the point that they are stalking or harassing another person. Teach your child that healthy, mature relationships are reciprocal and respectful.

- Make sure your child is fully aware of the potential dangers of the internet, and knows how to use the internet safely (see Chapter 8, **Sexual Relationships**, and the **Useful Websites** section at the back of the book). Be prepared to supervise your child's use of the internet. Note that whilst some of the websites and links recommended at the back of the book may be explicit, they are accurate and educational, and therefore far more appropriate than any pornographic sites your child may inadvertently visit.

- If you have a disagreement with your teenager, stay calm and *listen* to his or her point of view. Be prepared to compromise.

- Choose your battles; some things simply aren't worth fighting about.

- Offer guidelines, set reasonable limits, and stick to them. Within these limits, allow your child to make decisions. Although they may make some mistakes, your child will benefit from the opportunity to experience consequences, and to prove that they are a capable young person.

- Above all, stay light-hearted. A good sense of humour goes a long way to helping discussions about sexuality run smoothly.

In conclusion

A book such as this can be a great tool. Whether you choose to use it as a reference when certain topics arise, or leave it with your child to absorb at his or her own pace, the important thing is to show that you approve of the book. Indicate clearly that you are happy to discuss what is in it, answer questions, share relevant anecdotes and expand on information.

Obviously, a book can't do the job on its own. It certainly can't replace open, forthright, warm communication with a trusted adult. Nor can it impart the values, attitudes and beliefs about sexuality that are important to you. What it can do, though, is allow your child to digest some of the information alone, and perhaps help them to overcome any initial embarrassment. Once they are less self-conscious, they may become more willing to talk with you. A book can act as a trigger for discussion on certain topics, help to introduce more difficult issues, such as sexual feelings and masturbation, and can provide facts where there is a shortfall in your own knowledge. Sometimes the written word has a certain authority that your own words may lack as far as your sceptical teenager may be concerned.

But the real job of this book is to augment the messages that your child receives about sexuality from their most important sexuality educator – you!

1

Your Body

This book is about growing up and sex, and this chapter about your body will concentrate on those body parts that are particularly to do with sexuality – namely, the reproductive organs.

The reproductive system is one of several intricate body systems that interconnect to keep your body working – and it is the very last one to become active. Most of the systems are active well before birth: your skeletal and muscular systems, for example. You have bones and muscles before you are born, and can move your body while you are still inside your mother. Some of the other systems start to function properly once you are born; the respiratory system, for example, kicks into action when you take your first breath, and your digestive system starts to work properly once you begin to feed. But your reproductive system is different – even though all the body parts are there already, it isn't until puberty that it begins to function properly.

There are lots of reasons why you need good information about the reproductive or sexual parts of your body. First, it helps you to feel comfortable about your own body. This, in turn, helps you to feel less embarrassed, better able to ask questions if you need to, and more likely to respect and appreciate your body. When you feel good about yourself, you are more likely to take care of yourself and look after your own health. And last, it is not until you respect your own body that you can begin to respect other people's bodies – and this is especially important when you start to have sexual relationships, and also if you choose to have children of your own.

Whether you are a boy or a girl, it is good to know about the sexual parts of both males *and* females. Not only does this help you to understand and accept all the changes that will happen to your own body as you go through puberty, it also helps you to be more sympathetic towards people of the other sex, since you will understand what they are going through, too.

The female body

A female's sex organs include some that are on the outside of her body; that is, her *breasts* and her external sex organs (*genitals*), otherwise known as the *vulva*, and some that are inside her body and can't be seen – the internal sex organs.

Breasts

The main biological reason women have breasts is to produce milk to feed a baby. Breast milk is the very best food for a young baby, containing exactly the right nutrients, at the right temperature, and is available at any time without the need to sterilize bottles. You can read more about newborn babies and breast-feeding in Chapter 10, **Fertilization, Pregnancy and Birth**.

Breasts are also an important *secondary sexual characteristic*; that is, they may be considered to be sexually attractive by other people, and because they can be quite sensitive, many women enjoy having their breasts touched by their sexual partner.

Inside...

Inside each breast are around 15–25 *milk glands*, which increase in size during pregnancy, and begin to produce milk due to the release of a hormone, *prolactin*, once the baby is born. The milk then passes into the *milk ducts*, which store the milk until the baby is ready to feed. The milk is drawn from the ducts as the baby sucks on the area around and including the *nipple*.

The milk glands and milk ducts are surrounded by fatty tissue, which protects them and gives shape to the breast. There is also some fibrous connective tissue, which helps to maintain the breast shape. When a woman has bigger breasts, it is because she has more fatty tissue; a woman who has very little body fat will tend to have smaller breasts. But the size of her breasts does not affect a woman's ability to breast-feed her baby if she chooses to; a woman with small breasts is just as able to do this as a woman with larger breasts, as it is the presence of milk glands and ducts that is important, not the amount of fatty tissue.

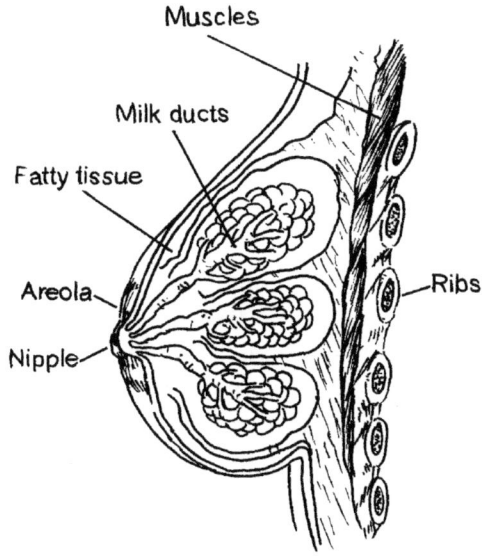

There are muscles that lie under the breasts, against the ribs, but no muscles in the breasts themselves, so even if she wants to, a woman can't increase the size of her breasts by doing exercises.

...and outside

The *nipple* contains tiny holes through which milk can flow when the baby sucks during breast-feeding. It is the most sensitive part of the breast, as it is supplied with many nerve-endings. There are thin muscle fibres around the nipple that enable it to become erect, both when it is cold, and in response to touch. Nipples vary in appearance between one woman and another, with some sticking out, some being almost flat, and some others turning inwards rather than outwards. All these are perfectly normal and healthy.

A darker, pigmented (coloured) area surrounds the nipple. This is called the *areola*; the size and colour of this varies from one woman to another, but in all women it tends to become darker during pregnancy, and to stay a little darker afterwards. The areola contains many tiny nerve and muscle fibres that help the nipple to stiffen and become erect. There may also be some hair follicles on the areola, and it is quite usual for there to be a few hairs on the breasts. Some small bumps on the areola are quite normal, too. These are called *Montgomery's glands*, and during breast-feeding they produce an oily substance that helps to cleanse and lubricate the nipple, and protect it from infection.

You can read more about the growth of your breasts, and how to choose a bra, in Chapter 2, **Puberty**.

The external sex organs

The *genitals* are those sex organs in both males and females that are outside the body. The correct name for the female genitals is the *vulva*. Because it is situated between her legs, it isn't all that easy for a girl to see her own vulva. The best way is for her to use a mirror. This is not rude, but it is private, so if you choose to do this, make sure that you are by yourself and not about to be disturbed.

Remember, the vulva is just another body part, and, as with all body parts, there are individual differences between one person and another. Your vulva probably won't look exactly the same as any picture or diagram you see, but you will be able to work out which are the different parts if you refer to a diagram while you are looking in a mirror. The vulva includes the *outer* and *inner labia*, the *clitoris*, the *urethral opening* and the *vaginal opening*. The *anus*, which is the opening into the digestive tract through which solid waste (faeces) leaves the body, is also close by, though is not part of the vulva.

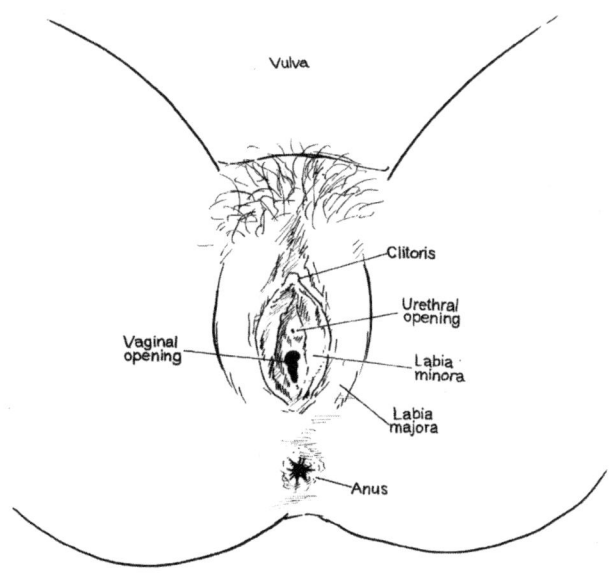

Outer labia (labia majora)

These are the fleshy folds of skin, or 'lips', that close over the inner parts of the vulva and protect them. They become covered with pubic hair at puberty.

Inner labia (labia minora)

These are thinner 'lips', and more sensitive to touch than the outer labia. In a young girl, they are hidden by the outer labia unless she has her legs apart. As she grows, the inner labia grow a little too, and sometimes stick out from between the outer labia. There are glands in the inner labia that produce a lubricating fluid to keep them moist.

The clitoris

This is a small (pea-sized), very sensitive organ situated at the front of the vulva, where the two inner labia join at the top. Its function is to provide pleasurable sexual feelings. Only the tip of the clitoris can be seen – most of it lies inside the body. It is well-supplied with nerves, and has the capacity to engorge with blood, in the same way as the penis. This causes it to swell a little, and become firmer and more visible, when the woman is sexually aroused. The size and shape of the clitoris varies from one woman to another.

Urethral opening

This is the opening of the urethra, which is the tube that carries urine from the bladder to the outside of the body. Because it is so small, it can be quite difficult to see. It is just above and in front of the vaginal opening.

Vaginal opening

This is the opening to the vagina, which is the passageway leading up inside the body to the internal sex organs. It is larger than the urethral opening, and easier to see.

THE HYMEN

This is a thin layer of skin that often, but not always, covers part of the vaginal opening in young girls. As a girl grows, and become more active, her hymen stretches and tears quite naturally and painlessly (she wouldn't even notice it happening), so that the vaginal opening becomes slightly larger; this is even more likely to occur if she uses tampons during her period. Even if the hymen doesn't tear much during childhood, there are always enough holes in it to allow menstrual (period) blood to pass through. You can read more about periods in Chapter 2, **Puberty**.

Internal sex organs

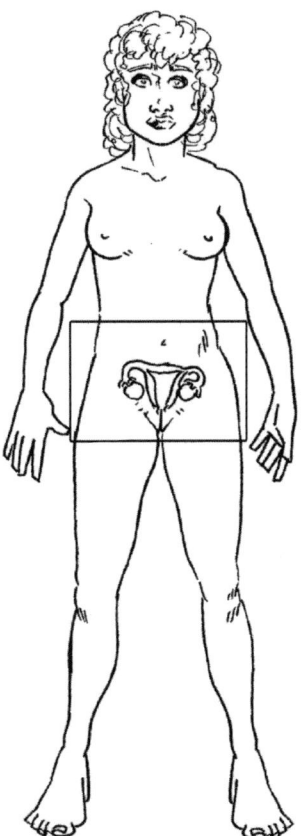

The internal sex organs

The internal reproductive organs are situated low down in the abdomen, between the hip bones. The diagrams illustrate what these would look like if you could see inside your body; you would be able to see the *vagina*, the *uterus*, two *Fallopian tubes* and two *ovaries*.

The vagina

The vagina, which slopes upwards and slightly backwards, is the passageway between the uterus and the outside of the body. It is a muscular tube, about 8–10 cm (3¾–4 in.) long, with convoluted walls. Normally

Female sex organs – internal (front)

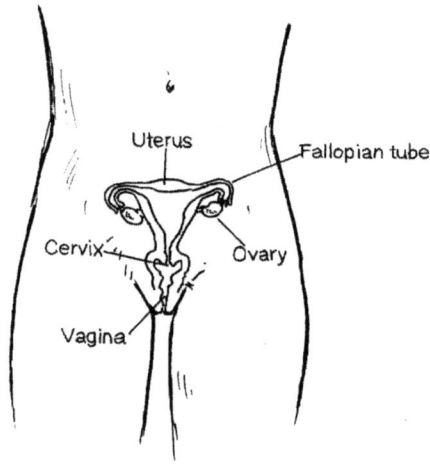

Female sex organs – internal (side)

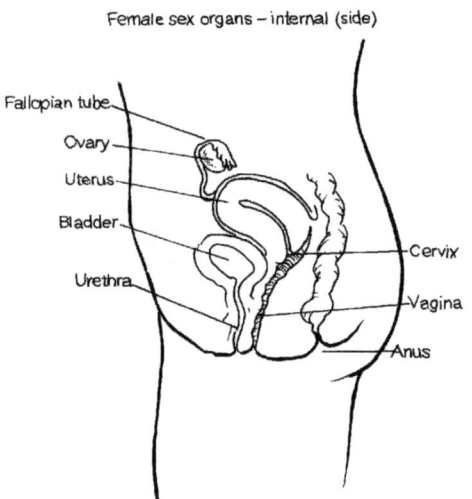

these walls lie close together, touching each other, but are very stretchy, and can stretch enough to allow a baby to pass through during childbirth. Blood also passes through the vagina during the period, and tampons can be held firmly in place by the strong muscles. The vagina is where the penis fits during sexual intercourse (see Chapter 7, **Sex**).

There are glands in the vaginal walls that produce a lubricating fluid to keep the vagina moist, clean and healthy.

The uterus

Sometimes known as the *womb*, this is a muscular organ, shaped rather like an upside-down pear, and approximately the size of your fist. It is situated just behind the urinary bladder, and at the top of the vagina. The opening at the base of the uterus into the vagina, the *cervix*, is very tiny, and normally only opens just enough to allow menstrual blood to pass through during the period; but during childbirth, it opens up to allow the baby to pass through. There is a small cavity inside the uterus, which is where the developing baby (*foetus* or *fetus*) grows during pregnancy. As the pregnancy progresses, and the foetus grows bigger, the uterus stretches to accommodate it (see Chapter 10, **Fertilization, Pregnancy and Birth**).

The Fallopian tubes

These two thin tubes extend from the top of each side of the uterus towards the ovaries, which are on either side of the uterus. They are approximately 7–14 cm (2¾–5½ in.) long, and lined with very fine hairs, called *cilia*. The end of each Fallopian tube is funnel-shaped with finger-like tendrils, called *fimbria*, which surround the ovary but don't quite touch it. When an *ovum* (egg) is released from the ovary, it is drawn into the Fallopian tube by the fimbria, and propelled along towards the uterus by the wave-like motion of the cilia.

The ovaries

These are two walnut-sized organs situated either side of the uterus, at the end of the Fallopian tubes. The ovaries have two functions: to store and release *ova* (eggs) into the reproductive system; and to produce the female hormones, *oestrogen* (or *estrogen*) and *progesterone*. These hormones control the development of the female body characteristics at puberty, such as breasts and body shape; they also regulate the menstrual cycle and pregnancy. As a female baby develops in the uterus, each of her ovaries contains more than a million immature ova. By the time she reaches puberty, the number of ova has dropped considerably, to about 350,000 in each ovary.

From puberty onwards, under the influence of hormones, one ovum (or sometimes two) matures, and is released from one or other of the ovaries into the Fallopian tube, in a process called *ovulation*. A mature ovum is tiny – about the size of a pinprick, and not really visible without the aid of a microscope. Ovulation happens on a regular basis, each month, until the woman reaches the age of about 50. At this point, the release of ova and production of hormones stop, and the woman no longer has periods. This time in a woman's life is called *menopause*.

The male body

In males, the major sex organs are on the outside of the body, and this means that most boys tend to be much more familiar with their external sex organs than girls are with theirs. There are, however, some important structures inside the body that, along with the penis and testicles, make up the male reproductive system.

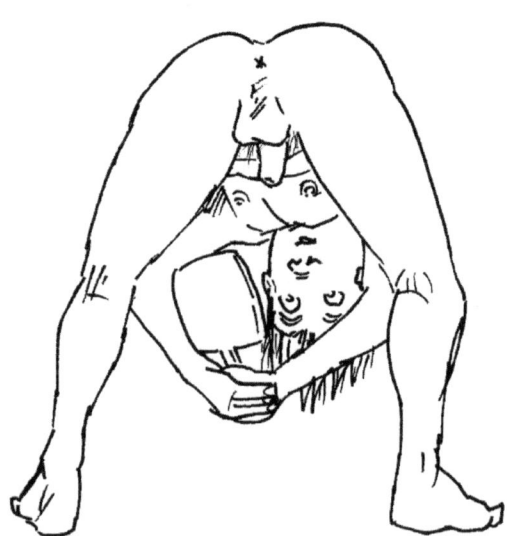

The external sex organs

The male genitals, or external sex organs, consist of the *penis*, the *scrotum* and the *testicles*. The *anus* is also close to this part of the body, and serves the same function in males as it does in females; it isn't part of the reproductive system.

Male genitals

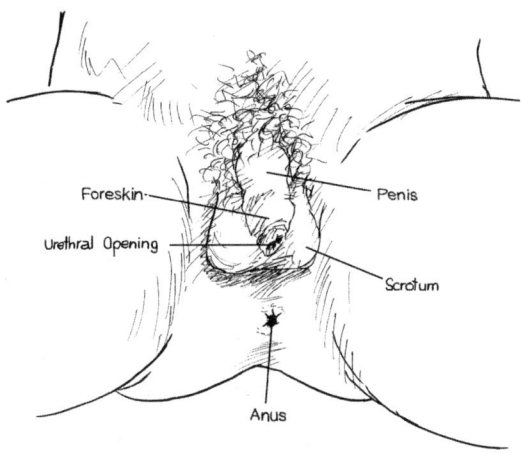

The penis

The penis, which is made of soft, spongy tissue and blood vessels, has three functions: to allow the passage of urine from the bladder; to allow the passage of semen and sperm; and to provide pleasurable sexual feelings. The end, or head, of the penis is also known as the *glans*, and is very sensitive. The glans is covered by a loose fold of skin called the *foreskin*. The long part of the penis, from the glans to where the penis joins the body, is called the *shaft*. Usually, the penis is fairly small and soft, but when the male becomes sexually aroused, the spongy tissue, which is also known as *erectile tissue*, fills with blood so that the penis

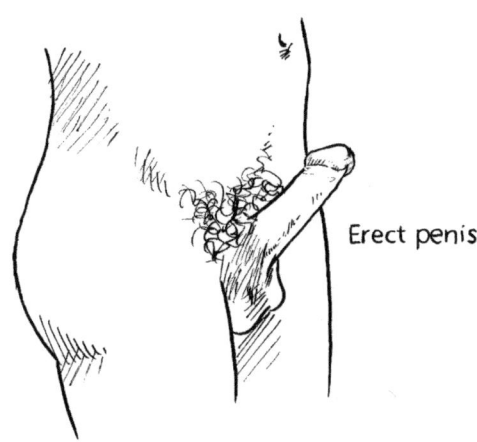

Erect penis

expands (rather like a sponge expanding as it absorbs water). It becomes longer, stiffer and slightly darker in colour and stands away from the body. This is called an *erection* (see Chapter 2, **Puberty**). An erection enables the penis to fit inside the female's vagina during sexual intercourse (see Chapter 7, **Sex**).

CIRCUMCISION

Sometimes the foreskin is removed surgically from the penis, for cultural, religious or health reasons. This operation is known as *circumcision*. Usually it is performed soon after birth, but in some cultures may be done around the time of puberty, as part of a ceremony to signify adulthood. Some people believe that a penis will be easier to keep clean and will be less likely to become infected if the foreskin is circumcised. This is because some small glands under the foreskin secrete a whitish substance called *smegma*, which lubricates the foreskin, and helps it to slide back over the glans. If smegma isn't cleaned away regularly, it can become smelly, and in rare cases cause an infection. However, if a boy cleans under his foreskin every day by pulling it back gently and washing with mild soap (or a gentle cleansing bar if soap is irritating) and water, his penis should be perfectly clean and healthy (see Chapter 3, **Caring for Your Body**). If he does experience any discomfort or infection under the foreskin, he should go to the doctor.

Uncircumcised   Circumcised

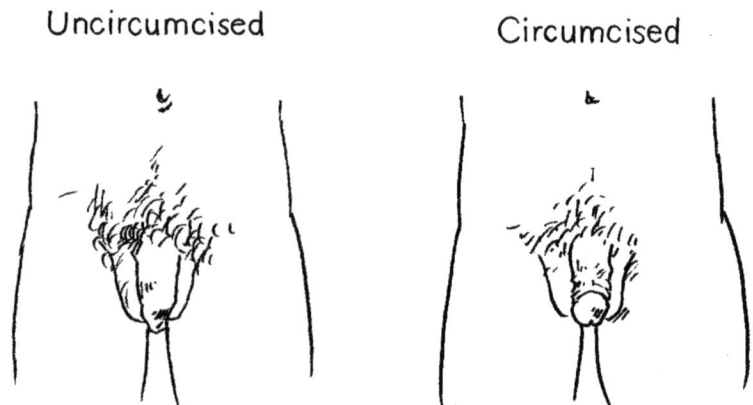

The scrotum

This is the loose sac of skin and muscle containing the two testicles, located between the penis and the anus. Its function is to regulate the temperature of the testicles. The testicles hang outside the body so that they can stay a little cooler than the internal body temperature, as sperm are only produced at this slightly lower temperature. To achieve this, the scrotum shrinks up and pulls the testicles towards the body when the outside temperature is very cold (e.g. if the male jumps into cold water) and hangs down further away from the body when the outside temperature is very hot, or if the male has a fever. The testicles are also drawn up towards the body in response to stress, such as when the male is frightened (this is probably an evolutionary response in order to protect the testicles in a fight).

The testicles

These two glands are the equivalent of the female ovaries, in that, from the time of puberty onwards, they produce both reproductive cells and hormone; the male sex cells are called *sperm*, and the male hormone is called *testosterone*. In a fully grown male, the testicles are about the size of small plums (though they do vary slightly in size between one male and another), and one tends to hang a little lower than the other, which prevents them from knocking against one another.

Each testicle contains very fine, coiled tubes called *seminiferous tubules*. These tubules are lined with a layer of specialized cells that produce sperm cells. The newly formed sperm cells, which look like tadpoles, are able to propel themselves by beating their tails. They travel along the tubules to the *epididymis* (a coiled tube on the back of the testicle), where they continue to mature for around two weeks. Mature sperm cells are microscopic – about $1/600$ in. (0.05 ml) in length. The whole process of sperm production takes a little over two months, and is a continuous process, with about 70 million sperm being produced every day. A man goes on producing sperm, though in slightly smaller quantities as he gets older, right through into old age.

The male hormone, testosterone, is also produced in the testicles from the time of puberty onwards. Testosterone is responsible for the process of sperm production, as well as bringing about the changes that happen to a boy's body at puberty. It is also responsible throughout life for maintaining the man's sex drive, as well as the male characteristics, such as bigger muscles, deeper voice, and facial and body hair.

The Internal sex organs

The vas deferens

These two thin tubes, which are 30–50 cm (12–20 in.) long, connect the epididymis on each testicle to the urethra. Fluid from two small glands, known as the *seminal vesicles*, and from the *prostate gland*, joins with the sperm, providing nourishment and lubrication. This combined fluid is called *semen*, and only a small part of this is sperm – most of it is a mixture of various substances, including vitamins, salts, sugars and enzymes.

Male sex organs

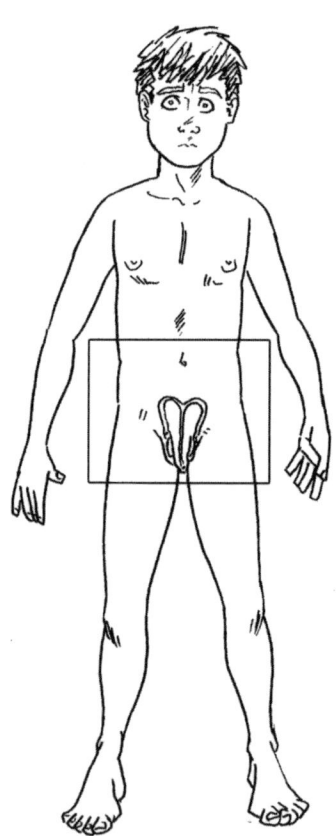

Male sex organs (front)

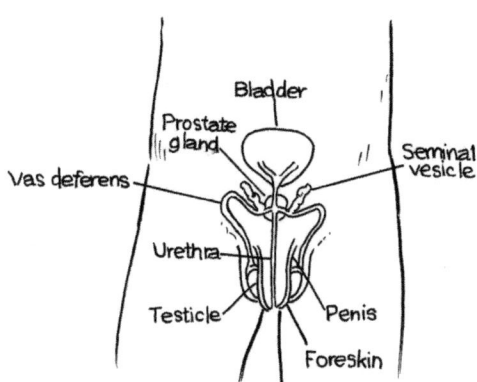

During sexual excitement, about 3–5 ml of semen (containing about 200–500 million sperm) is squeezed out of the seminal vesicles and along the *urethra* by muscular contractions, and squirted out of the tip of the penis in small spurts. This process is called *ejaculation.*

Male sex organs (side)

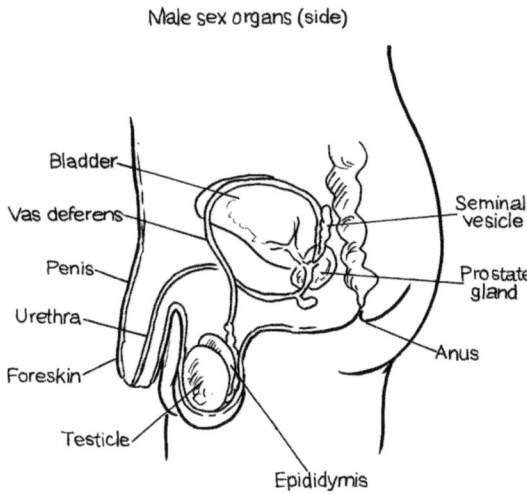

The urethra

This is a long narrow tube that has two functions: the first is to carry urine from the bladder to the outside of the body, and the second is to carry semen during an ejaculation. Owing to tightening of some muscles at the base of his bladder, a male cannot urinate and ejaculate at the same time, even if his bladder is full. In fact, most men have to wait a few minutes until their erection has subsided before they can pass urine.

Public and private

There's no doubt that it's a good thing to know the names of your body parts, and how they work; but it is also really important to recognize that the sexual parts of the body are considered to be private. This means that they are not generally displayed when we are in a public place, or even talked about, except in particular circumstances. Let's look more closely at what this means.

Public and private places

First, what do we mean by a public place? Simply, it's a place where there are other people around, so this means places such as the street, shopping malls, the classroom, school playgrounds, parks, beaches, buses, trains and so on – even your living room. These are all places where people can come and go without asking your permission. None of them are private places, although the living room could be, if you were home all alone, and no one was likely to come in.

So where are private places? The most usual ones are your bedroom, the bathroom and the toilet, as long as the door is shut and you are there by yourself. It is important to note here that public toilets (bathrooms) are *not* private places. When you are in a private place, other people should not come in, unless you give them permission to do so. For example, you might be happy for a family member or good friend to come into your bedroom, but only if you have said they can. Equally, if you are just cleaning your teeth or washing your hands, you might be okay with someone else coming into the bathroom. Some families are very open with each other, and may well share the bathroom, even when they are naked – this all depends how relaxed they are seeing each other's bodies. But if you want to be private while you are in the bathroom, then you are entitled to say so, and no one should come in without your permission. And of course, you should always close the door while you are using the toilet.

Private body parts

Very young children are allowed to show the private parts of their bodies in public, and not many people would object. For example, you may well see two- or three-year-old children running around naked in their house or garden, and even at the beach. Nobody minds, because the child is so young – and sometimes they are at the stage of learning to toilet train, so it can be a lot easier not to have nappies (diapers) on them, since this enables them to get to the potty more quickly!

But you will notice by the time they get to around five or six years old, most children prefer to wear pants in public – they have reached a stage where they recognize that bottoms, vulvas and penises are private, and should be covered up. Interestingly, little girls of this age often choose to cover their chests, too, so you will see them in one-piece swimsuits or bikinis, rather than just pants. This is because they are identifying with, and copying, older females, who do usually cover their breasts.

There are exceptions about the privacy of certain body parts, depending where you live in the world, and what culture you belong to. First, there are some tribal societies where people wear very little clothing, and women never cover their breasts – breasts are not considered to be a sexual or private part of the body. And there are some Western countries where people are very relaxed about their bodies, and may go naked on the beach. At the other extreme, there are cultures where it is considered inappropriate to show your arms or legs, or even your face, in public, especially if you are a woman. Although all this might seem a little confusing, the simple rule is to observe *what is normal* in the place that you are. Generally speaking, breasts, vulvas, bottoms, penises and testicles *are* considered to be private, and are covered up in public, even at the beach. If you follow this rule, you won't go far wrong.

When to talk about private body parts

Here is a true story.

> Emily was ten years old, in Year 5 (fifth grade). She and her class were having a sex education lesson about puberty, and the teacher was writing up on the board 'changes at puberty', while the children called out their suggestions. Many of them were adding information, such as, 'My big brother has acne'; 'My sister gets terrible mood

swings, and is always slamming doors' – even 'I get growing pains in my legs sometimes'. Other children were agreeing, and sometimes laughing at some of the stories. Emily was really enjoying the lesson, and felt quite involved. When someone called out 'pubic hair' as one of the puberty changes, she turned around to the class and announced 'I've got some pubic hair!' Suddenly, instead of agreeing or laughing, the other children looked at each other and rolled their eyes. Some of them pulled faces, and said things like, 'Oh yuck, Emily, that's disgusting' and 'Gross!' Emily looked quite confused by the sudden change of mood in the class.

What had Emily done wrong? Why was her contribution any different to those of the other children?

Simply, she had talked *publicly* about a *private* part of her own body. Most of the other children hadn't talked about themselves, but about someone else who wasn't in the class. And when they had talked about themselves, the bodily change they mentioned concerned a *public* body part – a part that everyone can see. During sex education, although private things are talked about in a public setting (in the classroom), they are talked about generally, rather than relating them to any individual in the room.

The simple rule to follow is, only talk about private body parts to someone you trust and know very well, and only do this when you are in a private place together. So, in other words, even if you are with your mum, if you want to talk about the fact that you need to change your sanitary pad, or your testicles are itchy, make sure no one else can hear you – a crowded train probably isn't the place for this kind of conversation!

Public and private behaviours

Private body parts should only be touched when you are in a private place – so it is not okay to adjust your bra or underwear when other people can see you, for example. When people choose to masturbate or have sex (see Chapter 7, **Sex**), they must do this in a private place. Masturbating, touching the private parts of another person and having sex are all private activities, so doing any of these in public is considered to be offensive, and is, in fact, against the law.

Other sexual behaviour between people doesn't always have to be in private – it depends what it is. Holding hands, linking arms and hugging are okay, because these involve public body parts. Kissing is a bit more difficult to make hard and fast rules about, as some kissing in public is fine – a kiss on the cheek, for instance, or even a quick kiss on the lips. Most people would agree, however, that passionate kisses should be done in private.

It's very important that you understand the difference between public and private in terms of body parts, places and behaviours. Society isn't very forgiving of someone who gets this wrong. At the very least, you could be laughed at or even rejected by other people for talking too loudly or inappropriately about private things in a public setting. At the worst, you could be in trouble for breaking the law for exposing a private body part in public. Talk with someone you trust about the information you have just read, and make sure you are very clear about the rules that exist so that you can be confident you are doing and saying the right thing.

2

Puberty

Puberty is the time when your body changes from being the body of a child to the body of an adult. It is normal and healthy and happens to everyone. You will experience changes in the way you look, think and feel, and many of these changes happen quite quickly. By the time puberty ends, your growth will be complete, and you will look more or less the way you are going to look as an adult.

If you aren't well prepared for puberty, it can all be rather confusing, embarrassing and even a little scary sometimes, which is why it is worth learning a bit about it. Things are a lot less worrying if you know what to expect.

What does puberty mean?

The word comes from a Latin word, *pubertas*, which means the 'age of maturity'. In fact, it is the time when your body becomes *sexually* mature. Your reproductive organs become fully developed, which means you are capable of reproducing – in other words, creating a baby. Just because you can reproduce doesn't mean you should, of course. Most young teenagers don't have babies, and even as adults some people are unable, or choose not, to have babies.

The other feature of puberty, apart from the maturing of the reproductive system (see Chapter 1, **Your Body**), is the development of *secondary sexual characteristics*. These include features such as breasts (for girls), facial hair (for boys), underarm hair and pubic hair (for boys and girls) – in other words, the body characteristics that make a young person look more like an adult, and can make them sexually attractive to another person. We will explore these in much more detail in a moment.

Puberty or adolescence?

Adolescence is the time between childhood and adulthood, and includes the development of your thinking processes and emotional maturity. *Puberty*, as just mentioned, is more specifically about the physical changes and the maturing of the reproductive organs, and it happens in the first few years of adolescence. Sometimes you will hear the words 'puberty' and 'adolescence' used interchangeably, and in many ways it doesn't really matter.

When does puberty happen?

It is a change that takes place over a few months or years (not overnight!). It usually starts some time between the ages of nine and 16 years. Girls or boys who are quite young when it begins (nine or ten) may find that they take a little longer to go through all the changes than someone who is a bit older at the start (15 or 16); these older boys or girls will probably go through the whole of puberty in a matter of months. By 17 or 18, nearly everyone has gone through puberty and has developed the body of an adult.

Typically, most girls begin around ten or 11 years old, and most boys around 12 or 13. But changes can begin as early as eight, or as late as 17. Everyone is different, and it's very important to remember this. Whenever you go through your changes is exactly right for you, and you needn't compare yourself to anyone else. Even two children in the same family can begin puberty at completely different ages, though quite often the age at which your parents began can give you a bit of a clue, as there seems to be a hereditary factor.

Going through puberty earlier or later than someone else doesn't make either of those people better or worse than each other. And don't take too much notice of the terms 'early developer' or 'late developer' – such phrases can make you feel abnormal, when this is not the case at all. The age at which you reach puberty doesn't affect how you will be as an adult. Sooner or later, each person's body will reach maturity, some quickly, some more slowly. The end result will be the same for everyone – a mature, adult-looking body.

What causes puberty to happen?

The simple answer is hormones! Hormones are chemical substances secreted by a number of glands in your body. Their job is to bring about a change in the function of other glands or cells in your body. The pituitary gland in the base of your brain releases several hormones into the bloodstream. These hormones act on your ovaries, if you are a girl, and your testicles, if you are a boy, which in turn produce hormones of their own. These are called the sex hormones; the female hormones are *oestrogen* (or *estrogen*) and *progesterone*, and the male hormone is *testosterone*. Both boys and girls have some of all these hormones, with the ovaries producing mainly oestrogen and progesterone, but a little testosterone, and the testicles producing mainly testosterone, and a small amount of oestrogen and progesterone.

The action of the sex hormones is to stimulate the testicles and ovaries to continue growing and maturing, and also to stimulate the development of the sex cells within the testicles and the ovaries. In a boy these are called *sperm*, and in a girl, *ova* (eggs). At the same time, the hormones also bring about the development of those secondary sex characteristics mentioned earlier, such as breasts, body hair, muscle growth, skin changes and so on.

What happens at puberty?

The changes that happen at this time are not just physical, but emotional and social, too. Some of these changes happen to boys only, and some to girls only. Quite a number of the changes, however, happen to both boys and girls. As you can see, there are a lot of changes, most of which will eventually make you look, feel and function more like an adult.

Both boys and girls experience:

- a spurt of growth
- a tendency to be a little clumsier
- an increase in weight

- a slight change to the shape of your face
- a deepening of your voice (more noticeable in boys)
- the growth of pubic hair
- the growth of underarm hair
- an increased oiliness of your skin, with the possible development of pimples
- increased body odour
- moodiness
- sexual feelings
- changes in the way you feel about your friends and family.

Boys only:

- a darkening and roughening of the scrotal skin (the sac containing the testicles)
- an increase in the length and thickness of the penis
- an increase in the size of the testicles
- increased leg hair
- the growth of facial hair
- a 'flattening' of the skull at the back
- muscle development
- broadening of the shoulders and chest
- an increase in the frequency of spontaneous erections
- the production of semen and sperm
- wet dreams
- (sometimes) slight breast changes.

Girls only:

- breast development
- widening of the hips
- (possibly) some light facial hair

- slight increase of leg hair
- increased fat deposits on thighs
- a darkening of the genital area, which also becomes fleshier
- vaginal secretions
- the start of periods (menstruation).

Physical changes at puberty

The growth spurt

Growth at puberty is different for everyone. Some people grow very quickly, while others just seem to grow slowly and steadily, with a much more gradual increase in their height. Your eventual height is not affected by the age at which you begin your growth spurt, but more likely by heredity, so the height of your parents may give you some idea of how tall you will eventually be.

The pattern of growth is slightly different for boys and girls. Girls may begin their growth spurt at the beginning of puberty, usually around the age of ten or 11, and it is likely to be one of the first changes they notice. Boys, however, begin their growth spurt towards the end of puberty, when many of the other changes have already occurred.

From the age of two, most children grow about 5 cm (2 in.) each year, until puberty. This slow, steady growth is caused by growth hormone. The growth spurt at puberty, however, is caused by testosterone, and once it begins, boys can add as much as 9 cm ($3\frac{1}{2}$ in.) or more each year to their height, while girls may grow 8 cm (3 in.) or more each year. The very fast rate of growth usually only lasts for one or two years, and then slows down. However, some growth continues until 18 years old in girls, and 20 in boys.

As you know, men are often (though not always) taller than women. There are two reasons for this: one is that because boys start growing later than girls, they have the advantage of an extra two or three years of regular childhood growth before their growth spurt begins. Second, boys grow faster at their peak rate, as already mentioned, because of the higher levels of testosterone.

The growth of your body happens in a pattern, from the 'outside in'. Your hands and feet grow first – you will notice that you need new shoes more often. Then your legs and arms grow longer, so that your sleeves and your trousers always seem to be too short! Following that, your spine grows so that your torso (your body from your neck to the top of your legs) lengthens; and finally, boys' chests and shoulders broaden, and girls' hips and pelvises become wider.

Clumsiness

The rate of growth accounts for the clumsiness that many young people seem to experience. First of all your feet seem rather too big for a while, which takes a bit of getting used to. Then your limbs grow before your torso, which makes you appear a little more awkward. It can take a while for your brain to get used to your big feet and longer arms and legs, and you may find yourself tripping up or knocking things over rather more often than you would like to. Eventually, of course, you do get used to your 'new' body, and become more co-ordinated.

Face changes

Even your face changes at puberty! All the bones in your body are growing, and this includes those of your skull. Often your nose grows first, so that some people worry that their nose is too big for a while, but the rest of your face does catch up. Your face will become longer and a little more angular – more like an adult's face, in fact. In boys, the shape of the skull at the back of the head changes, too, becoming flatter.

Weight gain and appetite

You are supposed to gain weight at puberty. Not only are you becoming taller – and longer bones weigh a lot more – your muscles grow accordingly (particularly in boys), and muscles are quite heavy, too. In addition to this, girls are putting on extra fat around the hips and thighs, and on the breasts, that is both attractive, in that they develop female 'curves', and essential if they are to function as a healthy female. Some people do find that they seem to put on weight very quickly, and may even feel a bit too fat for a while. It can be that they are 'filling out' before 'growing up', and they may well find that once they have their growth spurt, the extra weight is naturally absorbed, and they look slimmer again. Some other people grow fast but seem to gain very little weight, and for a while may look particularly gangly and thin. Again, it is a matter of being patient and waiting for your body to sort itself out. Eventually these very thin people will find that they do 'fill out'. It is, of course, worth remembering that everyone is different anyway, and that some people are naturally a little thinner or fatter than others. It's a good thing we aren't all the same – how boring would that be!

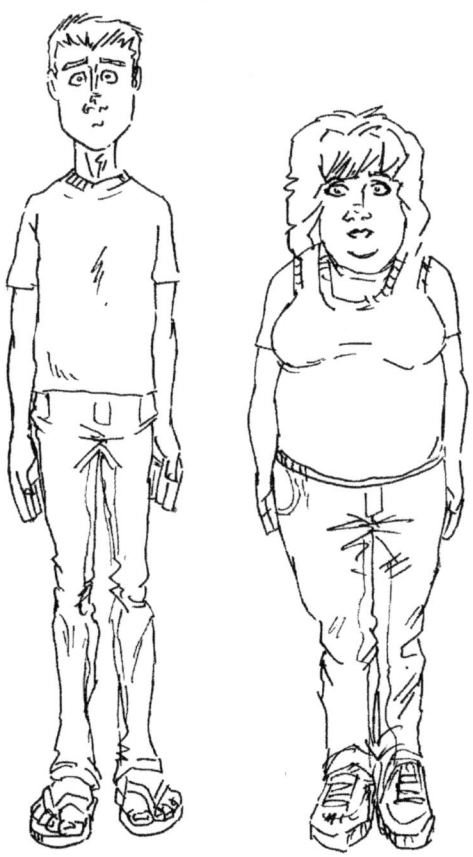

While you are growing so quickly, you will find that you become very hungry. Most adolescents eat more at this time of their lives than at any other time. For a while, some boys are able to eat as much as a grown man who does manual work and needs a great deal of food. It is important to eat as well as you can at puberty in order to be as healthy as possible, so that means choosing your food sensibly. To read more about healthy eating, see Chapter 4, **Making Healthy Choices**.

Deepening of the voice

This is a change that is more usually associated with boys, and it is true that in boys it is much more obvious. But there is a slight deepening of the voice in girls, too. (Compare the voice of one of your female teachers to the voice of any eight-year-old girl, and you can recognize the difference.) In girls it is a very gradual, almost imperceptible change.

For boys, though, the change can be very obvious indeed. What is happening is that the *larynx* (voice box) is growing, and the *vocal cords* are becoming longer and thicker. This means that when the air from the lungs passes between the vocal cords (which is what causes the sound), they vibrate at a lower frequency. This produces a lower sound. But during this time of growth it can be quite difficult for a boy to regulate the actual sound that he makes when he talks. If he shouts, or talks suddenly, his voice can come out as a squeak before it deepens to the pitch he was anticipating. Sometimes people refer to this as the voice cracking or 'breaking', but of course it isn't really breaking! It can, however, be a little embarrassing, as other people sometimes laugh (which is silly, really, as it happens to most boys from time to time). The trick is to talk steadily and carefully, not make too many sudden sounds, and the unexpected 'squeaks' can be minimized. But, remember, this cracking of the voice happens to just about every boy at some point, and is definitely not worth worrying about. Soon the larynx and vocal cords finish their growth, and your voice will settle into its adult pitch.

Body hair

Body hair increases generally at puberty, growing in some places where it has never been before, and increasing in amount in some other places. Hairiness tends to run in families, so take a look at your family if you want some idea as to how hairy you might eventually be. Usually, men are more hairy than women, and their hair tends to be thicker and coarser than women's hair. Depending on their culture, and on fashion, people sometimes like to remove the hair from certain parts of their body. It is important to remember, though, that your body hair is natural and okay, and doesn't need to be removed unless you want it to be. If you do choose to shave or wax any part of your body, it's important that you know how to do it safely and properly. You can read more about this in Chapter 3, **Caring for Your Body**.

PUBIC HAIR

This is the hair that grows around the genital area, on the vulva in girls, and above the penis in boys. Even when you are a child, you have some hair there, but it is very soft and fine, and almost invisible. At puberty it begins to change, gradually becoming a little longer, coarser and darker. Eventually it forms a sort of upside-down triangle, covering the pubic area.

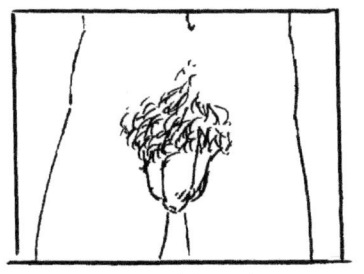 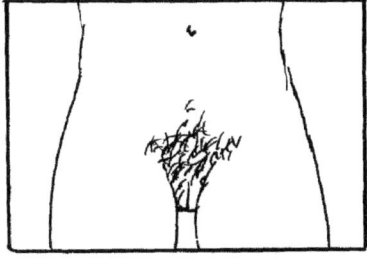

Male pubic hair   Female pubic hair

Usually the hair is slightly curly, and most often darker than the hair on your head. The amount of hair varies from one person to the next, as some people are more hairy than others. So some people may find that their pubic hair is never very thick, whilst others will notice that not only is the hair quite thick, but it also extends onto the top of their thighs, and in a line up to their navel. Either way, the amount of hair you have is right for you, and it is certainly nothing to worry about.

UNDERARM HAIR

This is the hair that grows in the armpits, in both men and women, usually appearing a year or two after the pubic hair begins. Again, it tends to be a little darker than the hair on your head, and the amount varies from one person to another, depending on how hairy that person is in general. In some cultures, women choose to shave or wax underarm hair to get rid of it. However, it is important to remember that it is natural, and having it there makes no difference in terms of odour or use of deodorants. Whether you like the look of underarm hair or not (particularly on women) depends to some extent on what you are used to seeing.

OTHER BODY HAIR

- *Legs and arms*: both boys and girls will experience some increase in the amount of hair on their legs and arms, though it is much more noticeable on boys. In fact, the increase in the amount of hair on their legs is one of the first puberty changes that many boys notice.

- *Face*: you may be more familiar with the idea that boys develop facial hair, though, in some cases, some girls may find that they do get a very fine growth of hair on their top lip – again, nothing to worry about, although some women do choose to get this removed (see Chapter 3, **Caring for Your Body**, for more information on this). For boys, the growth of a beard and a moustache is one of the later changes of puberty, usually occurring after many of the other changes. Growth of hair begins on your top lip, followed by some hair on your cheeks, and finally on your chin. To begin with, the hair is soft, though it becomes coarser over time. You may or may not choose to shave as soon as your facial hair becomes obvious – that will depend how you feel about it. Some boys can't wait to shave, as they see it as a sign of being grown up! And some boys choose never to shave, and to grow a beard and moustache (though this may not be allowed if they are still at school!). Again, everyone is different – some men, who are slightly less hairy, may find they only need to shave every two or three days, while others have such fast regrowth, they are almost ready for a second shave by the end of the day (they have what is sometimes called a 'five o'clock shadow').

- *Chest and back*: this is the last of the body hair that boys develop, often not until they are in their late teens or twenties. Some men never develop this at all, or only a little on their chest. It is also quite normal for girls to have occasional stray hairs growing from the areola, the area around the nipples. In this case, if they don't want them there, they can pluck out the hairs with tweezers, or trim them, but should never shave them, as the area is very sensitive.

Skin changes

You have oil glands (known as *sebaceous glands*) under the surface of your skin. Their job is to produce a substance called *sebum*, which lubricates and protects your hair and skin. At puberty, testosterone acts on the sebaceous glands, causing them to produce more sebum. This results in your skin and hair becoming more oily than usual during this time. Sometimes the extra sebum can clog the pores (tiny openings in your skin), which, if you do not wash your skin regularly with mild soap and water, can become infected. This results in pimples – otherwise known as *acne*.

Acne tends to occur mainly on the face and neck, and sometimes on the back, because the sebaceous glands are more numerous in these areas. It tends to be worse for boys than for girls, though just about everyone gets pimples from time to time. Good skin care and regular hair washing are essential at this time. For more information about this, see Chapter 3, **Caring for Your Body**.

It helps if you have a good diet. Although eating fatty or sugary food doesn't directly cause acne, it makes sense to eat less junk food and more fresh, nutritious food to help with your general good health. A good immune system helps to fight the infection that causes acne.

Acne is nearly always a temporary problem, and most people have grown out of it by the time they become adults. Some girls and women get an outbreak of pimples during their periods; and some people find their skin is sensitive to certain conditions, such as too much heat or cold, or even too much sunlight. However, if you feel your acne is particularly bad and it is distressing you, it is worth going to the doctor, as there are medical treatments that can help. Remember, though, it is how you feel about yourself and how you behave that is important, not what your skin looks like, and as long as you feel okay about yourself, most other people won't worry about your pimples.

Sweat glands and body odour

Even the way you smell changes at puberty! This is because there are some sweat glands in your body, in the armpits and groin area, which are not active until puberty. Just about all of your body is covered in sweat glands, especially the palms of your hands, soles of your feet and your forehead. These glands, which have been active since you were born, produce sweat that is made up mainly of water and salt. Its purpose is to help in the process of regulating your body temperature by cooling your body down as the water evaporates from your skin. But the sweat produced by the glands in the armpits and groin also contains proteins and fatty acids. The sweat itself has no odour, but bacteria that live on the skin metabolize (eat, digest and excrete) the proteins and fats, and it is this process that produces an unpleasant odour – which is what we know as 'body odour' or 'BO'.

The proteins and fatty acids in the underarm sweat also give it a milky or yellowish colour, which is why underarm sweat stains on clothing appear yellowish in colour.

It is thought that the purpose of body odour is to make someone sexually attractive to another person. However, this is really referring to the almost imperceptible smell of fresh sweat, not sweat which has been there for hours – there's no doubt that a person who is unwashed and sweaty for too long does not smell attractive to anyone!

So the important thing once you get to puberty is to wash carefully every day, particularly those areas that are more prone to body odour (underarms, groin, back of the neck and feet), and use a deodorant or anti-perspirant under your arms to minimize the sweating and reduce the odour. To find out more about keeping clean and the use of deodorants, see Chapter 3, **Caring for Your Body**.

Boys only...

But girls can (and should) read this as well. It is useful to have an understanding of the things that happen to the other sex, as it can sometimes help explain the way they might be behaving or feeling – and in any case, it's just interesting.

The penis and testicles

One of the early signs of puberty is that your testicles start to enlarge. You will also notice, around the same time, that the skin of your scrotum is becoming rougher, and turning a slightly darker, 'reddish' colour. Pubic hair usually appears a few months after the testicles have begun to grow, though in some boys it can happen first.

Some people refer to the 'balls dropping' ('balls' is a slang term for testicles. For other slang terms to do with sexuality, see Chapter 11,

Sexual Language). However, this isn't strictly true. The testicles descend from inside the groin to the outside before birth in most cases. At puberty they appear to 'drop' because they gradually get bigger and hang lower. And you will notice that one testicle usually hangs a little lower than the other. This is simply to make it easier for you to walk around without them knocking together, which would be painful.

Your penis also starts to grow, first in length, then later in thickness. Your final penis size is reached about four to six years after the testicles first start to enlarge (in fact, a year or two after you have reached your full adult height). As you can see, it is not a quick process, so it gives you plenty of time to get used to your 'new' body. Since puberty happens at slightly different times for everyone, and since everyone changes at different rates anyway, there is no point comparing the size of your penis to anyone else's, since they are sure to be different. Even in adults, penis size varies considerably between one man and another. Nevertheless, you are very likely to hear boys and girls making jokes about penis size, and implying that, unless a man has a really big penis, he isn't a 'real man'. This is, of course, untrue. But because this kind of ignorance can be very unsettling, here are some facts that might be helpful.

PENIS FACTS

- The function of the penis is to: allow the passage of urine from the bladder; allow the passage of semen and sperm; and provide pleasurable sexual feelings; if a penis fulfils these functions, then it is just right.

- The penis reaches its full adult size one to two years after you have finished growing.

- The size of your penis is determined by genetics, not by the size of your feet, your hands, or even your height.

- A penis can appear slightly smaller if a man is very overweight, as layers of fat on the lower abdomen can obscure the first few centimetres of the penis.

- *Flaccid* (soft) penises vary in length between different men and may be anything between about 5 cm and 12 cm (2–5 in.), once a man is fully grown.

Some different penises...

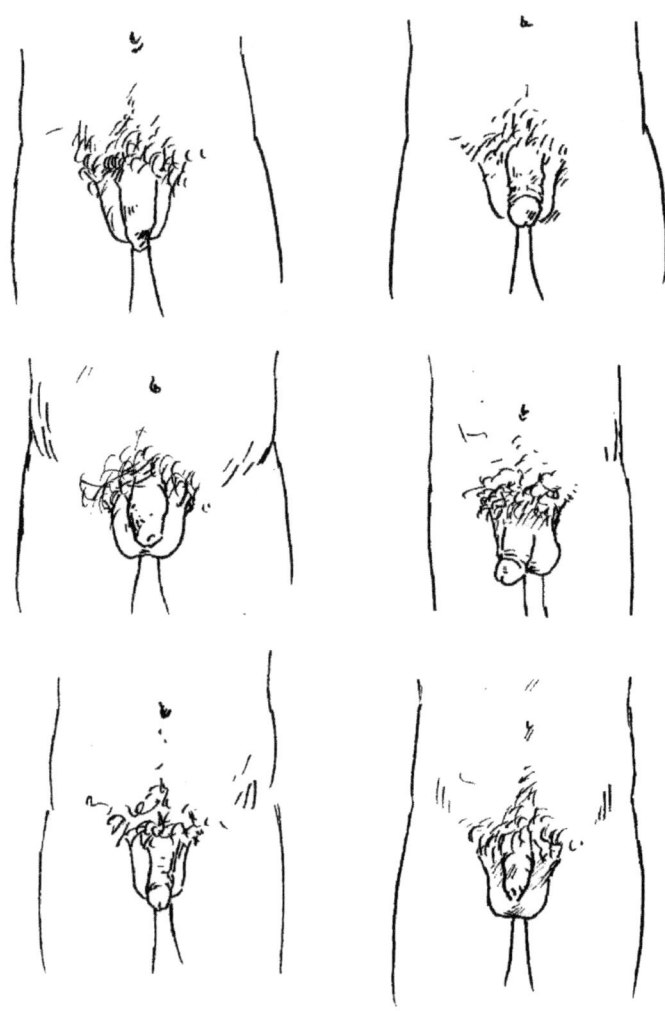

- *Erect* (stiff) penises also vary in length from one man to another, and can be anything between about 10 cm and 21 cm (4–8¼ in.) once a man is fully grown.

- Generally, a penis that is slightly smaller when soft tends to grow proportionally more when it becomes erect than one that is slightly larger when soft.

- It is not necessary for a man to have a large penis in order to have a successful sexual relationship. How he behaves towards his partner, and the love and respect they have for each other, are far more important than how big his penis is. (For more information about sex, see Chapter 7, **Sex**.)

- Some men have a penis that bends slightly to one side when it is flaccid. And sometimes, erect penises can have a slight bend in them. This is perfectly okay – it doesn't stop them functioning normally.

ERECTIONS

An *erection* (stiffening) is a normal, healthy function of the penis. In fact, your penis has had this ability since before you were born. Ultrasound scans have sometimes shown baby boys in the uterus to have erect penises, and from time to time during childhood, you would have found your penis becoming erect, especially if you touched it and it felt nice. And throughout your life it is quite normal to wake up in the morning with an erection. This may be because you are relaxed, or have had nice dreams, but is often because your bladder is full, which stimulates the nerves at the base of the penis. In fact, you get several erections while you sleep, related to your sleep cycle, but, of course, you are not aware of them. (For more information about the physiology of the penis, and exactly how erections happen, see Chapter 1, **Your Body**.)

At puberty, however, erections happen a lot more frequently (sometimes several times a day), due to the increased levels of testosterone, and you certainly are aware of them! You may find your penis becoming erect because of the sensation of clothing rubbing against it, or because of the vibrations of the engine of the bus or the train on your way to school. Or you might be wrestling with your brother or sister and find that you have an erection. Sometimes erections happen because you have a thought about someone you find sexually attractive, or you catch sight of a picture that you think is sexy.

But sometimes you will have erections for no reason that you can recognize. These are called *spontaneous erections*, and they happen a lot during puberty. You might be sitting in class or out in the playground, and suddenly become aware that you are getting an erection. It's almost as if your penis has 'a mind of its own'. Because this can be embarrassing, it's important to know how to deal with it (see below).

Rest assured, this phase of puberty doesn't last for very long. Eventually you will stop having so many spontaneous erections, and it will feel as though your penis is much more under control!

DEALING WITH SPONTANEOUS ERECTIONS

- Don't say anything about it! Other people don't need to know or see that you have an erection.

- Stay seated if you can, or, if you are standing up, make an excuse to sit down. It's a lot easier to disguise if you are sitting down.

- Quietly wait for it to pass, which it will do, all by itself, in a minute or less.

- Try not to think about it, as this will help it to go away more quickly. Try to think of something fairly uninteresting and unrelated instead, such as what you were just learning in class, or you could try doing some mental arithmetic.

- Wear clothing that disguises erections. Close-fitting underwear is better than boxer shorts, for example, as the tighter fabric helps to hold your penis closer to your body, so that even when it becomes erect, it doesn't stick out. Then have your long pants or shorts a bit baggier, which helps to disguise any slight lumps or bumps.

The production of semen and sperm

Testosterone stimulates the production of the male sex cells, *sperm*, in the testicles (see Chapter 1, **Your Body**, for more detail about the production and function of sperm and semen). Once puberty begins, you will make millions of sperm cells in each testicle every day. By the time you become an adult, your testicles will be manufacturing sperm at a rate of about 75 million a day (that is about 1000 a second!).

This production of sex cells continues all through your life. This is not the same for women, however. Their supply of *ova* (already in the ovaries at birth) runs out when they reach the menopause, at around 50 years old.

In their journey from the body, sperm are nourished and transported by *semen*, a whitish, slightly sticky fluid, which also starts to be produced at puberty. Semen, containing millions of sperm, leaves the erect penis in a series of little spurts, which is known as *ejaculation*. You may experience your first ejaculation during *masturbation* (see the section at the end of this chapter), or during a *wet dream*.

WET DREAMS

Around the age of 13 (perhaps a little earlier or later), you may experience your first wet dream, or *nocturnal emission*. This is when you ejaculate some semen and sperm while you are asleep. Sometimes your dream may be about something you find sexy, and sometimes it isn't – and sometimes you won't remember your dream at all – but you will experience pleasurable feelings, and then wake up and find that you have produced a small amount (2–3 ml) of semen. This isn't enough to make much of a mess, of course, though it may well make a little wet patch on your pyjamas or boxer shorts – or on your sheets if you don't wear anything in bed. You can sponge off the semen with a wet cloth, or put your clothing or bedding into the wash. Semen doesn't have much of a smell, and, once the sheets or clothing have been washed, it shouldn't leave a stain. It's quite a good idea to have some tissues beside the bed, so that it's easy to clean up. Just remember to throw them away when you have used them!

The frequency of wet dreams varies. There will be times when you seem to have quite a few (perhaps two or three a week), and other times when you hardly seem to have any. Some boys only ever experience one or two wet dreams. How often they happen is probably related to the levels of testosterone in your body. It is also related to whether or not sperm are leaving the body for some other reason; for example, someone who masturbates regularly may have fewer wet dreams, and an adult who is in a sexual relationship may hardly ever have them.

Wet dreams are normal and healthy, and a reassuring sign that your body is producing sperm, and changing in the way that it should. You tend to grow out of wet dreams by the time you become an adult, though there are some men who report that they still experience them occasionally.

Developing muscles and a broader chest

The broadening of your shoulders and chest is the very last stage of your bony growth, finishing around the age of 20. Men develop larger hearts and lungs than women, relative to their size, and the slightly larger chest cavity allows for this. The heart, which has approximately 40 per cent more muscle than a woman's heart, contributes to men's added strength, by pumping more blood around to the muscles.

The muscles themselves become bigger and stronger. This is thanks to testosterone, which increases the levels in the blood of a substance called *haemoglobin*. Haemoglobin delivers oxygen to your muscles, so, with testosterone levels increasing in a big way as you go through puberty, your muscles are getting much more oxygen than before. This enables the muscle fibres to increase in both length and width, so that your overall strength increases.

This change in your strength can be unexpectedly rapid. You might suddenly find yourself being a bit too rough in a wrestle with someone, or punching something a little too hard when you are in a bad mood. This is when you find adults telling you that you 'don't know your own strength'. In a way this is true, and it is worth being extra careful until you do become used to your stronger muscles.

Breast changes

Around half of all boys experience some breast changes early on in puberty. It begins with some tenderness and slight swelling under the nipple (usually both nipples, but sometimes it is only on one side), with some boys going on to develop some breast tissue. The main things to understand about this change are first, that it is temporary – it usually disappears within 12–18 months – and second, you are not turning into a girl! It happens because there is a temporary imbalance of hormones. Once the balance settles, then, in most cases, the 'breasts' disappear. Meanwhile, if you are feeling self-conscious about the situation, wear loose clothing, and wear a T-shirt when you go swimming. If you are really concerned, it might be helpful to talk to a doctor, who will be able to reassure you.

Girls only...

But boys should read this, too. As mentioned before, it is important to have an understanding of what happens to the other sex – and you might find it interesting!

Breast development

The beginning of breast development is one of the first visible signs of puberty for a girl, though the changes take several years to complete. A girl may be around 17 or 18 – sometimes even older – before her breasts are fully grown, and even then, they will continue to change slightly throughout her life.

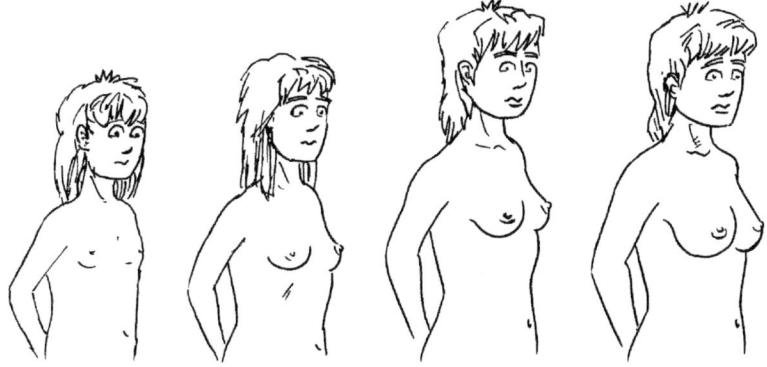

Stages of breast development

The development of the breasts, caused by the female hormone *oestrogen*, happens in stages. To begin with, the milk ducts start to grow, and a small amount of fatty tissue is laid down. This causes the area beneath the nipple to swell slightly, and the *areola* (the slightly darker area of skin which surrounds the nipple) to enlarge a little. This stage is known as 'breast budding', and can begin as early as eight years old. But because the timing of puberty is so variable, some girls may be 13 or 14 when they first notice these changes.

During the next stage of development, the breasts start to become slightly rounder and fill out a little, and the areola begins to darken. Quite often, during these first two stages of development, the breasts may feel very tender, sometimes even sore, and the surrounding skin may be a little itchy. Don't worry, there is nothing wrong – this discomfort is temporary, and is due to the fluctuation of hormones.

During the next year or two, the breasts become fuller and more rounded, reaching their adult size and shape around the age of 17 or 18.

BREAST FACTS

- Breasts are mammary glands, and, as in all mammals, their purpose is to provide milk for an infant. In addition to this, many women enjoy their breasts being touched by a sexual partner; and many people consider breasts to be sexually attractive.

- The whole process of breast development takes about 3–5 years, but can be much longer than this for some girls, even taking as long as ten years for some.

- Breast size is determined mostly by heredity. So look at your mother, grandmother and other female relatives, including those on your father's side of the family, to give you some idea of how big your breasts may eventually be.

- Breast size is also to do with your body type, and how much body fat you have. Thinner girls tend to have smaller breasts, and fatter girls tend to have larger breasts, as breasts consist partly of fatty tissue. Girls who are more athletic (and therefore probably have less body fat) tend to have smaller breasts.

- Once you have reached the stage of breast buds, your menstrual periods will probably begin within two years (see later section).

- It is quite normal for one breast to develop before the other, so that they can seem a little 'lop-sided' for a while. Mostly they even out as you grow, though some women always have breasts that vary slightly one from another, in either size or shape. In most cases this difference is not noticeable to other people.

- Some girls and women have 'flat' nipples. Most flat nipples start to 'stick out' more during pregnancy.

- The size of a woman's breasts is unrelated to whether or not she will be able to breast-feed her baby. Women with small breasts are just as successful at breast-feeding as women with larger breasts.

Some different breasts...

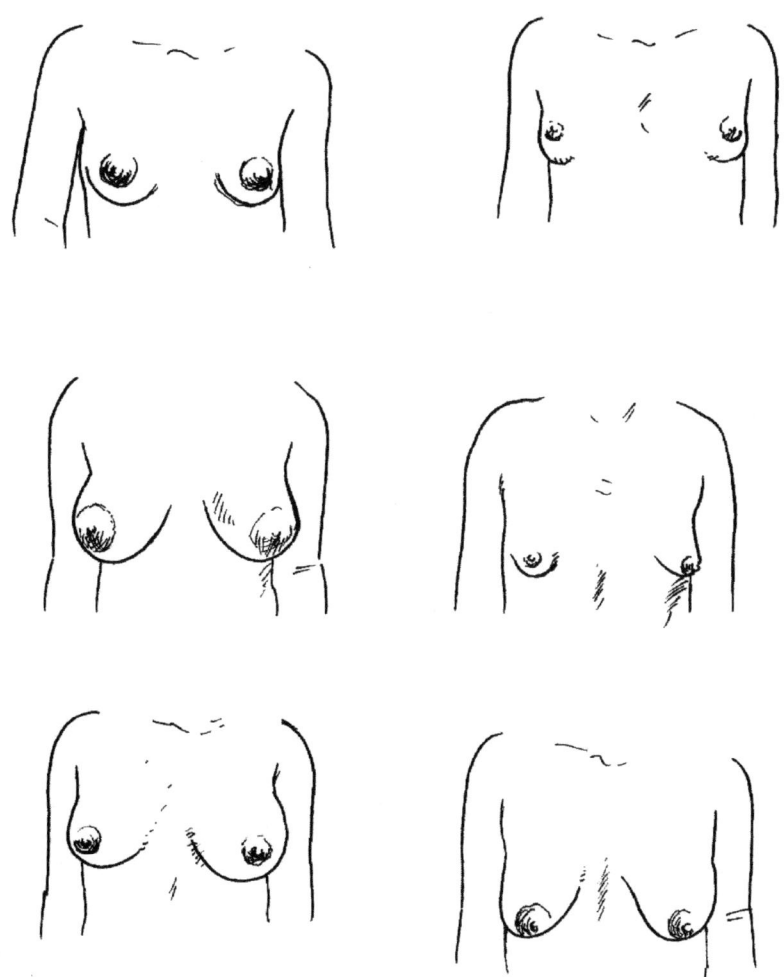

It is very important to recognize that breasts vary significantly in size and shape between different women. Be careful about being 'brainwashed' by the media into thinking a certain size or shape is desirable. Our attitude to breast size is influenced by fashion, which, as you know, changes all the time. In the 1920s it was considered desirable to have very small breasts – almost flat chests – which led many women to strap their chests in an attempt to make their breasts appear smaller. Small breasts became fashionable again in the 1960s. Now, it is fashionable to have fuller breasts, and to show them off in revealing clothing. But, unless someone has plastic surgery, there is no way to significantly change the size of your breasts. Certainly, there are no exercises or creams that can do this. Your breasts will look their best if you have a well-fitting bra or properly fitting clothing.

In short, relax and try to be happy with what you've got. Your breasts, once they have finished growing, are almost certain to be perfect for you, and as long as you are happy, everyone else will be.

CHOOSING A BRA

- It is not essential that you wear a bra in order for your breasts to be healthy. However, many girls and women choose to wear one at least some of the time, for example at school or work, and when playing sport.

- Some girls feel self-conscious about their breast development as soon as the nipples start to stick out a little (at the breast bud stage). If this is the case for you, consider wearing a 'crop top' or soft training or sports bra.

- As soon as your breasts begin to feel a little heavier, or uncomfortable when you run, you might want to consider buying a bra.

- You will need help when choosing a bra. Take your mother, an older sister or an adult you feel comfortable with when you first go to buy a bra.

- You will need help to select a bra that is a good fit – if you go to a reputable store, the assistant will be able to measure you and make sure that you get a bra that is exactly the right size.

- A bra should be comfortable, as you will be wearing it for many hours each day. Make sure it doesn't feel too tight, and that the material doesn't feel scratchy or irritating to your skin.

- It is essential to try a bra on, even when you think you know your size. Individual bras vary in size, so unless you are buying an exact repeat of one you have had before, you won't know whether it will fit properly until you try.

- When trying bras, remember to move around, jump up and down and raise your arms above your head! This sounds a bit strange, but it's the only way you will know that the bra will stay in place and still be comfortable when you move around.

- The straps shouldn't dig in, the bra should not ride up at the back, and your breasts should be comfortably contained, and not squeezing out at the edges.

- Try putting a T-shirt on over the top while you are in the changing room – this will give you a good idea as to how the bra looks under clothing.

- For lop-sided breasts, buy a bra that fits the slightly bigger breast, and use a padded insert to help the other breast to fill up the bra cup.

- Remember, your breast size is constantly changing for a few years, so it's a good idea to buy only two or three bras at a time.

Widening of hips

The widening of your hips and narrowing of your waist are the changes (along with breast development) that give you your attractive 'female' shape. The pelvic bones widen for a biological reason, and that is to allow a baby enough room to pass through during childbirth (see Chapter 10, **Fertilization, Pregnancy and Birth**).

You will also gain a little weight around your hips and thighs – this is what is known as the 'female distribution of fat'. It is healthy, and essential, as it helps in the production of the female hormone, oestrogen. It is very important that you don't ever diet or exercise so much that you lose this essential fat, as it is vital for the continuation of menstrual periods. In short, enjoy your healthy, curvy shape.

A change to the vulva and vagina

As you start to go through puberty, you will notice a very slight darkening in the colour of your vulva, in particular the inner labia (see Chapter 1, **Your Body**). You develop a pad of fat beneath the mons pubis, just above the vulva, so that it becomes a little more rounded than before, and the inner and outer labia become fleshier. The inner labia sometimes grow slightly bigger than the outer labia, and may stick out from between the outer labia. Pubic hair begins to grow on the outer labia, eventually spreading to cover the pubic area (see section on pubic hair).

VAGINAL SECRETIONS

Once you have started puberty, you will notice that you have some secretions that come from your vagina, leaving a slight yellowish stain in your underwear. Don't worry, it is not urine, and you are not wetting your pants! All women experience this. It is a mucous that is secreted by the cervix (see Chapter 1, **Your Body**) to keep your vagina clean and moist. In the same way that saliva helps to keep your mouth healthy, these secretions keep your vagina naturally clean, without you having to wash inside your body.

Vaginal secretions tend to start a year or two before your first period (see next section), and usually increase in amount just before the period begins. Once you have started periods on a regular basis (and this can take a year or two), you will notice that the secretions vary in amount and consistency at different times of the month. Sometimes the secretions are slightly thicker and a bit sticky, and at other times they are thinner, and almost 'slippery'. Sometimes you will notice hardly any at all.

Healthy vaginal secretions are whitish in colour (usually darkening a little as they dry, so that the stain on your underwear is slightly more yellow in appearance), and may have a slight (but not unpleasant) smell. Any prolonged itchiness or discomfort around the vagina or vulva, or a change in the smell or colour of the secretions (e.g. a smell that is very strong or unpleasant, or a greenish or brownish look to the secretions) may mean that you have an infection. This *doesn't* mean you have done anything wrong, and you needn't be embarrassed about it. It's important to tell a trusted adult about it, so that you can arrange to have a check-up with the doctor. Vaginal infections are very easily treated.

Generally, as long as you wash your vulva carefully (see Chapter 3, **Caring for Your Body**), and change your underwear every day, you will not smell, and your vagina will be perfectly healthy.

Periods

All women, all over the world, get periods. A *period* (also known as *menstruation*) is a monthly event, when a small amount of blood leaves your body through your vagina for a few days. Periods begin during puberty, and continue, approximately once every month (unless you are pregnant, when they stop temporarily), until the age of about 45–50, which is called the *menopause*. Once your periods begin, it shows that your body is healthy, fertile and working properly.

WHY DO PERIODS HAPPEN?

It's all thanks to hormones! Once a month, under the influence of the female hormones, oestrogen and progesterone, one or other of the ovaries releases a mature ovum (egg) into the Fallopian tube. This is known as *ovulation*. In the two weeks or so leading up to ovulation, the lining of the uterus (the *endometrium*) has been thickening and increasing its blood supply in preparation for a possible pregnancy. Once the ovum is in the Fallopian tube, it can become fertilized by a sperm, if the woman has had sexual intercourse. If this has happened, the fertilized ovum moves along the Fallopian tube and into the uterus, where it embeds itself into the nourishing lining. This is the beginning of a pregnancy. (For more on this, see Chapter 10, **Fertilization, Pregnancy and Birth**.)

However, a lot of the time the ovum does not meet with a sperm, either because the woman has not had sex – or if she has, she was using contraception (see Chapter 9, **Looking After Your Sexual Health**), or she had sex at a time when there was no ovum in the Fallopian tube. So instead, immediately after ovulation, the ovum makes its way along the Fallopian tube unfertilized. And because fertilization has not taken place, the thickened lining of the uterus is not needed to support a pregnancy, so it gradually peels away and leaves the woman's body through her vagina, along with the unfertilized ovum and menstrual blood. Soon afterwards, the lining begins to thicken again, ready to receive a fertilized ovum the following month. This whole process, which happens month after month, is called the *menstrual cycle*, and the gradual loss of blood and uterine lining through the vagina is called the *period*.

During pregnancy, when the uterine lining is needed to nourish and support a developing baby, the woman does not have any periods.

Stages of menstrual cycle

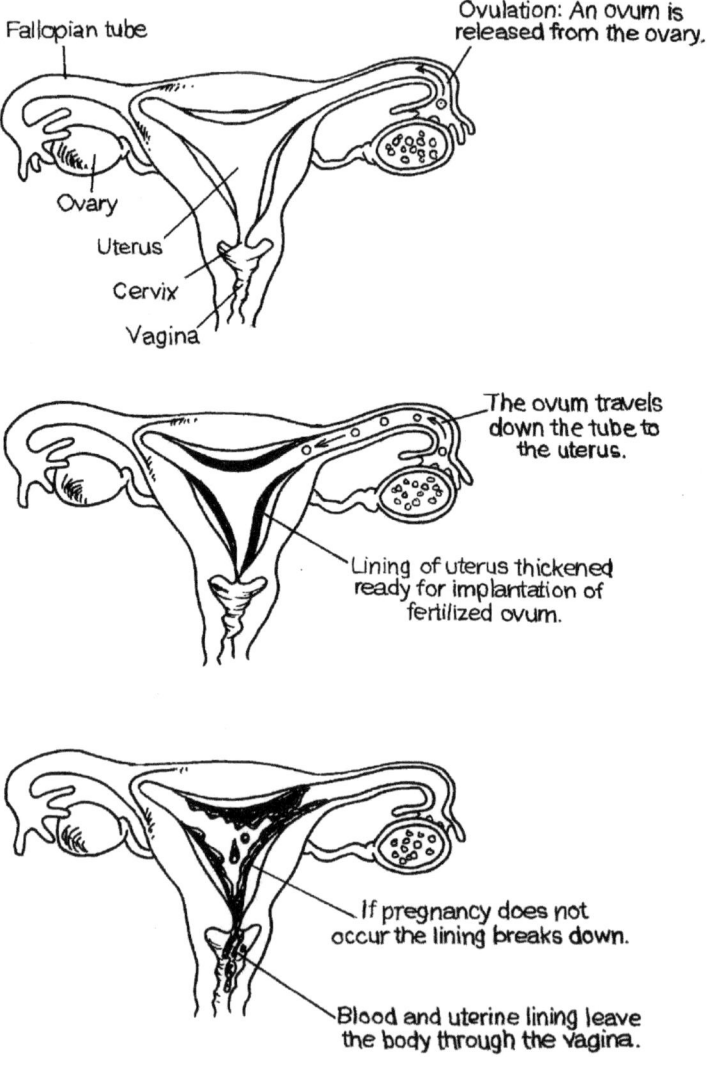

WHEN DO PERIODS BEGIN?

The average age for periods to start is somewhere between ten and 14 years old. Very occasionally, a girl may be a little younger or older than this. Usually, your first period happens about one to two years after you first notice changes in your breasts (see the earlier section on breast development). Whatever age you are, you will probably have experienced several of the other puberty changes too, such as a growth spurt and weight gain, a change in your shape (wider hips, narrower waist), oilier skin and hair, and the growth of pubic and underarm hair. Most girls will also experience mood swings, which often become slightly worse immediately before the first period.

To begin with, periods are almost always irregular. That is, they don't happen once every month, like clockwork. Most girls will find that their periods will take some months, even years, to settle into a regular, predictable pattern. So you might have a period lasting for a few days (anything between two and eight days is perfectly normal), and then not have another one for two or three months. Or the next one could come only two or three weeks later. It is very unpredictable at first – and this can go on for the first year or two at least.

Eventually, however, it is very likely that your periods will become regular, almost to the point that you will be able to predict when you will have your next one. For most women, their regular cycle is somewhere between 21 and 32 days. The length of a cycle is the number of days from the first day of one period to the first day of the next one.

KEEPING TRACK OF PERIODS

You will need to use a calendar or diary to do this. Simply record when you start a period each time, and eventually you will be able to see whether there is any pattern. You can record more detail if you want, such as how many days the period lasts, how 'heavy'* it is (i.e. how much blood loss there is), and any other details, such as how your mood is on each day, and whether you experience any pain or discomfort (see next section). If you do this for a few months, the information you gather can help you see what is normal for you, and certainly helps you to be prepared for your period each time.

WHAT HAPPENS DURING A PERIOD?

A small amount of blood slowly leaves your body through your vagina, for a few days. Although it may feel like a lot, the amount of blood and uterine lining that leaves your body is probably only about the equivalent of half to one cupful over the whole period, and only about three tablespoons of this is blood. The rest is uterine tissue and secretions.

Often, it begins with a few 'spots' of brownish-coloured blood, which gradually become redder and increases in amount during the next two or three days. Some girls begin straight away with a trickle of red blood. In both cases, it eventually decreases in amount, until it completely disappears after about five days. However, as already mentioned, some girls only bleed for two days, while others have a much longer period – perhaps seven or eight days. It can vary from one month to the next even in the same girl, though most girls eventually settle into a pattern that is typical for them, and tend to have periods that last for roughly the same number of days each month.

There is very little feeling as the blood leaves your body, though on the 'heavier' days, you might be aware of a slight trickling sensation.

DEALING WITH PERIOD PAIN

Some girls may experience *period pain*, which is a certain amount of discomfort, usually at the beginning of the period, for a few hours, or even for the first day or two. This can be a slight cramping sensation in your lower abdomen, or sometimes a backache. In most cases, the discomfort

---

*   Whether a period is 'heavy' or 'light' is very much a matter of individual opinion. Most women experience their greatest blood loss in the first two or three days of their period. For some this may mean using super pads or tampons, which need to be changed every two to three hours. Other women have much lighter flows, and may only ever need to use regular or mini pads or tampons, even during the first two or three days.

is not enough to interfere with your normal activities. Some girls find that taking a mild painkiller (such as paracetamol or some of the medication specifically for period pain available from the pharmacist) is enough to help them deal with the cramps. If you are at home, then sitting with your knees curled up or holding a hot water bottle to your abdomen can be soothing. Some girls find that doing some gentle exercise is helpful, while others prefer to sit still and relax. It is a matter of trial and error, and finding what works best for you. If the pain is bad enough to interfere with your normal activities, then it is advisable to see the doctor, as there may be other treatment that he or she can recommend.

PRE-MENSTRUAL SYNDROME

You may find that in the few days leading up to your period you feel especially tearful, tired or tense, perhaps becoming irritated very easily, or maybe you suffer from headaches or a feeling of bloatedness in your abdomen. All these are possible symptoms of *pre-menstrual syndrome* (PMS), and are due to the changing levels of hormones in your body at this time. Not all women experience PMS, but those who do report a wide range of symptoms, from clumsiness and forgetfulness to pimples and breast tenderness, and even food cravings. For a few women, the symptoms can be quite severe, though in most cases they are mild, and may even go unnoticed. In nearly all cases, symptoms of PMS disappear quite suddenly once the period starts.

Managing PMS

There are steps you can take to minimize some of the more common symptoms of PMS.

- You can ease bloatedness and breast tenderness, which are often caused by fluid retention, by reducing salt in your diet.
- Drink plenty of water.
- Try to eat healthy, regular meals, keeping the portions fairly small. If you want to snack in between meals, make these healthy too – fresh or dried fruit and unsalted nuts make good snacks. Try to avoid too much salty, fatty or sugary food.

- Some people find that vitamin supplements are helpful – the pharmacist will be able to advise you about these.

- Get plenty of exercise. This really helps the more emotional symptoms, such as mood swings, anxiety and even tiredness.

- Try to get enough sleep and relaxation as well.

All of these measures are good for your general health every day, but will certainly help to reduce any symptoms of PMS. Remember, most women manage very well, and don't find that PMS interferes with their lives very much at all. If you find that your symptoms are very severe, and interfering with your life, then it is a good idea to go to the doctor, who will be able to suggest some treatment.

MANAGING PERIODS

These days it is very easy indeed for girls and women to manage their periods. All it requires is for you to protect your clothing by wearing either a *sanitary pad* (otherwise known as a pad, a napkin or a towel) or a *tampon.*

Sanitary pads

These are disposable pads made of absorbent cotton that are worn inside your underwear, against your vulva. They are backed with plastic to prevent blood leaking through to your underwear, and usually have an adhesive strip to attach them to your underwear and keep them in place. Once in place, a pad will absorb the blood as it leaves your vagina.

Using sanitary pads:

- You will need to change the pad every four hours or so (it may be more often while your flow is heavier, and less often once it has begun to ease).

- Go to the toilet, making sure you take a new pad with you.

- Remove the used pad, and wrap it in toilet paper before throwing it in the bin (wastebasket). In public toilets, and school toilets, you will find a disposal bin next to the toilet. In private houses, you will need to find out where people keep their bin – sometimes there is one beside the toilet or in the bathroom, but sometimes you will need to take the wrapped-up pad out to the

Sanitary pads

Pad with wings

Pad without wings

Wrapped pad

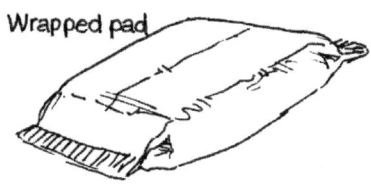

garbage bin. If you are too shy to ask someone where the bin is, then take the wrapped-pad home with you – but don't forget to dispose of it once you get home!

- *Never* try to flush the pad down the toilet. It will block the toilet and require someone to call the plumber – this can be very awkward, possibly embarrassing and almost certainly expensive.

- Fit the new pad. This is easy – simply unwrap it, remove the backing paper from the adhesive strip, and attach the sticky side of the pad to the crotch of your underwear. Throw the paper into the bin – or you can use the paper from the new pad to wrap up the old one before you throw it away.

Fitting a Pad

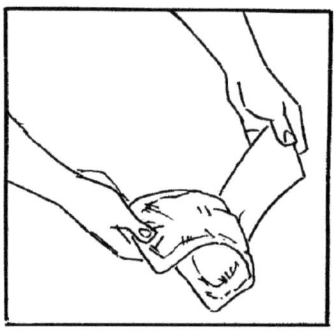

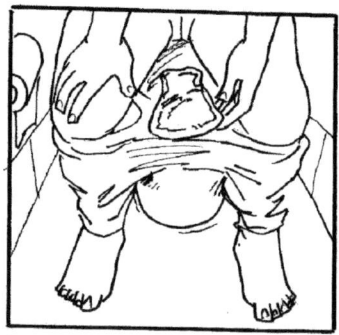

Sanitary pads are generally thin enough that no one will know you are wearing one (though it probably would show under tight jeans, or in a leotard or similar tight clothing for ballet or gymnastics, in which case you might consider wearing a tampon). And as long as you change your pad regularly there will be no unpleasant odour.

Pads come in a variety of thicknesses and sizes, to suit your flow. There are mini, regular, super and overnight pads, and all of these have an 'ultra-thin' option if you want. They also come with or without 'wings', which are extensions on the side of the pad to wrap around the crotch of your underwear (the purpose is to prevent any leaking of blood on to the elastic of your underwear). The overnight pads are longer and more absorbent, so that you don't have to worry about leaking on to the sheets while you are asleep.

It is really only by trial and error that you will work out exactly which style and size of pad suits you best, and is the most comfortable for you. You may want a couple of different sizes, to suit your flow on different days of your period.

Tampons

These are small, compacted wads of absorbent cotton, shaped a little like a lipstick, which are used inside your vagina to absorb the blood before it leaves your body. They are inserted into your vagina with an applicator, or by using your finger. There is a string attached very firmly to the end of the tampon to assist removal. Once a tampon is correctly in place in the vagina, you can't feel it. Sometimes girls worry that a tampon might get lost inside them. This is impossible! As you know from Chapter 1, **Your Body**, the vagina is only about 8–10 cm long, ending at the cervix (the opening to the uterus), which is only a tiny opening – about the width of a matchstick. There is no way that a tampon can pass through the cervix.

Tampons come in different sizes and absorbencies to suit your menstrual flow (mini, regular and super – and in some countries, super-plus), so you don't need to worry about blood leaking. However, if you are concerned that you might leak (perhaps because you are out somewhere,

Tampons

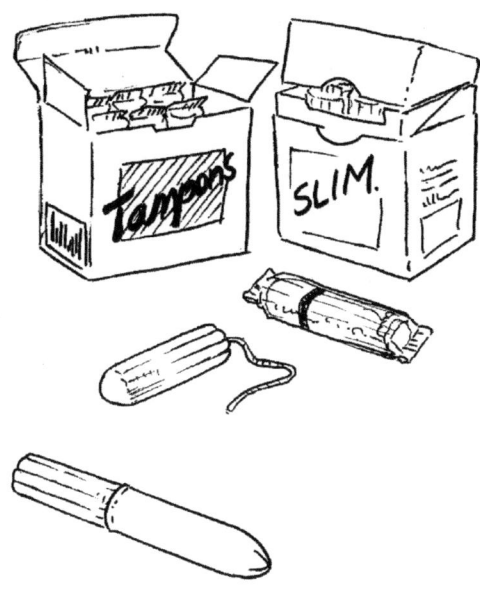

and might not be able to get to the toilet when you need to, for example), you can always wear a mini pad as extra protection. It takes a bit of trial and error to discover which size of tampon is best for you at each stage of your period, but the general rule is to use the smallest one that does the job, to avoid the possibility of getting a condition called *Toxic Shock syndrome* (see later section).

Inserting a tampon:

- Tampons need to be changed every four to six hours. Never leave one in for longer than eight hours; again, this is important in order to minimize the possibility of Toxic Shock syndrome.

- Wash your hands before inserting a tampon, especially when you are using your finger. This means that, if you are using the toilet

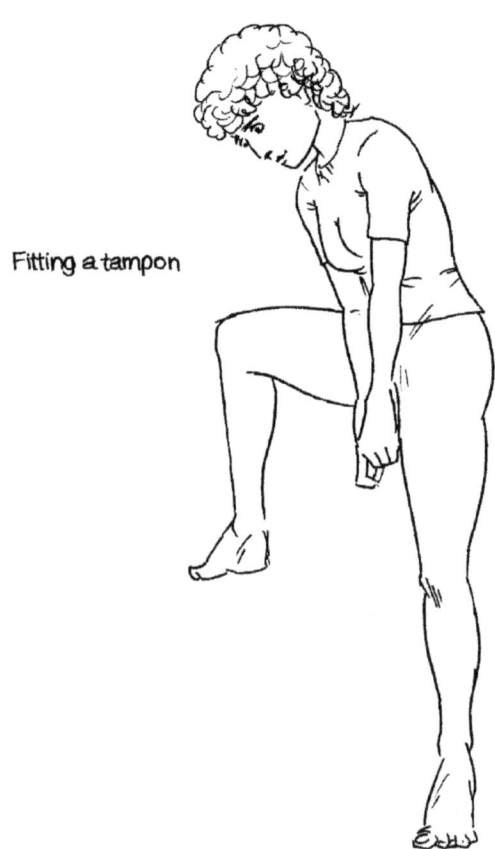

Fitting a tampon

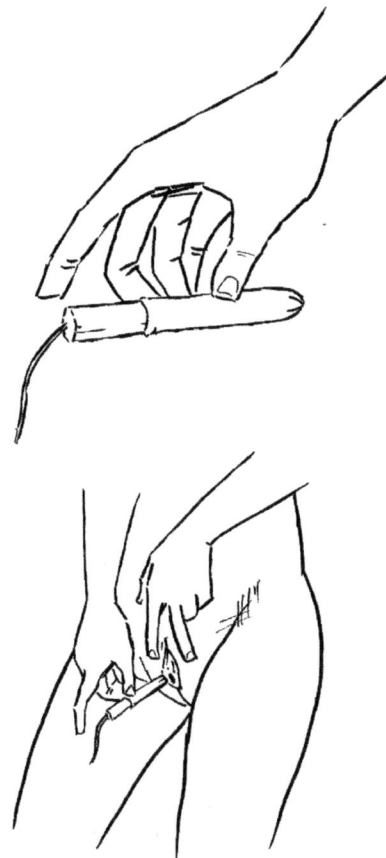

after you have removed your tampon, you should wash your hands before inserting the next one.

- Remove the outer wrapping of the tampon and throw it in the bin.

- *To insert a tampon that has an applicator:* find a position that is comfortable (some girls sit on the toilet, others find it easier to stand, perhaps with one leg up on the toilet seat) and insert the cardboard tube of the applicator about 2 cm into your vagina. Gently push the inner tube into the outer tube as far as it can go, which then places the tampon comfortably in the right position in your vagina. Remember, your vagina slopes slightly backwards, so you push the tampon in as if towards the small of your back, not straight up towards your chin.

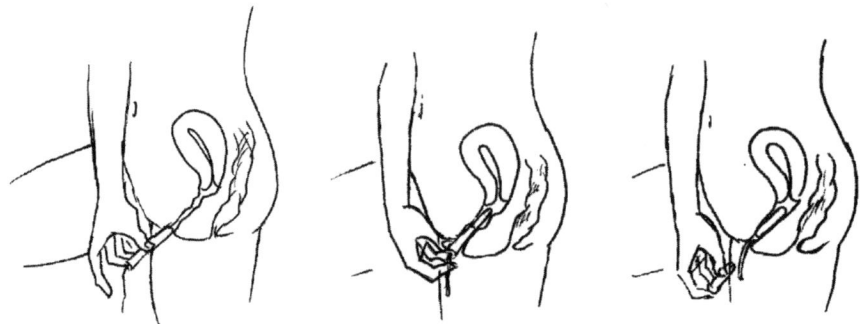

- Once the tampon is in place, pull back the cardboard applicator tube and throw it in the bin.

- *To insert a tampon with your finger:* find a position that you find comfortable, as above, and insert the end of the tampon gently into your vagina. Unravel the string from the bottom end of the tampon, and then with your finger push the tampon upwards and slightly backwards as far as it will go, until you can't feel it.

With both applicator and non-applicator tampons, you will see the string coming out of your vagina. This makes it easy to remove the tampon later on.

You might be a little nervous about inserting a tampon the very first time. If this is the case, remember it will be easier if you are as relaxed as possible. Take your time (don't choose to fit a tampon for the first time if you are in a rush to go somewhere), and make sure you have plenty of light and can see what you are doing. All tampons come with an easy-to-use instruction leaflet, so you may find it helpful to refer to the diagrams.

If your vagina feels a little dry, and you feel as though the tampon won't go in, wait until your menstrual flow is greater, as your vagina is more open and well-lubricated then. Otherwise, you could try lubricating the end of the tampon with a little saliva (spit), petroleum jelly or a drop of lubricating gel, such as *K-Y Jelly*, available from the chemist (drugstore). If you don't succeed the first time, don't worry. Try again when you feel more relaxed. It takes practice to insert tampons, but eventually it becomes very easy.

Removing a tampon:

- Simply pull gently on the string. If it doesn't come out easily, and feels very dry, it may not have absorbed very much blood, and can probably be left in a little longer (as long as it hasn't already been in for more than about six to eight hours). This is why it is important to use the smallest tampon you can that does the job. For example, you almost certainly won't need a super tampon towards the end of your period – it would only absorb a very small amount of blood relative to its size, and would be very dry and difficult to remove. A mini tampon would be much more appropriate at this stage. Again, you will discover through trial and error what size of tampon suits your needs best at different stages of your period.

- Wrap up the used tampon in toilet paper, as you would a pad, and dispose of it in the bin. Although tampons can be flushed down the toilet, this isn't ideal from an environmental point of view, and definitely shouldn't be done if the toilet flushes out to a septic tank.

Are pads or tampons better?

This is very much a case of personal preference. Many women use both, at different times of the period. For example, you might use tampons most of the time, but a pad at night; or you might prefer pads most of the time, but wear a tampon for sport, swimming or dancing. Many girls start off wearing pads until they become more confident about their periods. However, there is no reason why you can't wear tampons from the beginning, if you choose. (See Table 2.1 for comparison.)

Once you become familiar with them, both pads and tampons are comfortable to wear, hygienic, and easy to use and dispose of.

Toxic Shock syndrome

This is a very rare, but serious, bacterial infection. Anyone can get *Toxic Shock syndrome* (TSS), including men and children. It can occur when bacteria are able to enter the body via a wound or surgical incision, but it has also been found to occur in women who use high-absorbency tampons, or who have left a tampon in for too long while having their period.

Table 2.1 Comparison of pads and tampons

	Advantages	Disadvantages
Pads	• Easy to use, especially when you are just starting • Allow you to become familiar with the amount of blood you may lose at different times of the period • Can be more comfortable than tampons if you get cramps • Some women prefer not to insert something into their vagina	• Bulkier than tampons to carry around • You can't wear a pad with very tight clothing, such as tight jeans or leotards • You can't go swimming while wearing a pad • Slight risk of odour if pads aren't changed frequently enough
Tampons	• Very comfortable once you are confident about using them (you can't feel them at all if they are inserted properly) • Small and therefore easy to carry around, even fitting in something as small as a coin purse • Don't show at all under clothing • You are able to swim while wearing a tampon • Much less chance of body odour, because the blood is absorbed into the tampon inside your body	• Take more practice to get used to • Can be uncomfortable if you suffer from menstrual cramps • Very slight risk of Toxic Shock syndrome

The symptoms of toxic shock include a high fever, vomiting, muscle aches and pains, headache, a rash and diarrhoea. Any woman who experiences these severe symptoms while she is having her period (and using tampons) should remove the tampon immediately and see her doctor.

The best ways to avoid the risk of TSS (and remember, it is very rare) are to change your tampons regularly, be careful about hygiene and always use the smallest tampon you possibly can. There is no need to use a super-absorbency tampon unless you have a particularly heavy flow.

And remember to remove the last tampon that you wear during your period. This one can be easy to forget, as you have almost finished bleeding and therefore won't be reminded by any blood leaking past the tampon.

BEING PREPARED FOR PERIODS

Before periods begin

You may not have started your periods yet, but are perhaps wondering when you will, and what to do to be prepared. Remember, periods are usually one of the last changes of puberty, following breast development, the growth of pubic and underarm hair and the widening of your hips. In the weeks leading up to your first period, you will have a surge of hormones. This has the effect of causing more noticeable mood swings, skin changes (lots of women get an outbreak of pimples just before a period) and an increase in vaginal secretions. In other words, if you are observant, you will see the warning signs.

Talk to your parent or carer if you think your periods may be on the way. The chances are they will have noticed the obvious changes in you, and be thinking the same thing! Go out together and buy a supply of pads: get a couple of different types (e.g. mini and regular pads) and some overnight pads. Keep a supply in your school bag, together with some clean underwear, and perhaps a travel pack of wipes. So that you can keep these in your schoolbag as discreetly as possible, you may choose to use a zip pencil case or a plastic lunchbox, but a toiletry bag would do just as well.

Even before periods start, it can be very helpful to practise wearing pads from time to time, both during the day and over night. This helps you to get used to the feeling of them, and also gives you the opportunity to learn how to fit and dispose of them.

Getting caught out

However well-prepared and organized you are, there are sure to be times, for whatever reason, when your period begins and you don't have any sanitary supplies with you. What can you do?

- Borrow from a friend.
- Buy a pad or tampon from a dispenser in a public toilet.

- Call home and get your parent or carer to bring you what you need.

- Go to the school office or sick room, where they will almost certainly keep emergency supplies. If you are embarrassed about telling the teacher, office staff member or school nurse, write it down on a piece of paper – 'I've just started my period. I need a pad'.

- Use a wad of folded toilet paper temporarily. This will help, but not for very long. You will still need to organize getting a pad fairly quickly.

- Best of all, try to always have some sort of sanitary wear with you at all times. A panty liner (or an ultra-thin pad) is very small and discreet, and can even fit in your wallet.

- Be aware of your body changes and try to be prepared for the start of your periods (see above section). If you have already started periods, keep track of them in a diary so that you are aware when your next one is due.

What to do if you leak

You are bound to experience occasions when you leak some blood – all women do; perhaps your period begins unexpectedly, or is heavier than you are prepared for. Sometimes you can't get to a toilet quickly enough to change your pad or tampon. Here are some hints for avoiding or dealing with these situations.

- Change your pad or tampon just as soon as you can, to prevent any more leakage.

- Always change your pads or tampons regularly.

- Consider wearing tampons together with pads, especially on heavy days.

- If you have leaked onto your clothes, try to change them as soon as possible. Blood comes out of clothing more easily if it has had less time to set.

- Blood stains are removed most effectively with *cold* water (hot water sets the stain).

- If you can't change your clothes immediately, and you have a mark on your skirt or pants, tie a jumper or jacket around your waist to hide the stain.

- Wear darker-coloured clothing and underwear during your period. This helps to disguise any leaks if they do happen.

Emotional and social changes at puberty

There is so much happening to your body as you go through puberty, it is easy to forget that hormones have a big effect on how you feel as well. Adolescence can be a time of intense feelings, with most boys and girls experiencing mood swings, feelings of uncertainty and insecurity, and changes in the way they feel about their friends and families. Many young people will also experience strong sexual feelings for the first time. But it is important to be aware that, just as with the variation in the timing of physical changes at puberty, emotional changes are not the same for everyone, nor do they happen at the same time. If you don't experience some of the changes in the way they are described in the next few sections, don't worry. Everyone is different. It can be helpful, in any case, to have an explanation as to what might be happening to your friends and classmates – at least you can understand why the world seems to be going mad around you!

Mood swings

Your mood is very much affected by your hormones, and as the levels rise and fall, so does your mood. One moment you may be feeling cheerful, confident, energetic and full of life and laughter; then suddenly, almost without warning, your mood dips, leaving you feeling sad, uncertain, tearful and angry. This can be difficult for other people to deal with, but it is especially difficult for you. Unfortunately, you have very little control over this, and there isn't a lot you can do other than recognize what is happening, 'go with the flow' and enjoy the times when you feel 'up'. A bad mood will pass of its own accord, though there are a few things you can do to hurry it along a bit. Some of these ideas are discussed in Chapter 5, **Understanding Emotions**, and include things such as taking time out to be by yourself, vigorous exercise of some sort or even hitting your pillow or a punch bag. Look at the suggestions on pages 153–154, and see if you can come up with any more ways to manage your mood swings.

Independence

As you go through adolescence it is quite likely that you will want to become increasingly responsible for aspects of your life. You may want to be able to choose what time you go to bed, what clothes you will wear, who you go out with, where you will go and so on. Sometimes this desire for independence causes clashes with your parents, who are worried about whether you are ready for certain responsibilities. It can make you angry and resentful when they say 'no' to some requests. Usually this is not because they want to make your life difficult, but because they are concerned for your safety and well-being. Having a tantrum, being rude and slamming doors is not the way to get what you want if you're looking for independence – it is more likely to prove to your parents that you are definitely *not* ready! Alternatively, by discussing issues calmly and sensibly, and perhaps reaching some sort of compromise, you can demonstrate to your parents that you *are* ready for a certain amount of responsibility. It takes time for parents to adjust to your readiness for independence. It is said, jokingly – though there is often some truth in it – that, when it comes to the issue of independence, young people see themselves as two years older than they really are, while parents see them as two years younger than they are. You can see how this results in conflict.

Changing feelings towards parents

Many young people, particularly in early adolescence, feel irritated and often very embarrassed by their families, especially their parents. Not everyone feels this way, but many do. Everything your parents do or say makes you annoyed, and suddenly it is not okay for them to come to school, certainly not to enter the classroom. It is not okay to be seen with your parents in public – and it is *especially* not okay for parents to show physical affection towards you in public. You may be like many other young people, and find everything your parents do or say deeply embarrassing (though, interestingly, you will probably find you are not at all embarrassed by someone else's parents!).

This stage does serve a function – it is a way for you to 'grow away' from your parents, to achieve independence. But even though you will inevitably be in conflict with your parents from time to time, don't dismiss them altogether. They have a good knowledge of life and sexual matters, and can be the best people to turn to when you have questions or concerns about growing up. Don't forget they were teenagers once, going through many of the things you are going through now. Try asking them about their own experiences of growing up. This not only helps you to understand them better, it also reminds your parents how it feels to be an adolescent, which can make them more understanding of you.

Whether you talk to your mum or your dad is a matter of personal choice. There is no rule that 'girls must talk to mum' and 'boys must talk to dad'. The best thing is to talk to the parent you feel most comfortable with – and when it comes to sexual issues, this can be the parent who is most at ease with this topic.

Once you are through puberty and adolescence, any embarrassment or anger you may have felt about your parents tends to disappear, and arguments and conflicts become fewer and fewer. By the time you become an adult, you will probably find plenty of common ground with one or both of your parents, and be able to form a close, mature friendship with them.

Changing friendships

You will find that, gradually, as you go through adolescence, your attitude to friendship changes. Bit by bit you will notice that you and the people around you are becoming more interested in friends as emotional support – someone to talk to about one another's worries and concerns – than simply someone to play with because you like the same activities.

However, these developments happen at different times for different people (just like all the changes at puberty), which means that some young people 'grow apart' from their friends. While you, for example, may still want to play the same games and pursue the same interests, your friends may be wanting to 'hang around' with other friends, just talking and joking. A lot of young teenagers at this stage enjoy spending most of their free time simply communicating with friends – text messaging, phoning and talking to friends online. If you are not yet at this stage, this can seem quite pointless and boring.

In addition to this increasing interest in seemingly endless communication with each other, many young people are also showing an interest in having a boyfriend or girlfriend. This is partly a result of the increased levels of sex hormones in the body, which can cause quite strong sexual feelings (see following section).

All of these changes can mean that some friendships break up, because two people who were friends find they are no longer interested in the same things – but new friendships form. You may find yourself wanting to spend more time with older or younger people who may show more of an interest in the things you like. It can be a difficult time, when you may feel insecure, and sometimes even jealous of your friends because of the way they are moving on, or confused as to why they are no longer interested in the same things as you.

The important thing is to be aware that most young people go through times of insecurity, and very few people are as confident as they might appear. Try to find someone you can talk to, such as an older brother or sister, or a parent – or someone you trust and feel comfortable with. They will be able to help you understand what is going on with your friends and classmates, and help you to feel good about yourself, especially when your friends seem to be giving you a hard time.

For more information and ideas about friendships during adolescence, see Chapter 6, **Friendships**.

Sexual feelings

Although some people don't experience sexual feelings, and some others don't become aware of them until much later in adolescence, a lot of young people first experience these new and unfamiliar feelings during puberty. They are caused by the increased levels of sex hormones in your body at this time. Some young people have described them as 'tingly' or 'squirmy' feelings, particularly around the genital area, and in the lower abdomen, often accompanied by general feelings of excitement. For a boy, sexual feelings usually result in an erection of his penis, which makes it quite obvious to him what is happening. For a girl, though, the signs are less obvious, though she might be aware of a slight 'wetness' at the opening to her vagina. To read more about sexual feelings, see Chapter 7, **Sex**.

SEXUAL ATTRACTION

Puberty is the time when many young people experience 'crushes' – those 'tingly' feelings of sexual attraction to another person – for the first time. You may find that when you are around a particular person, you feel extra aware of them, and slightly nervous or excited. Sometimes you may find particular parts of their body fascinating and attractive (e.g. breasts, legs, eyes, hands or hair). You may find yourself thinking about this person all the time, and perhaps even thinking you might be in love with them. Very often these feelings don't lead to anything, and you don't need to mention them to the person you are attracted to (although you may choose to tell your closest friends or someone in your family). It can be good just to enjoy these feelings privately and be reassured that you are a normal, healthy adolescent.

Crushes are a very normal part of early adolescence. You can have a crush on someone without it developing into a relationship, yet, at the same time, it can be a good way to explore these unfamiliar feelings of attraction. Sometimes you might have a crush on someone you are never likely to meet or get to know – such as a music or sports star. You may simply enjoy daydreaming about this person, or admiring their poster on your bedroom wall – and, of course, it's easy to end the 'relationship' when you are no longer interested in them – you just take down the poster!

As you get older, these feelings of attraction can motivate you to get to know the other person better. This may result in you developing a genuine friendship with them, or it may even become a sexual relationship. For more ideas about what is involved in a relationship, and how to start one, see Chapter 8, **Sexual Relationships**.

SAME-SEX ATTRACTION

Don't be concerned if you find yourself becoming fascinated by, and developing a crush on, a person of the same sex as yourself. This might be a friend, or someone older, such as a school leader, or a friend of an older brother or sister. Often the attraction starts because you admire this person in some way. Perhaps they are particularly talented at something, or have been especially nice to you. You may find yourself daydreaming about being in a friendship or relationship with them. Usually, a same-sex crush doesn't turn into a real (sexual) relationship, though sometimes a friendship may develop.

Same-sex crushes are very common during puberty, and do not predict whether you will be heterosexual or homosexual when you grow up (see Chapter 7, **Sex**). They are really just part of your developing sexual feelings, and a normal part of growing up for many people. They allow you to experience sexual feelings and fantasies in a safe way, without having to negotiate a real relationship.

It is worth noting here that if these strong same-sex feelings continue, and you start to believe that you may be *gay* or *lesbian* (the commonly used terms for male and female homosexuals), it is a very good idea to talk to an adult you trust about your feelings. Sometimes it is best to talk to a professional who is sympathetic to homosexual issues. School counsellors can be very helpful, as can telephone help-lines for young people (check your local telephone directory).

MASTURBATION

Masturbation is when a person touches his or her own genitals (particularly the penis or clitoris) in a way that feels very nice to them, in response to sexual feelings and thoughts. (See Chapter 7, **Sex**, for more details about masturbation.)

Because it is a very private activity, you need to work out where it is okay to masturbate. A lot of people choose to masturbate alone in their bedroom, with the door closed, making sure that no one is likely to come walking in suddenly. If you share a bedroom with someone, it is *not* okay to masturbate while they are in the room, even if you think they might have gone to sleep! It may be that the only private places to masturbate are the bathroom or the toilet – again, it is very important to make sure that you really are in private, and that no one is going to disturb you. Most important, remember that you must *never* masturbate in a public place (and this includes public toilets, which are *not* considered to be private places) where other people are likely to see you, as this is against the law.

There is no 'normal' frequency for masturbation. Some young people go through a stage of having very strong sexual urges for a while, probably because there are very high levels of hormones in their bodies at this time, and they may want to masturbate every day. Other people don't get such strong urges, and may only masturbate very occasionally, or perhaps never.

Masturbation is a very normal activity for men and women, boys and girls, and is not rude or dirty. However, some people have strong personal or religious beliefs that it is not okay, and therefore they may choose never to do it for this reason. The American comedian, Woody Allen, is reputed to have said 'Masturbation is safe sex with someone you love'! It certainly *is* safe – but because it is private, it is something you would rarely talk about with other people. It is, however, a very healthy way to release sexual feelings, and a great way to learn about your own body, and what you like sexually, as you are growing up.

3

Caring for Your Body

It's quite easy to be clean and healthy when you're little – all the decisions are made for you. But once you get to puberty, all sorts of responsibilities that used to be your parents' or carers' become yours – such as washing, keeping your hair looking good, choosing your own clothes, deciding what you want to eat and when you want to go to bed and so on. Of course, your parents continue to have some say in all this while you are getting used to becoming more responsible. And mothers are very good at telling you that you look a mess, or that you don't smell nice! But your personal hygiene and your appearance have to become your responsibility eventually.

In addition to personal hygiene, there are other factors involved in how you look – such as whether or not you shave, wear make-up or even have a tattoo or a nose stud. There can be a great deal of peer pressure among young people about these matters, and almost certainly strong opinions from your parents and carers. It can be quite difficult to know how to make these decisions sometimes.

Many of these choices affect the way you feel about yourself, and can even affect your health, so it's important that you choose wisely. This chapter is about all these choices, and how you can make the healthiest choices possible to keep you looking and feeling good.

Keeping your body clean

Most people like to shower or bath at least once a day, and these days that's quite easy to do, as nearly everyone has access to good washing facilities. Regular washing isn't just a good idea because your mother tells you it is. It's essential for your good health. Every day you are exposed to dirt and dust in the air, and your skin sheds dead cells all the time. In addition to the dirt and skin cells that accumulate on your body every day, you also have sweat, secretions, and even traces of urine and faeces from when you go to the toilet. You can see that all of this needs to be washed off on a regular basis if your skin and hair are to be healthy, and you are to look and smell good.

Your body is covered with millions of glands that produce sweat in response to heat. As the sweat, which consists mainly of water and salt, evaporates from your skin, it has the effect of cooling you down. But as we learnt in Chapter 2, **Puberty**, at puberty the sweat glands under your arms and in the groin area become active. They respond to sexual arousal, nervousness and anger, as well as to heat. This sweat is made up of proteins and fatty acids, and, although not unpleasant smelling when it is fresh, quickly becomes unpleasant, due to the action of bacteria. This is the smell that is commonly referred to as *body odour*, or *BO*.

It may be that you can't really see the point of worrying about whether you are clean and pleasant-smelling or not; *but other people do care*, and you may be rejected by your friends and become the target of teasing or bullying if you smell bad. If you care about being included, and having friends, or even a girlfriend or boyfriend, then one very simple thing you can do to help this process is wash yourself thoroughly every day.

Managing body odour

The parts of your body that need particular attention when you wash, in terms of body odour, are the back of your neck, your underarms, your groin area and your feet. This means that it isn't enough to just stand in the shower, letting the water cascade over you, and then pretend to yourself that you have had a proper wash! You have to actively wash yourself, using soap and probably some sort of washcloth (though it's possible to wash most of your body just using your hands – and soap).

ALL OVER YOUR BODY

There is a huge range of toiletries available for washing, including regular soap, cleansing bars, liquid body washes and so on. It's easy to find one that you like the feel and smell of, even if you have sensitive skin, along with washcloths, sponges or washing mitts to apply the soap. Rub the soap all over your body, not forgetting the back of your neck, and then take care to rinse it all off before you climb out of the shower or bath.

UNDERARMS

When your underarm area is washed and dry, you will need to apply deodorant. There are various types available, including sticks, roll-ons, crystals and sprays. Some of these are straightforward deodorants, which means that they act to remove or disguise the smell of body odour; and some also include an anti-perspirant, which is a substance designed to minimize the amount of perspiration (sweat) you produce. There is also a huge variety of scents available in deodorants – some are quite highly perfumed and some are unscented. The only way you will know what works best for you is to try different ones until you find one you really like. But even if you find one with a scent you enjoy, it's important to understand that you can't expect to smell nice if you apply deodorant to sweaty, smelly armpits. It only works properly to minimize the smell of body odour if your armpits are clean when you apply it.

If sweating is a problem for you, in addition to washing carefully and using an appropriate deodorant you might want to consider the type of clothing you wear. It's best to wear loose-fitting clothes made from natural fibres, such as cotton, wool or silk, as these allow your skin to breathe, and keep sweating to a minimum. Synthetic fabrics and tight-fitting clothes, on the other hand, don't allow your skin to breathe and tend to make sweating worse.

GROIN

You need to take particular care with this part of your body. Some people are quite sensitive to soap, and find they become itchy if they use it. An alternative is a mild, unscented soap, baby soap, or a mild cleansing bar.

Even plenty of warm water, without any cleansing product, can work well. The main thing is that you wash gently but thoroughly around your genitals at least once every day.

- *Boys*: you need to wash your penis and scrotum. If you are not circumcised, you should pull back the foreskin gently, to wash stale smegma (see Chapter 1, **Your Body**) from the head of the penis. Wash the pubic hair thoroughly, as traces of urine can linger here after you have been to the toilet. Don't forget to wash your anus and around your buttocks as well.

- *Girls*: you should wash carefully in between the folds of the labia to clean away vaginal secretions and any residue of the smegma that is produced by the glands around the clitoris. Wash your pubic hair, and also your anus and around your buttocks. It is especially important to be thorough with your washing when you have your period, as your genital area can sweat a little more when you are wearing a pad, and dried blood can have a slight odour as well. Some girls and women like to freshen up with baby wipes, or the specially designed wipes that will flush down the toilet. You can use these at any time, not just when you have your period. Just be careful *not* to use highly perfumed sprays, or even the sprays and deodorants that are supposedly designed for use around the genital area. These are quite harsh, and can cause a change in the delicate balance of the good bacteria that keep your vagina healthy, and this in turn can lead to an infection.

- *Wiping yourself after the toilet*: it may seem strange, but if you are female there is a proper way to do this! When you have used the toilet, you should wipe with toilet paper from the front to the back, rather than the other way round. By doing this, you will avoid transferring bacteria from the anus to either the vagina or the urethra; this minimizes the risk of both urinary tract and vaginal infections.

- *Boys and girls*: whether you are a girl or a boy, your groin area will sweat a lot less if you wear underwear that is made of natural fibres, such as cotton. Underwear made from synthetic fibres not only increases sweating, which can make you feel itchy and uncomfortable, and more likely to smell, but in girls and women it can be one of the contributing factors to a fungal infection called *thrush* (see Chapter 9, **Looking After Your Sexual Health**). You may not be able to avoid wearing synthetic fabrics against your groin sometimes; for example, you may have to swim a lot, or play sports. Panty-hose (tights) can also be irritating to some women. The main thing is that you don't spend all day in synthetic clothing if you can avoid it. Try to give your body a chance to 'breathe' for a few hours each day. When you go to bed, you can wear very loose cotton pyjamas or boxer shorts, or even nothing at all!

FEET

Lots of young people suffer from smelly feet, and find that parents, brothers and sisters – even teachers! – are forever complaining about it. It's quite natural to have sweaty feet, because this is where the majority of your sweat glands are situated, and they do become particularly active at puberty. What happens is that the excessive sweat attracts bacteria. These bacteria eat the sweat and excrete waste; it is this waste that produces the unpleasant odour.

Although it is a natural process, there are things you can do to help minimize the bad smell.

- Wash your feet at least once a day, taking care to wash in between the toes. If you have a serious problem with smelly feet, use an anti-bacterial soap. You might need to consider washing your feet more than once a day, especially in hot weather, and if you play sports.

- Dry your feet properly after you have washed them, especially in between the toes. This helps to prevent itchiness and fungal infections.

- There are foot powders that you can shake onto your feet and in between the toes to keep your feet dry, and help reduce sweating. You can even shake a little inside your shoes.

- If you are putting on socks, make sure they are clean.

- If possible, don't wear the same shoes every day. If you have a real problem with smelly feet, it's really helpful to have two pairs of shoes that you alternate. Give each pair at least 24 hours to air before wearing them again.

- There are anti-bacterial sprays you can apply to the inside of the shoes while they aren't in use.

To reduce the amount of sweat you produce try the following.

- Wear well-ventilated leather shoes. Because leather is natural, it allows your feet to 'breathe', whereas plastic or other synthetic materials don't, and cause your feet to sweat more.

- Always wear socks when you are wearing closed-in shoes – preferably cotton ones.

- If you are putting socks on after you have washed your feet, always make sure they are clean – don't re-use the ones you just took off.

- Put 'odour-eater' inserts into your shoes.

- Spray your feet, after you have washed them, with a foot anti-perspirant.

All these measures should help to reduce foot odour, and perhaps help to stop people complaining about your smelly feet all the time!

Caring for your skin

This section refers mainly to the care of the skin on your face, though the skin on the rest of your body might need special attention, other than just washing it, from time to time.

Coping with acne

Your face is a very important part of your body when it comes to caring for yourself, as it is the part most on show to the rest of the world. It is also the part most likely to suffer from a condition known as *acne* (spots, pimples, zits). Over 80 per cent of young people experience an occasional outbreak of acne, mostly on the face, and most often during their teenage years, although it can happen at any time of life.

The reason it occurs mostly during adolescence is that your sebaceous glands, which are in the hair follicles just below the surface of the skin,

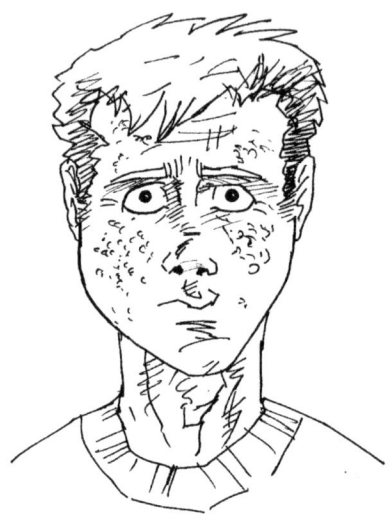

react to testosterone by producing excessive amounts of oil, or *sebum*. As you may remember from Chapter 1, **Your Body**, testosterone is the male hormone responsible for the changes that happen to boys at puberty. But girls also have a certain amount of testosterone, which is why both girls and boys can get acne, though it is slightly more common in boys. Most of the time, the sebaceous glands produce just the right amount of sebum to lubricate your hair and skin. But when the glands become overactive at puberty, the excess sebum, together with dead skin cells, can clog the pores (tiny openings in the skin).

There are different types of pimples, depending on how much sebum is produced, and whether a small infection results. A *whitehead* is when the trapped sebum remains below the skin surface. It results in a small lump that tends to heal up within a couple of days. Sometimes the sebum and dead skin cells break the surface of the skin, and react to the air by turning black. These small spots are known as *blackheads*, and it's very important to understand that the black colouring is not dirt, but darkened oil. When the area becomes infected by bacteria, a small reddish lump may result, sometimes with some pus at the opening of the pore. This is what is most usually referred to as a *pimple*. Sometimes the infection spreads beyond the follicle, under the skin, causing a *nodule*, which is an infected, painful cyst, bigger than a pimple.

Acne can be mild, in that you might get only the occasional outbreak of blackheads or whiteheads, and sometimes a few pus-filled pimples. A number of young people, though, have more severe acne, where they seem to have a continuous outbreak of various types of spots, at different stages of development.

The good news for the majority of people is that acne tends to clear up altogether by the time you become an adult. A few people do continue to have outbreaks occasionally, even as adults; and many women experience pimples just before their period each month.

SOME FACTS ABOUT ACNE

- Acne is not caused by dirt, and the black spot in blackheads is not dirt, but discoloured sebum. In fact, most people with acne are especially diligent about washing their face, and usually have very clean skin.

- Overwashing the face, especially too vigorously, can make acne worse, by drying the skin too much, which stimulates the sebaceous glands to produce more sebum to compensate.

- Acne is not caused by eating fatty or sugary food. However, if that's all you eat, you're not doing yourself any favours. A good, balanced diet, with plenty of vitamins, minerals and proteins (see Chapter 4, **Making Healthy Choices**) may help reduce your acne, and is good for your general health. If you notice that certain foods seem to make your acne worse, try cutting out these foods, and see whether this helps.

- Stress, particularly if it is severe or prolonged, may be linked to new outbreaks of acne, and can worsen existing acne.

- Plenty of sleep, enough exercise and a few glasses of water each day help to keep your stress levels under control, and boost your immune system. Such measures won't necessarily get rid of acne altogether, but they may help the lesions to clear up more quickly.

- Squeezing and picking pimples doesn't actually spread them, though it will probably damage the underlying tissue. This makes it more likely that you will end up with small, permanent scars, so avoid picking and squeezing if you can.

- Excess sweating and humidity may cause acne to flare up in some people. This may be because water, which is present in the sweat, swells the sebum in the duct, causing a complete blockage, which then becomes infected with bacteria. It may be helpful to wash your face after exercise, especially if you have sweated a lot.

- A little bit of sunshine is good for your skin and general good health, but too much causes your skin to become dry or irritated. This has the effect of causing the glands to produce more sebum, thus making the acne worse. Therefore, you should limit your time in the sun, and *always* protect your face with an oil-free sunscreen.

WHAT CAN YOU DO ABOUT ACNE?

First, it is important to keep your face clean to prevent the oil build-up that can contribute to acne. Wash your face each morning and evening with a mild soap and warm water. Be gentle – harsh rubbing may feel like the right thing to do, especially if you are frustrated, but it will actually make things worse.

Don't be brainwashed by all the advertising of skin care products, and feel that you have to have a shelf full of bottles and jars in order to have good skin. Products such as toners and fresheners are unnecessary, as well as expensive – and be aware that when it comes to expense, the cheaper brands from the supermarket are often just as good as more expensive brands.

Some of the cleansers and creams specifically for the treatment of pimples, which are available from the pharmacy, can be helpful, particularly for mild acne, but everybody is different – what works for one person may not work for another. Experiment with different products, but be sure to follow the instructions, and never use more than you are supposed to. You also need to give a cleansing regimen time to work – several weeks at least – rather than chopping and changing every few days, so be patient.

Keep your hair clean and off your face, as long hair falling against your face can irritate the skin, and oil from your hair can clog the pores on your face. Some hair sprays and gels can clog pores, too, so keep these away from your face and try to use make-up and sunscreen that is labelled 'oil-free' or 'non-comedogenic' (i.e. it won't clog your pores and worsen the acne). If you are in doubt, ask the assistant or the chemist when you are buying products. You should change your pillowcase every two or three days, since dirt and oil can settle in it when you sleep. Equally, make sure that you change your towel regularly, and always pat your face dry, rather than rubbing it.

If your acne is moderate or severe, or you are worried about it, it is a good idea to see your doctor. There are various medical treatments available, and no one needs to suffer or feel miserable because of acne. Just remember that most people really don't like having pimples, even when they know they are temporary, so *never, ever* tease anyone about having acne.

The rest of your body

Some people have dry skin, which means that it tends to feel a little 'tight' after your bath or shower. If you find that it's beginning to look dry – a bit flaky, perhaps – you might consider using a body moisturizer, and apply this to the affected areas once you are dry. Moisturizers come in a variety of consistencies and perfumes, including unscented ones. Some are very thick and oily, for very dry skin; others are more milky and are absorbed more easily into the skin. As with any product, it's a matter of reading the label carefully and trying out a few different ones until you find something you like.

If you have a more oily skin, it's unlikely that you will need to use a moisturizing cream. However, you may be prone to getting pimples on your back and shoulders, as there are numerous sebaceous glands under the skin of this part of your body. Washing these areas with an anti-bacterial soap can be quite an effective way to keep these under control, though they can take longer to disappear than pimples on your face. Be gentle when you wash any pimples, whether they're on your back or your face, as harsh scrubbing can actually make them worse.

PROTECTION FROM SUN

Whatever type of skin you have, it needs to be protected from strong sun, as harsh sunlight is known to cause not just premature ageing of the skin, but various types of skin cancer. If you are in a very hot climate where the sun is intense, it's best not to be out in full sun during the middle of the day (even on holiday): the best times are before 10 a.m. and after 3 p.m.

These days, a tanned skin is considered to be sun-damaged, rather than attractive. It is especially important to avoid getting sunburnt, as this is the most damaging to your skin. When you are out in the sun, *always* apply sunscreen to the exposed areas of your skin, making sure it has a high protection factor. If you are swimming, you will need to use a waterproof sunscreen, and be sure to re-apply it regularly. If you live in a very hot climate, and are exposed to strong sunlight every day, you should probably wear a T-shirt or special sun-protection clothing at the beach or swimming pool. And don't forget sunglasses and a hat with a brim that will shade your face.

Sunlight isn't all bad though, and you shouldn't be too paranoid. A certain amount is actually good for you. Vitamin D is produced naturally by the body when the sun's ultraviolet B (UVB) rays strike the skin. Vitamin D is essential for building strong bones and teeth, and for strengthening the immune system. It may even help prevent some cancers.

So, as with so many things in life, it's a matter of moderation. Do get out in the sun sometimes – at least half an hour each day, at a time when the ultraviolet isn't at its most intense – and enjoy it!

Healthy hair

Your hair is most healthy when you eat a good diet, get enough exercise and protect it from too much sun. Getting regular haircuts is another good way to keep your hair looking healthy. Even if you have long hair, or are trying to grow it, a haircut can protect the ends from splitting and becoming damaged. And whether you wear your hair long or short, it looks its very best if it's clean!

Looking after your hair
HINTS FOR HAIR WASHING

- Use enough shampoo to create a good lather. Massage your scalp well to remove oils, dirt and flaky skin.

- Rinse your hair thoroughly in clear water.

- You don't really need conditioner, but it can be helpful if you have long hair, as it makes it easier to comb through.

- Use a wide-toothed comb for wet hair, as it's easier to pull through.

MANAGING OILY HAIR

If you have oily skin, you will probably have oily hair, too. You may find it helps to wash your hair every day, using a mild shampoo specially formulated for oily hair. You probably won't need to use conditioner, but if you do, make sure that it is oil-free. When applying the shampoo, massage your scalp very gently, and leave the lather in for about five minutes. It's okay to do two washes if your hair is very oily.

Don't brush or comb your hair too frequently, as this can stimulate oil production. Avoid contact with your scalp when you are brushing, and be gentle.

If you have acne, keep your hair clean and away from your face, so that hair oils don't clog up the pores on your face.

In most cases, oily hair is a temporary phase of puberty. After a while, your body becomes used to the changed hormone levels, and the oiliness in your hair will settle down.

MANAGING DRY HAIR

If you have dry hair, wash it less frequently – perhaps only once or twice each week. Use a shampoo and conditioner specially formulated for dry hair. Heat is particularly damaging to dry hair, so don't overdo the use of hair dryers or other appliances, and always protect your hair from strong sunshine when you are outdoors.

DEALING WITH DANDRUFF

All people have a certain amount of flakiness on their scalps, as the old, surface skin is shed. Normally these flakes of skin are tiny, and hardly noticeable, and washing or brushing your hair gets rid of them. Sometimes, though, particularly when you begin to produce more oil at puberty, and possibly due to the action of a particular yeast or a fungal infection which irritates the scalp, these flakes of skin are held together to form larger, more noticeable flakes. Along with an annoying, itchy scalp, this condition is known as *dandruff.*

If simply washing your hair gently with a mild shampoo to get rid of the flakes of skin and the extra oil doesn't solve the problem, then you might need to use a special anti-dandruff shampoo. Talk to the pharmacist to get advice about what might be the best product for you. Whatever you buy, make sure you follow the instructions carefully to get the best results. If your dandruff is very severe and prolonged, see your doctor.

In addition to washing your hair, other things you can do to help control dandruff are avoid products such as hair gels and dyes, eat a good, healthy diet and spend just a little bit of time in the sun.

EXPERIMENTING WITH YOUR HAIR

It can be fun to experiment with different styles, and even with getting your hair permed (curled), straightened or coloured. Some of these things can be done at home; others have to be done by a professional hairdresser. Chat with a friend or family member you trust (and whose opinion you value) about what might make your hair look good – not forgetting, of course, that sometimes the natural colour and a simple cut can be as good as anything else.

Caring for your teeth

Your teeth are vital to you, as you can't chew your food or speak clearly without them. So it's important that you know how to care for them, and keep them as healthy as possible.

There are bacteria in the mouth that feed on sugar, and form a coating on your teeth called *plaque*. Plaque contains an acid that, if left in contact with the teeth for too long, gradually destroys the enamel (the hard coating). Normally, your saliva helps to wash away and neutralize the acid, just so long as you don't continually consume sugary food or drinks. If you do, the saliva doesn't get a chance to do its job, so that eventually the acid will cause tooth decay (holes in your teeth).

Gum disease happens when plaque is left too long, and forms a hard substance called *tartar* close to the gums. This can irritate the gums, and eventually lead to the gums pulling away slightly from the teeth, allowing even more plaque and tartar to become trapped. Teeth can become infected and wobbly, and sometimes need to be taken out.

When you don't brush and floss your teeth frequently enough, tiny particles of food can become trapped. Bacteria are attracted to and break down these particles, which creates an unpleasant odour. This is one of the reasons for bad breath.

To keep your teeth and gums healthy, and to have fresh-smelling breath:

- brush at least twice a day (the last time just before you go to bed)
- use a fluoride toothpaste, which helps to strengthen your teeth and prevent tooth decay
- brush up and down, or round and round, rather than across, so that the bristles can get into the gaps between your teeth; be gentle – if you are too vigorous, you can wear away the enamel
- make sure you brush all surfaces of your teeth, including the back of your teeth
- never use anyone else's toothbrush
- learn how to use dental floss to get in between the teeth
- rinse with mouthwash, rather than water, after brushing
- visit your dentist regularly (he or she will tell you how often you need to visit)
- try to avoid too many sugary foods or drinks; if you are snacking in between meals, then fruit, nuts, vegetables and cheese all cause less decay than foods that contain refined sugar (sweets, biscuits, ice cream, soft drinks and so on).

Caring for your nails

Clean hands and nails are a lot more hygienic, and attractive, than dirty ones, so it's important to wash your hands regularly, especially after you have been to the toilet. Use a nailbrush occasionally to scrub around and under the nails of your fingers and your toes.

Your toenails should always be kept short, and cut straight across; shaping them can cause them to grow into the flesh at the side of the nail. This is called an *ingrowing* (*ingrown*) toenail, which can become very painful, and may require medical attention.

Your fingernails can be longer if you like, though if they tend to break easily you may find it more practical to keep them short. You can trim your nails with nail clippers or nail scissors, and then file them to a smooth shape with an emery board.

About half of all adolescents bite their fingernails, most often as a nervous habit, and usually they are barely aware that they are doing it. If your fingernails are bitten down to the flesh you can't pick up small things or even scratch an itch satisfactorily. But mostly they just don't look very nice, and if you bite them too low, and break the flesh at the tip of your fingers, or around the edges, you can get an infection, and they will become very sore. The other thing to think about is where your hands might have been before you put them in your mouth. It's not a particularly nice thought, is it? If you would like to be able to stop nail-biting, but are finding it difficult to break the habit, talk with someone you trust. They might be able to help by giving you a quiet reminder each time they see you biting your nails. Another alternative is to buy some special, bitter-tasting nail polish that you apply to your nails and fingertips. The idea is that this tastes so horrible that you can't bite your nails, and eventually you get out of the habit.

Shaving – and other ways of removing unwanted hair

As you go through puberty, you get an increase in the amount of hair on your body. Both boys and girls get more hair on their legs, and under their arms; boys get facial hair – and it's not uncommon for girls to get some hair on their faces, as well; and pubic hair can spread across the top of the thighs and up to the belly button in some people.

Depending on how you feel about the extra hair on your body, you may or may not want to get rid of it. How you feel about it may depend on what is normal in your family, culture or religion. Sometimes you may not be able to make a choice; for example, in some religions, the men aren't allowed to cut or shave their hair. In some societies it's quite normal for women to keep the hair under their arms, while in others shaving is the norm. But quite often people are influenced by fashions, which come and go, so that sometimes it might be considered cool or trendy for men to have stubble, or a beard or moustache, while at other times a clean-shaven look is the thing; or girls may want to have smooth, hairless legs, because the fashion is for short skirts. But really, as long as you are not required by your religion to follow a certain trend, it is up to you to decide.

Even though it may seem that everyone else is starting to shave or wax, and perhaps teasing others who don't, it's important to remember that hair removal, however it's done, is a personal choice. Your body hair is perfectly natural, so don't feel pressured by other people to remove any of it if you don't want to.

If you do decide that you would like to remove some of your body hair, it's a good idea to know how to do it properly. Check first with your parents or carers before you start using razors, tweezers, wax or hair-removal creams, to be sure that they approve of what you want to do. You also may need to engage their help, as you can do yourself some damage if hair removal is not done properly.

Shaving your beard

While some girls may have a few stray hairs on their face, this bit is mainly for boys, obviously! (Girls, see later sections). You can start to shave just as soon as there's hair on your face, if you want to. Because people develop at such different rates, there's no set age when this might be. Some boys have enough hair on their face to shave by the time they are 13 years old; others may be 18 or 19 before they begin. There's no rush, and it isn't a competition, so don't worry about it. The main thing is that when you do shave, you do it properly, and avoid cutting your skin, making it raw, or giving yourself pimples.

Electric razors are faster and easier to use than manual razors, but they are harsh on young skin, and can leave you looking raw and sore.

A *manual shave* can be done as follows.

- You can buy razors at the chemist or supermarket. There is quite a large range available.

- Wash your face with warm water.

- Apply shaving foam, and rub it gently but thoroughly into your face.

- Shave downwards (i.e. in the direction of your hair growth). Going against the grain can cause redness, and you may nick the skin. Rinse the razor after each stroke.

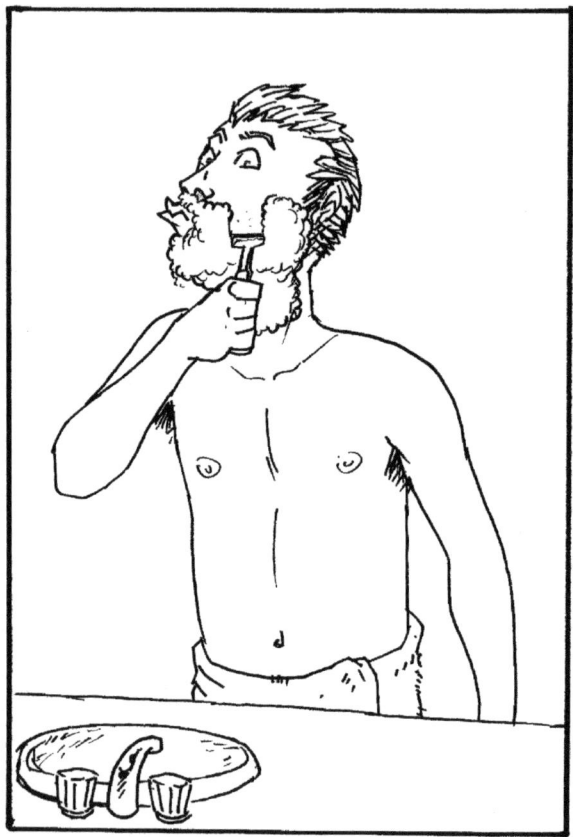

- Begin at the sides, then do the moustache area on your top lip, and shave the chin last. This is a good habit to get into, as once you are an adult, the hair on your chin will be a lot tougher than the rest, and needs more time to soften in the shaving foam.

- If you have acne, make sure your razor is very sharp. Work gently, and only pass over each area once or twice to minimize the risk of damaging the pimples.

- Rinse your face with warm water, and pat it dry.

- Splash with cold water to close the pores. Aftershave, though it can smell nice, is too harsh. Apply moisturizer to the shaved area.

Shaving underarms and legs

This is usually for girls, though some boys like to remove the hair on their legs to participate in certain sports:

- use a regular, manual razor
- lather with a mild soap and warm water (never do a dry shave with a manual razor – it's too harsh on the skin)
- using the razor slowly and carefully, shave downwards for armpits, upwards for legs, taking care around your knees, ankles and shins, as these are areas where it is particularly easy to cut yourself
- rinse the razor after every few strokes.

An electric shaver (used on dry skin) may also be used for underarms and legs, the advantage being that you are unlikely to cut yourself. However, the shave isn't quite so smooth or close.

The rate at which the hair grows back depends on how hairy you are. It usually comes back in a few days, a bit prickly, but can be shaved again. It is a myth that shaving causes the hair to grow back thicker or darker, or that it changes the rate of growth. However, the short hair shaft may be more noticeable because the tip of the hair is blunt rather than tapered.

Waxing

This method uses hot or cold wax, which is spread over a patch of hair, allowed to set for a moment and then pulled off quickly, removing the hair that is trapped in it. Home kits are available, though they can be quite messy and difficult to use. Lots of people go to a beauty salon and have waxing done professionally. Although waxing is more expensive than shaving – and is much more painful – the hair takes a lot longer to grow back. Waxing also has a smoother finish than shaving, and eventually reduces the amount of hair that grows in the area.

Waxing is suitable for most of the body, including the top lip on women; it is also suitable for the pubic hair that spreads on to the top of the thighs and up towards the navel. Women often get this done so that there is no hair visible when they are in swimwear.

Use of tweezers

Tweezers can be used to remove stray hairs anywhere on your body.

They are used by gripping an individual hair firmly and pulling sharply in the direction of the growth of the hair. It can be quite painful, especially as the areas where you are likely to be doing this are very sensitive (e.g. eyebrows, top lip, nipples). The hair will grow back. Take particular care not to overdo it if you choose to pluck your eyebrows to re-shape them. It is very easy to be overenthusiastic and pluck too much, leaving you with very thin, unnatural looking eyebrows.

Hair removal cream (depilatories)

This is another method that can be used at home. The cream is applied to the skin, left for a few minutes, and then washed off. It sounds simple; however, the cream is made of chemicals that dissolve the hair at the surface of the skin. As these chemicals can be harsh, it is very important to follow the instructions carefully, to avoid damaging the skin and causing an irritation. Hair-removal cream is unlikely to be suitable for you if you have sensitive skin.

Electrolysis

This method has to be carried out by an experienced practitioner. An electric current is applied through a fine needle inserted into the hair follicle. This kills the follicle, thus preventing any more hair growth. Each follicle is treated individually; therefore the treatment is slow and expensive, and really only used for very small areas of hair, such as eyebrows and the upper lip or other areas of a woman's face.

Laser hair removal

Again, this treatment has to be carried out in a specialist salon. A laser (a type of light) is used to destroy the hair. Although the treatment is not permanent, it does slow down the growth of the hair significantly, and the effects last for several months. It is quick treatment, but expensive.

Use of make-up

The decision to wear make-up is a very personal one. If you look around you, you will notice that there are lots of women who do wear make-up, and lots who don't. Some women only wear make-up for special occasions, while others wear it every day. What you will also notice is that quite a few young girls who are going through puberty are beginning to wear make-up.

The first thing to be aware of is that it is *not compulsory* to wear make-up. The choice should be yours. We will look briefly at some of the more obvious reasons why people may choose not to wear make-up, and then at the reasons they do – then you can perhaps decide for yourself whether or not it is for you.

Some reasons for not wearing make-up:

- you can look fresher and more natural without make-up
- if you are too young, make-up can look wrong; it makes you look older than you really are, and may attract inappropriate sexual attention
- if it isn't cleaned off properly, it can clog your pores and cause pimples, or make them worse
- it doesn't look attractive when it is applied badly or too heavily
- it takes time to apply
- it is an added expense
- it can 'run' in the rain, or when you play sport; 'panda eyes' are never a good look!
- it may be against your school rules.

You, or your parents or carers, may feel very strongly about some of these points. They may be the reason you choose never to wear make-up. However, many women do wear it, even just a very small amount (e.g. just a little lipstick or mascara), or on rare occasions. Let's look at some of the factors that may influence some women to wear make-up.

Some reasons for wearing make-up:

- *To cover up blemishes or features you're not happy with*: make-up can be quite effective in covering up blemishes and marks that you might be unhappy with, such as birthmarks, dark shadows under the eyes, scars and pimples. If your skin is pale, it can be given more colour, and you can look healthier, with the use of make-up.

- *To enhance certain features*: make-up is often used to enhance facial features. For example, you can make your eyes look bigger and more defined with eyeliner, and your eyelashes longer and darker with mascara. You can enhance the colour of your eyes with various coloured eye shadows, and emphasize your cheekbones with blusher. You can make your lips look fuller and more defined with lip liner and lipstick.

- *To make yourself look older*: if you are very young, your features are already well-defined, and don't need make-up to achieve definition. However, if you do wear make-up, it will make you look older – more like a young woman. A lot of young girls can't wait to be older, and, along with higher heels and fashionable clothes, make-up helps them to feel that they are already grown up.

- *To make yourself look younger*: this isn't, of course, why *you* might choose to wear make-up, but it may be the reason your mother or grandmother does! As we age, our features lose some of their definition. Our skin becomes less smooth, more uneven in its colour, with blotches and blemishes often caused by exposure to sunlight. Our lips become paler and lose their definite outline, blending in more with the surrounding skin. When older women wear make-up, it can smooth out the skin, and add colour and definition to their lips and eyes, which makes them look brighter and younger.

- *To fit in with everyone else*: no matter what age we are, we can be influenced by advertising, fashion and what the people around us are doing. Many people enjoy following fashion – it helps them to feel that they are part of the group, and that they fit in. Sometimes, other people can be dismissive of, or even make fun of, people who choose to be different and not follow fashion, so the pressure to do the same as everyone else can be quite strong. Lots of young girls start wearing make-up just because 'everyone else' is.

Deciding to wear make-up

If you do decide you would like to wear make-up, be sure your parents or carers approve. It's not worth having big fights about it. Your parents could be reluctant for you to start wearing make-up because they fear it will make you look older than you really are, so that you could get into trouble by mixing with people who are too old for you. Sometimes parents are just worried about you growing up. It may require you to be very calm and reasonable (rather than having a tantrum and slamming doors!) to prove that you *are* mature enough to wear make-up. Usually, a compromise is all that is needed: for example, you might agree to wear just a touch of eye shadow and a light lipstick rather than a lot of heavy make-up.

Buying make-up

The range of make-up available is huge, and very confusing. You can get some idea of what you might like by reading magazines for teenage girls, or by going with a friend or a trusted adult to the cosmetics counters at some of the big department stores. The assistants will be happy to go through with you what products are available and what will suit you. You don't have to buy what they suggest, and, in fact, might find something similar, but cheaper, at the pharmacy or supermarket once you have got an idea of what you want.

Make-up and acne

Remember, if you have trouble with acne, always buy products that are marked 'oil free' or 'non-comedogenic', as these will not clog the pores. Also avoid any strongly fragranced products.

Applying make-up

Since make-up doesn't look good if it isn't applied properly, you will need advice to start with. Your mother, older sister or a friend that you trust can be really helpful in giving you some ideas and showing you what to do to begin with. Mostly, make-up looks best when it is applied lightly, so that it is subtle and gently enhances your features.

Body art

You will have noticed that body piercing and tattoos are quite popular. You may even think that these would be fun things to get done for yourself. In most countries there are rules about how old you have to be to make such a decision for yourself. Generally, you can't get a tattoo without the consent of your parents or carers until you are 18. In some countries you can't get a tattoo at all if you are below 16, even with parental consent. The rules for body piercing vary, but are less restrictive. In the UK, for example, there is no lower limit on the legal age at which you can get a piercing, although some piercers have their own practice guidelines. If you are thinking seriously about getting either tattoos or body piercings (or both), have a chat with someone you trust about your idea. Find out the rules that apply where you live, about the age at which you're allowed to get body art, and where the most reputable places are (it's very important that they have modern, sterile equipment and experienced practitioners).

Tattoos

Tattooing is an ancient practice, dating back at least 6000 years. It was originally a symbol of status, used only for royalty or tribal chiefs. In the middle of the twentieth century, it began to be popular in Western countries, initially among sailors, then among criminals and members of bike gangs, which led to the perception of tattoos being only for rough, uncultured people. Towards the end of the century, tattoos started to become more acceptable, and by the end of the 1990s were very popular with both men and women.

Tattoos are created by placing coloured pigments below the surface of the skin, with a needle. Because the dye is injected into the deep layer of skin (the *dermis*), tattoos should be considered to be permanent.

Getting a tattoo can be a very slow, and usually very uncomfortable, procedure, depending on how large the tattoo is and how many colours are being applied. As with any puncture wound to the skin, there is a risk of infection. They are not easy to get removed if you change your mind; removal is done by laser (not always successfully), takes just as long, if not longer, than getting the tattoo in the first place, and costs a lot more.

If you aren't quite sure about getting one, but would like to see how one might look, it is possible to get temporary tattoos, which last anything from a few hours to a couple of weeks. In this way, you can decide how you feel about it before you make the choice to have something you will have to live with for the rest of your life.

Body piercing

Body piercing is very popular, and has also been practised for thousands of years. The most usual areas for piercing are the ears, lips, nostrils, eyebrows, belly button, tongue and cheeks. It involves a piercing into the chosen part of the body with a needle; a piece of jewellery is then inserted into the puncture.

Because it involves a puncture wound, infection is always a possibility, and special care must be taken to keep the wound clean and disinfected for a few weeks after the procedure. Mouth and nose piercings are particularly vulnerable to infection, because there are millions of bacteria in these parts of the body. Tongue piercing can eventually damage the teeth, and cheek and lip piercing can cause gum problems.

Before you decide to go ahead with a body piercing of any sort, talk it over with someone you trust. If you happen to have a condition such as diabetes, an allergy or a skin disorder, check with your doctor before you get any piercing at all.

Unlike tattoos, body piercing isn't permanent, so if your wound won't heal, and you get an infection – or even if you just change your mind, and don't like it any more – you can always remove the piece of jewellery, and the wound will heal up, although in some cases it may leave a small scar.

4

Making
Healthy Choices

This chapter is about 'lifestyle' choices – what you eat, how much you exercise, the amount of sleep you get and whether or not you choose eventually to become involved in smoking, drinking or drug-taking. Everyone feels their best when they get the 'balance' right. For example, if you eat more food than your body can use up, you will put on weight, but if you exercise sufficiently you will burn up some of this energy and maintain a healthy weight. Adequate sleep is essential if your body and brain are to function the best they can – if you are too tired you can't concentrate and you won't even feel like exercising or eating properly. If you smoke or take drugs or alcohol, your general well-being, as well as your appetite and your sleep cycle, can be affected. One thing affects another, and getting the balance just right can be quite a challenge.

But when you do get it right, your health will benefit, and you will look and feel really good. Read on to find out how to make the healthiest choices you can.

Healthy eating

Food is the body's fuel. It gives you energy to keep you active and functioning, enables your body to repair wounds, fight illness and infection, and helps you grow – especially now, as you go through puberty. And your body has a wonderful, automatic response when it requires food – you feel hungry!

So all you need to do is eat plenty of your favourite food, whatever that might be – chips, plain bread, curry, sausages… Right?

Wrong!

Your body is like a hugely complex, intricate machine made up of many parts. Each of these parts has a specific job to do, and requires a particular type of fuel to help it function at its very best. The wrong type of fuel, or inadequate supplies of the right sort, will eventually lead to that part not functioning as it should. It's rather like a car engine that requires premium unleaded fuel – you can put regular unleaded fuel into the petrol (gas) tank, and the engine will run, but not at its best. None of the parts will function as efficiently as they would do with the right fuel.

What fuel does your body need?

You need the right amount of protein, carbohydrates, fats, vitamins, minerals and water every day to ensure that your body functions as well as it can. Each food item that you eat will have some of these essential ingredients, in varying quantities, but no one food item has all of them, so in order to get just the right amount of these vital body fuels, you need to enjoy a wide variety of nutritious foods, and eat what is generally referred to as a *balanced diet* (more on that later).

KILOJOULES

A *kilojoule* is measure of energy (rather like a kilometre or a mile is a measure of distance). Food energy is measured in *kilojoules*, which is the internationally accepted term. It used to be *calories*. A calorie is the amount of energy required to increase the temperature of 1 g of water by 1 °C. One calorie has the same energy value as 4.2 kilojoules.

Different foods have different energy values, or kilojoules; in other words, some foods, such as fats, are energy-dense (and high in kilojoules), whereas others, such as lettuce, have very little energy value (and are very low in kilojoules). This means that in order to provide your body with the same amount of energy, you would need to eat only a very small amount of oil or butter, but a huge amount of lettuce.

The amount of kilojoules you need each day depends on how much energy you use up. While you are growing you use a lot of energy, which is why most young people, as they go through puberty, are always hungry. Boys, because they are usually bigger, require more food than girls, and as they go through their growth spurt, may need as much food as a fully grown, physically active man.

If you regularly consume more kilojoules than your body needs, the surplus energy is stored in your fat cells, and you put on excess weight.

PROTEIN

This essential nutrient has a very important maintenance and repair job to do in your body. It helps build up and maintain the health of your muscles, organs and glands. It also makes both haemoglobin, which is a compound in your blood that carries oxygen around your body, and anti-bodies, which are produced by the immune system, to recognize and fight infection; and it helps in the repair of your body, so that any cuts and sores heal up quickly.

Protein is found in red meat, chicken, fish, eggs, nuts, beans and lentils, and in dairy products.

CARBOHYDRATES

These are divided into two types: starches and sugars. Their job is to provide energy to all the cells in your body. Sugars are also known as 'simple carbohydrates' – these are digested quickly by your body so that you get a quick burst of energy that doesn't last very long. Starches, on the other hand, are known as 'complex carbohydrates': they take longer to be digested, but the energy they give you lasts much longer.

Simple carbohydrates are found in foods that have a lot of sugar, such as sweets, biscuits and soft drinks, but also in fruit (which is a lot better for you). Complex carbohydrates are found in bread, pasta, cereals and starchy vegetables, such as potatoes and carrots.

Carbohydrates are converted to glucose (a type of sugar) to provide the energy to the cells. Your body uses what it needs, and then stores the rest, in a converted form known as *glycogen*, in the liver. This store can be used to provide your body with energy even when you haven't eaten for a while.

But if you consume more carbohydrates than your body requires, so that the body cells have all the glucose they need, and the glycogen stores are full, the surplus is converted to body fat.

FIBRE IN YOUR DIET

Fibre is a carbohydrate found in cereals, fruit and vegetables. It is made up of the indigestible parts of plants, which pass straight through the stomach and intestines without changing much. Its main role is to make the muscles of your intestines work efficiently to keep the digestive system healthy.

People who don't eat enough fibre are more likely to suffer from constipation, and, in the long term, more likely to suffer from serious conditions such as bowel cancer.

In order to get enough fibre in your diet, eat:

- breakfast cereals that contain barley, wheat or oats
- wholemeal and multigrain bread, and brown rice
- plenty of vegetables
- fresh fruit, dried fruit and nuts.

When you eat enough fibre you also need to drink plenty of fluid, preferably water.

FATS

A certain amount of fat in your diet is essential. It helps to give you some of your energy, and keeps your skin and hair healthy. There are two types of fat in the food that we eat:

- *Saturated fat*: This is found in animal products, such as meat, dairy foods (butter, cheese, milk, cream and yoghurt) and most margarines.
- *Unsaturated fat*: This is found in fish, some vegetables, vegetable oils, nuts and some margarines.

You only need a small amount of fat in your diet to be healthy, and it is better (when you can) to eat slightly more unsaturated than saturated fat. Too much fat of any type can contribute to obesity (severe overweight), heart disease and other illnesses such as diabetes and cancer. It also spoils your appetite so that you don't eat enough of the other important foods, and this can make you feel unwell and lacking in energy.

VITAMINS AND MINERALS

Vitamins and minerals have several important functions in your body, including being involved in the chemical processes that make energy, keeping your cells and nervous system healthy, helping to fight infection and prevent cancer, and helping with blood clotting. As long as you eat a good variety of fresh, healthy food, including plenty of vegetables and fruit, you should get all the vitamins and minerals you need, without having to take supplements.

WATER

Water is even more vital to your body than food. It is involved in all your important bodily functions, including transporting oxygen and food around your body in the blood, and removing waste from your body in the forms of urine and faeces. You lose water from your body all the time, in your breath and in sweat.

As you start to go through puberty, you are probably losing about one litre of water each day, and this amount increases as you grow. An adult loses up to about two litres of water a day (more if he or she is involved in sport or strenuous activity which results in a lot of sweating), which needs to be replaced. When your body is lacking the fluid it needs, your saliva (also made of water) is reduced, resulting in a dry mouth – in other words, you feel thirsty. Thirst is your body's automatic way of drawing your attention to the fact that you need water.

HOW TO REPLACE THE WATER THAT YOU NEED

Some of the fluid that you need is in the food that you eat – fruit and vegetables have quite a bit of water in them already, for example. All the drinks that you have are made up of water, too – even milk and juice. However, soft drinks, although largely made up of water, contain too much sugar, which isn't good for you. Soft drinks won't really quench your thirst, and have too many kilojoules, so that they can cause you to gain weight. Some drinks, such as tea, coffee and some varieties of cola, contain a substance called *caffeine*. Caffeine has the effect on your kidneys of making them produce more urine (so that you go to the toilet a lot more). In other words, you excrete too much of the water that you are putting into your body. Therefore it's best to limit the amount of caffeine that you consume. The very best fluid that you can drink, of course, is water – several glasses a day, if you can.

What is a balanced diet?

The food that we eat has been divided into five groups, according to how good it is for us. You should eat the greatest quantity of food from Group 1, and the least from Group 5. In between are the foods you should eat in reasonable quantity, but not too much. A balanced diet is one that

includes all these foods in the right quantities, so that you get the nutrition you need for your body and your brain to function at their very best.

GROUP 1: BREAD, CEREAL, RICE, PASTA, NOODLES

Eat at least *five* servings from this group each day.

One serving is equivalent to two slices of bread, or half a cup of (dry) cereal, rice, pasta or noodles.

GROUP 2: FRUIT AND VEGETABLES (INCLUDING DRIED FRUIT AND FRUIT JUICE)

Eat at least *three* servings of vegetables and *two to three* servings of fruit each day.

One serving of vegetables is the equivalent of half a cup. A serving of fruit is the equivalent of *one* apple, *two* plums or a small glass of fruit juice; and a serving of dried fruit is *four* small pieces, or *one or two* tablespoons of raisins.

GROUP 3: MEAT, POULTRY, FISH, BEANS, EGGS, NUTS AND LÉGUMES

Eat *one* serving each day. One serving is equivalent to:

- small portion (65–100 g) of meat or chicken
- fish fillet (80–120 g)
- two small eggs
- one-third of a cup of nuts
- three-quarters of a cup of légumes.

To reduce the amount of saturated fat, trim the fat off meat and avoid eating chicken skin.

Iron is an important mineral that is found in all these foods, and is essential for healthy blood. Girls and women can become low in iron when they have their periods, and need to be sure to eat enough of these foods to keep their iron at a healthy level.

GROUP 4: DAIRY FOODS

Eat (or drink) *three* servings each day. One serving is equivalent to a glass (250 ml) of milk, a small tub of yoghurt or two slices (40 g) of cheese.

To reduce the amount of saturated fat in your diet these foods can be low-fat.

Dairy foods are particularly high in calcium, which is a very important mineral that keeps your bones and teeth strong and healthy.

GROUP 5: FATS (BUTTER, MARGARINE AND OIL)

You need very little of this – no more than about *one tablespoon* in a day. In fact, you already get most of the fats you require in your diet from other food, such as meat, eggs, cheese and nuts.

BISCUITS, CAKES, SWEETS, CHOCOLATE, CHIPS AND SOFT DRINKS

These are tasty but non-essential foods. You can have *one to two small portions* of these 'treat' foods each day, but no more if you want to be healthy.

It's much better to have fresh or dried fruit, nuts or cheese as a snack, rather than sweet or salty fatty food such as biscuits or crisps.

Why do I need breakfast?

Breakfast is probably the most important meal of the day. Even when you are sleeping, your body still uses energy – and during puberty, you grow while you are asleep, so it uses more energy than ever. By the morning, your body's energy stores are depleted, and need to be replaced if you are going to function properly throughout the day. (You literally need to 'break' your 'fast' – which is where the word comes from.)

You might find mornings difficult, and be in a rush to get to school. If you don't have a lot of time, you can have something simple but nutritious, such as cereal with milk and fruit. If you really have to eat on the run, a tub of yoghurt, a sandwich or even a banana will give you the energy to start your day.

Unfortunately, when people skip breakfast, rather than lose weight (which may be what they hope), they tend to snack on high kilojoule food during the morning, and end up gaining weight.

People who eat breakfast burn up their food more efficiently, and are less likely to gain weight. Breakfast foods such as cereals are typically high in carbohydrates and vitamins, which have been shown to improve your mood as well as helping you to think more clearly and concentrate better.

Fast food

Fast food is the term we use to describe ready-prepared, takeaway meals. It has become popular in many parts of the world because people lead such busy lives, and often feel they don't have the time to slow down and prepare a healthy meal. The problem is that fast food is usually very high in saturated fat, sugar and salt, and low in vitamins, minerals and fibre. Thus it is very high in kilojoules, but without any nutritional benefit. In fact, the typical fast food meal, along with a fatty dessert such as ice cream, would probably contain a whole day's worth of kilojoules, and almost certainly your ration of fat for the day.

Although many fast food restaurants have started to include healthier, lower-fat choices on the menu, it is still a good idea to see this type of food as 'occasional' rather than 'regular' – and that means no more than one meal of this type each week. If you do choose to eat a fast food meal, just make sure you balance your food intake that day with low fat, healthy food such as bread, cereal, fruit and vegetables.

Problem eating

It isn't difficult to eat well in most societies. The trouble is it's very easy to get into bad habits, which can become difficult to break. Eating fast food on a regular basis rather than occasionally is one of these bad habits. Getting fixated on one particular type of food is another. Although you might be very unadventurous, or really dislike certain

foods when you are young, once you get to puberty, it's time to start 'branching out' with what you eat. Not only does it make it easier to go to other people's houses, where you might be offered unfamiliar food, but you can eat out in restaurants without worrying, too. And in addition to this, you will get better nutrition, which will help your mood, your concentration and your growth.

GAINING WEIGHT (AND MAINTAINING A HEALTHY WEIGHT)

You are supposed to gain weight at puberty. Your bones are growing, you're getting more muscle, your internal organs are getting bigger and, if you're a girl, you're developing more essential body fat. It is normal and healthy for girls to have 20–30 per cent more body fat than boys after puberty.

If you eat more food than your body can burn up, however, you will gain more weight than you should. Although some young people 'grow out' before they 'grow up' (and often lose the excess fat once they begin to grow), lots of people don't like the feeling of being overweight, even temporarily.

You certainly should never, ever starve yourself, as this is bad for your health. 'Crash' diets never work, because your body cleverly adjusts to having less food, and the rate at which you burn up the food slows right down. Once you start eating again, you immediately put back the weight, plus extra, as your body doesn't burn up the food quickly enough.

What you can do, though, if you are concerned, is eat sensibly. Cut down on fatty foods, such as crisps, chips and takeaway meals, and sweet 'fillers', such as cakes, biscuits and chocolate. Cut out soft drinks, as they have no nutritional value whatsoever. Try to develop a liking for water (though weak cordial and the occasional fruit juice are okay) and snack on fruit and nuts. Try to recognize when you are satisfied, and stop eating at that point. There's no need to keep on eating when you are not hungry. One way to do this is to eat slowly, and enjoy your food, rather than gobbling it down. By taking your time, you give your brain a chance to recognize that your stomach is full. When you eat too fast, your brain doesn't register 'full' until you have eaten way too much.

If you eat sensibly, and get enough exercise (see later section), you will be the size and weight you are supposed to be. Remember, some people are naturally thinner and some people are naturally fatter. Variety is the spice of life!

EATING DISORDERS

People who have eating disorders are obsessed with food and with their weight, and are suffering from an emotional problem that also has serious physical consequences. Both girls and boys can be affected, but eating disorders tend to be more common in girls.

There are several possible reasons why eating disorders occur. They can be linked to the hormonal changes that happen at puberty, to pressure from other people (including the media) to be thin, and to stress. This stress can be about a range of emotional issues, including the need to be successful, anxiety about being bullied or teased, especially about appearance, or even a reaction to divorce or death or other worrying events in the family. It is thought that people suffering from eating disorders feel that by controlling their food intake, they can somehow take control of their lives.

There are two main types of eating disorder: *anorexia nervosa* and *bulimia nervosa*:

- *Anorexia nervosa*: people who suffer from anorexia nervosa become obsessed with losing weight. They develop a distorted body image and believe they are fat, even when they are not. They often exercise obsessively, and starve themselves to the point that they become dangerously thin.

- *Bulimia nervosa*: people who suffer from bulimia are often a normal body weight, sometimes even a little overweight. They are terrified of becoming fat, but are obsessed with eating. They binge eat (i.e. eat excessive amounts of food in a short space of time, often in secret) and then 'purge' themselves, which means either making themselves vomit, or taking laxatives. They believe that by doing this, they can avoid gaining weight. They often feel very guilty and out of control, and hate themselves for what they are doing.

There can be very severe health consequences for people with eating disorders, especially if these disorders are left untreated. Physically, sufferers may experience digestive problems, tiredness and weakness, loss of their regular menstrual cycle, calcium deficiency leading to weaker bones, long-term damage to important body organs and even death from malnutrition. Mentally, they can experience depression, poor concentration, withdrawal and loneliness, and interrupted schooling due to needing so much time off while they are ill.

If you suspect that you or someone you know is showing some of the signs of an eating disorder – for example, extreme weight loss, a preoccupation with food, including obsessive counting of kilojoules and a secretive attitude to food – it is very important that you seek help by talking to an adult you trust about the problem. The sooner symptoms are recognized and treatment begins, the easier it is to break the cycle and the better the outcome. Treatment may take a long time and involve several different specialists. While some people may need help on and off throughout their lives, many people recover completely.

Exercise

Have you ever noticed how much running around, jumping, swinging and tumbling small children do? They exercise quite naturally, without even thinking about it, in a way that humans are designed to do. In days gone by, exercise happened naturally for adults, too, while they cleaned the house and tended the garden by hand, chopped wood for fuel and walked everywhere. Today it's all very different. We use labour-saving devices such as dishwashers, washing machines, vacuum cleaners, lawn mowers and food processors to help us in our chores around the house. A lot of us have jobs that are sedentary (involve sitting for most of the time). We drive everywhere, park close to where we want to be, take lifts (elevators) and escalators rather than climb stairs – and even stay in our seats while we change the TV channel with the remote control device. On top of all this inactivity, most people eat more than they need to, as well. Is it any wonder that obesity is becoming a problem all over the world?

The importance of exercise

By doing the right amount of exercise, you burn up the kilojoules that you put into your body, and maintain a healthy weight. But exercise isn't just about avoiding obesity. As you can see from the following list, there are many other benefits, too.

BENEFITS OF EXERCISE

- helps you feel fitter, stronger and physically healthier
- helps you feel mentally healthy, too; each time you exercise for more than 20 minutes, your brain releases 'feel-good' chemicals called *endorphins*
- relaxes you and helps to relieve stress
- burns off anger and frustration
- improves your concentration
- improves your circulation, too, which results in nutrients and oxygen getting around your body faster
- burns up kilojoules, and maintains your body at a healthy weight
- increases the strength of your muscles, bones, heart and lungs
- improves your co-ordination
- gives you the strength and enthusiasm to do other things
- helps you sleep more soundly
- makes you look good.

Getting the exercise you need

Some of you may be thinking at this point 'But I hate sports' or 'I'm no good at throwing/catching/kicking a ball' or even remembering with a sinking feeling all the times you've been teased for being clumsy and dropping the ball, or for being too slow. Don't let these thoughts, or your previous experiences, put you off. Exercise doesn't have to be about being a sports whizz, joining a gym or being a member of a club or a team. It certainly can be if you want, and if you're good at that sort of thing – but you can get enough physical activity in your life without ever having to join the swimming club or go jogging.

INCIDENTAL EXERCISE

Think about your day – do you get a lift to school? Do you spend break times in the library? Do you head straight for the computer, snack in hand, when you get home? Do you then have a couple of hours in front of the TV, only moving your hand to operate the remote control device?

If you answered yes to any (or all) of these, you might be missing out on opportunities to benefit from *incidental exercise* in your day.

Incidental exercise is the sort of exercise people got in past centuries, just going about their normal business. In recent years, though, we have come to rely on cars and machinery, and tend to take the easy way out. Incidental exercise is about moving around more and sitting on your bottom less. Here are a few ideas. See if you can think of some more:

- if you don't live too far away, ride your bike or walk to school or to the local shops

- take the dog for a walk

- play active games with your little brother or sister

- offer to mow the lawn or wash the car

- bounce on the trampoline, or practise hitting a ball up against a wall, or kicking a ball round the yard
- encourage your mum or dad to park a little further from where you want to be, so that you can all walk a bit more
- walk up the stairs rather than take the lift or the escalator in shopping centres and public buildings
- help carry in the shopping
- offer to help out with household chores
- get up from the couch sometimes and change the TV channel by hand.

If you add even two or three of these activities to your day, so that they become part of your routine, you will start to feel much livelier and fitter (and you might, at the same time, get the half-hour of fresh air and sunshine you need for healthy skin and bones; see Chapter 3, **Caring for Your Body**). Certainly, you will be well on the way to getting the exercise you need to keep you healthy.

MAKING EXERCISE FUN

Exercise, whatever you choose to do, should always be enjoyable. If it's not, you won't keep it up. It doesn't have to be organized sport – it doesn't even have to involve anyone else. There are lots of things you can do by yourself if you want to, such as walking, riding your bike, skating, skipping, jumping on the trampoline, dancing to your favourite music, swimming...the list goes on (only limited by your imagination). It can be fun to do these things with other people, too. You can learn new things from each other, and you can often be more adventurous when you're with someone else.

ORGANIZED ACTIVITIES

Again, you don't have to be particularly accomplished to enjoy organized sports or activities. Depending on what your skills are, the possibilities are endless. If you are good at a particular activity, or keen to learn, check with your parents or carers whether you could join a group, club or team locally. It's a good way to meet people who enjoy the same things as you, to learn new skills and feel a sense of achievement.

As well as the more traditional social or team sports, such as football, tennis, cricket, netball, athletics and so on, there are many other activities that require different skills, for example martial arts, fencing, synchronized swimming, surfing, rock climbing, orienteering, rowing…the list goes on. You can look in the local paper or telephone directory to find out what happens in your area.

Sometimes, things such as scouts, guides or youth groups can be fun because they do a range of interesting activities, many of which are active and improve your physical and thinking abilities.

HOW MUCH EXERCISE?

Altogether, in any one day, you should get about 60 minutes of exercise. This may sound like a lot, but don't worry – it includes the incidental exercise mentioned previously, so that you can accumulate the 60 minutes throughout the day with a variety of activities.

When you are exercising, try to do some of it vigorously, so that your heart rate increases for at least 20 minutes, three to four times a week. If you are involved in some sort of sport or bike-riding, this should be easy to achieve, as you can challenge yourself to work harder or go faster for a few minutes. However, it is never wise to push yourself to the point of pain. Stop what you are doing if you are getting very tired, or if your body starts to hurt.

MUSCLE BUILDING

Some young boys love the idea of developing strong muscles so that they look toned and fit. Although it is impossible for you to look like a body builder while you are still going through puberty, weight training can be a very good way to build strength in your muscles and joints, whether you are a boy or a girl. However, it is vital that any exercise done with weights is supervised by a trainer or physiotherapist, and is designed specifically for you, so that you don't lift weights that are too heavy for you or use an incorrect technique. Both of these could cause permanent damage to your body.

BUILDING UP GRADUALLY

If you haven't been very active, make sure that you work gradually towards the ideal amount of exercise. Your muscles and joints need time to adjust, and you don't want to hurt yourself in the process of trying to become healthy!

By eating sensibly and doing enough regular exercise as described here, you will feel good, and your body will be exactly the weight and shape it is supposed to be – so you will look good too.

Sleep

Most young people need plenty of sleep at puberty, and throughout adolescence, because they are growing, and growing uses up a lot of energy. However, there may be some of you who find that your sleep cycle becomes particularly disturbed during puberty, so that you either have difficulty getting to sleep, or staying asleep. We will explore some ideas about how to get the rest that you need in a moment. First, let's look at the role that sleep plays in keeping you healthy.

Why do you need sleep?

Sleep is a time of recovery and repair for your body. Your heart rate decreases, your breathing slows down and your muscles relax. Growth hormone is active at this time, too, and this is when your body does most of its growing. It is thought that dreams also serve a function by helping you restore and repair your emotions.

If you have too little sleep, your immune system becomes weaker, and you are more prone to illnesses, coughs and colds – even to outbreaks of acne. Without sufficient sleep, your brain can't function properly, you will feel low and irritable, and you will have difficulty concentrating and making decisions.

How much sleep do you need?

There are obviously variations between one person and another, and even in the same person at different times, in how much sleep is ideal. It is generally thought that between the ages of ten and 14, you need about ten hours sleep each night; and between 14 and 18, about nine hours each night.

However, this isn't the same for everyone. The best way to tell what is right for you is to assess how you feel during the day. Do you get up feeling refreshed in the morning? Can you cope with everything you have to do during the day? Can you concentrate properly?

GETTING YOURSELF INTO A 'RHYTHM'

At the weekend, or when you have time to conduct this small experiment, allow yourself to wake naturally in the morning (no wake-up call from your mum or your alarm clock) and calculate how many hours sleep you had. Ideally, do this over a few days, until you can be sure of the number of hours that seems right for you. Then work out what time you normally have to get up for school, and work backwards from that to calculate what time you need to go to bed in order to achieve the number of hours of sleep that suits you best. You can then 'train' your body to get into a rhythm, where you go to bed at approximately the same time each night, and wake naturally, having had sufficient sleep, at the same time every morning.

Overcoming sleep problems

Some of you will probably be thinking, 'If only it was as easy as that!' because quite a number of young people do have problems getting enough sleep, for various reasons. There are solutions to many of the problems, and some of these are quite logical. However, everyone is different – some things work for some people but not for others. Take a look at this list of possibilities, think which might apply to you, and give it a try – it can't do any harm.

- Make sure you have burned off your excess energy by doing enough exercise and activity during the day. A very sedentary, inactive day could actually be keeping you awake. But don't exercise just before bedtime – this can be too stimulating and keep you awake, too.

- If you have a lie-in in the morning, this could be preventing you getting to sleep at night. You may need to readjust your sleep cycle by getting up a little earlier.

- Avoid eating too much immediately before bedtime. It's difficult to get to sleep while your digestive system is hard at work. Eat your last meal at least two or three hours before you go to bed. But don't go to bed while you are hungry, either. Warm, milky drinks, and herbal teas, such as chamomile, can be very soothing last thing at night.

- A firm, comfortable bed is important for a good night's sleep. If your mattress is sagging and not offering the support you need, you may need a new mattress. This can be expensive; however, a cheap option may be to place a sheet of plywood underneath the mattress. Make sure your sheets and pillowcases are washed regularly, too (at least once a week); it is much more restful to have clean linen.

- It may be helpful to have a simple bedtime routine. This can include having a warm bath or shower before bed, and winding down by reading a relaxing book. Try to avoid watching television, or reading anything too exciting just before you go to sleep.

- If you find it difficult to stick to a routine, and become easily distracted by other things in your room, have a 'to do' list of what needs to be done once you are in the bedroom. Clear guidelines can be comforting, and help to keep your level of anxiety down.

- If you have things that need to be ready in the morning – especially if you are particularly tired or disorganized in the mornings – get them prepared the night before, to make the morning easier. This will stop you needing to worry about this during the night.

- Have a list of 'things to do' for the next day. Again, this will mean that you don't need to lie awake worrying about or planning tomorrow's events.

- Listen to soothing music quietly on the radio or through headphones to help you settle down.

- If you are someone who needs darkness in order to fall asleep, make sure your room is dark enough. Block-out curtains can be very helpful if even a small amount of light is disturbing to you.

- Be sure that your room is free of sounds, smells or other stimulations that might be disturbing to you.

- On the other hand, you may be a person who is soothed by, and needs, a certain amount of stimulation in order to go to sleep. To help you settle down, you may need to have the light on, or the bedroom door open so that you can hear movement and activity around you.

WHEN STRESS IS PREVENTING YOU GETTING TO SLEEP

Stress may be interfering with your ability to get to sleep, or to stay asleep. Even though it is true that things can seem a lot worse at night when you're lying awake worrying, it is important that you deal with these concerns, no matter how small they may be. Try some of these ideas.

- Talk with someone you trust about what is worrying you. This is the smart way to ease the burden, and help you to see a different perspective. You may need to see a doctor, or talk to a professional counsellor if your level of stress is becoming too great.

- Make a list, on a piece of paper, of some of the negative things that are bothering you – then throw away the piece of paper. This can metaphorically 'get rid' of all your worries, so that you won't dwell on them at night.

- Learn some relaxation techniques. There are a few methods of relaxation that can be learnt and can be applied at any time of the day when you are feeling particularly tense. These methods can also be very helpful at bedtime, to relax your body and your mind when you are trying to go to sleep. See the section on Relaxation in Chapter 5, **Understanding Emotions**.

Managing on less sleep

If you are a person who genuinely gets by on less sleep than most other people (e.g. three, four or five hours' sleep each night), and you are able to function well in the day, then don't stress about this. You may need to get up in the night and occupy yourself, rather than lying in bed and stressing about not sleeping. However, talk with your parents or carers about what you can do while you are up. Be sure that you are very quiet, so as not to wake the rest of the household. Be sensible, and, above all, safe.

Smoking, drinking and drugs

Everybody knows that smoking cigarettes, drinking alcohol and taking illegal drugs can be bad for you – so why do people do any of them? And what can you do to ensure that you make wise choices about these things if and when the time comes?

Alcohol and tobacco (in cigarettes) are the most commonly consumed drugs in the world, but because they are legal, people don't usually think of them as 'drugs'. A drug is any substance that affects your physical or mental functioning. Alcohol and cigarettes certainly do this, and so do medications, whether they have been prescribed by a doctor, bought over the counter or obtained illegally. Any drug has the potential to harm a person if it is misused.

Drinking

As long as a person is grown up and fully developed, alcohol is usually harmless in small quantities. Many people like it, particularly in social situations, because it helps them to feel relaxed and confident.

The problem is that alcohol is a poison that can harm the body in many ways when it is consumed too quickly or in large quantities.

When people drink too much alcohol, their emotions can become exaggerated, so that they can say and do things they might regret later. It affects the co-ordination of their muscles, so that they become clumsy, have blurred vision and slurred speech. Their judgement becomes impaired, so that activities such as riding bikes, driving and swimming become very dangerous. They may vomit, or even lose consciousness.

Very large amounts of alcohol can make some people aggressive or violent.

Most people suffer from the after-effects of too much drinking. This is known as a 'hangover', and happens because alcohol causes the body to dehydrate (lose fluid). There are various symptoms, but most people feel very unwell and suffer from a headache, thirst, nausea (feeling sick) and sometimes diarrhoea. The symptoms of a hangover are worse the more the person has had to drink, and there is very little they can do, other than drink plenty of water, get some sleep if they can, and wait for the several hours it takes for the hangover to pass.

Alcohol is addictive for some people – this is known as *alcoholism*. These people crave alcohol, and become anxious and jittery as its effects start to wear off. They feel that the only way for them to relieve these unpleasant symptoms is to have more to drink. Alcohol interferes with their daily lives, sometimes leading to loss of jobs and breakdown of family and relationships.

In the long term, alcohol can cause permanent damage to the liver and other major organs. It affects a man's ability to produce healthy sperm, and even to get erections. The brain is also affected, so that not only is the person's mental capacity impaired, but they are also at greater risk of developing depression.

In most countries, alcohol is illegal until you are at least 18 years old, and for good reason – it is simply not good for you as your body is growing and developing. There are two things in particular to be aware of as you and your friends go through adolescence: *never* get into a car that is being driven by someone who is drunk; and try never to become involved in drinking games or 'binge' drinking, where huge amounts of alcohol are consumed in one sitting. This is an exceptionally dangerous way to drink alcohol.

Remember, it is not compulsory to drink alcohol – many people choose not to. But if you do choose to drink (once you are old enough), then, as with so many things, moderation is the safe and sensible solution.

Smoking

Every cigarette contains thousands of chemicals, and at least two of these are known to cause major problems, so smoking even occasional ciga-rettes is considered to be bad for your health.

Nicotine, which is one of the chemicals contained in cigarettes, is a stimulant drug that narrows the blood vessels and makes the heart beat faster, and may be addictive. Certainly, many people soon find, once they start smoking, that they look forward to and crave the next ciga-rette. Soon they reach a point where they can't go without one – smoking can become a habit very quickly.

Another major ingredient of cigarettes is tar. Tar irritates the mucous membranes of your respiratory system, narrows the air passages and damages the very fine hairs that line these passages (the job of these hairs is to trap dirt and germs from the air you breathe, keeping your lungs clean). So, eventually, a smoker who is inhaling tar and other chemicals day after day develops a cough, shortness of breath and is prone to chest infections.

Smoking affects the way you look: people who smoke regularly have dull hair, a 'grey' look to their skin, which becomes drier and develops wrinkles more quickly, and stained teeth and fingers. They have bad breath and they smell of stale smoke. Smoking affects their sense of taste, so that food doesn't taste as good. It also interferes with their sense of smell, which means they can't tell how bad they smell to other people.

But the worst consequences of smoking are to people's long-term health. The continual damage to the respiratory tract by smoke can lead to cancer of the lungs, mouth, nose and tongue. Other organs, such as the heart, pancreas and kidneys, can be affected by regular smoking. The narrowing of the blood vessels all over the body has a range of effects. First, it causes a light-headed feeling with the first puff on a cigarette (which a lot of smokers enjoy); but it is this constriction of the blood vessels that contributes to heart and lung disease. It also affects a man's ability to get an erection, and makes periods more painful for women. When a woman is pregnant, the narrowing of the blood vessels to the placenta reduces the flow of oxygen and nutrients to the baby, leading to low birth weight and potential brain damage for the infant.

However, the good news is that when people give up smoking, much of the damage to the body reverses itself – within a couple of months the lungs begin to repair themselves. Ten years after giving up, a person's chance of a heart attack is the same as someone who has never smoked. Although it isn't easy, even people who have been addicted to smoking for years can give up with help from their doctor, friends and 'Quit lines', but mainly by using a lot of willpower.

But it is so much easier never to start smoking than to have to try to give up. Just think of the benefits to your health and your looks, and how much money you will save.

Drugs

Drugs (including alcohol and tobacco) are chemical substances that change the way your body or mind work. All drugs can have unexpected side effects, no matter whether they have been prescribed by a doctor, bought over the counter or obtained illegally. The consequences of taking something that wasn't prescribed for you, or that your body doesn't need, can be extremely serious, even fatal.

Different types of drugs have different effects on the body and the brain:

- *Stimulants* act on the central nervous system to speed up the person's heart rate and breathing, and cause the person to feel nervous and excited. Drugs in this category include tobacco, cocaine, 'Ecstasy' and amphetamines ('speed').

- *Depressants* act on the central nervous system, too, but slow down the activity of the brain. They make a person feel relaxed and a bit sleepy. Drugs in this category include alcohol, heroin and other opiates, and tranquillizers.

- *Hallucinogens* are drugs, such as LSD and 'magic mushrooms', which act on the brain, distorting reality, or causing people to have experiences and see and hear things that don't really exist.

Another drug that doesn't quite fit into any of these categories, but is widely used by young people, is *cannabis* (also known as 'marijuana', 'dope', 'pot', 'weed'). It can make some people feel relaxed, though others can feel paranoid and panicky. It affects people's concentration and mental functioning, and there is a risk of mental illness if the drug is used frequently and heavily.

All drugs, whether legal or illegal, carry some risk, so there are some things you need to be aware of:

- it is never a good idea to take medication that has been prescribed for someone else

- never take too much of any medication, even when it has been prescribed for you, and don't mix medications

- illegal drugs are not manufactured to a standard, so you can never be sure exactly what is in them or how strong they are

- all drugs have potential side effects

- it is possible for people to become used to a certain dose of a drug, so that they need to increase the dose to get the same effect; this increases the risks associated with any side effects

- when a person finds that they can't cope without the drug, and suffers unpleasant symptoms when they try to stop, we say they have become *addicted*

- addiction to any drug has the potential to ruin a person's health, as well as their relationships and job prospects.

Making wise choices

Teenagers may try drinking, smoking or drug-taking for all sorts of reasons. They may be influenced by their friends and feel the need to fit in; they may want to rebel against their parents, or to look grown up; perhaps they are bored and think it will be fun; or they may simply want to satisfy their curiosity. Whatever the reason, you can see from what you have just read that the risks are very high. You can only make good decisions about all of this when you have all the information, so check out some of the health websites on the internet, and read some of the many leaflets that are available. Above all, make sure you talk about all of this with a trusted adult or good friend. Perhaps you could practise ways of refusing the offer of something you are unsure about. Although there may be quite a bit of pressure from other people your age to try smoking, drinking or drug-taking – they may even tease you for not joining in – just remember, you are never a fool if you choose to care for your health.

5

Understanding Emotions

A lot of people become very moody and emotional as they go through adolescence. This is partly to do with the rise and fall of hormone levels in your body, which tends to cause mood swings. But there are several other factors that have an impact on your emotions at this time of your life. We have already explored some of these issues briefly in Chapter 2, **Puberty**, such as the need for you to become more independent, which can at times lead you into conflict with your parents and carers. We also

looked at the way that your friendships tend to go through a process of change as well. All this can be very unsettling, adding to your feelings of uncertainty.

If you are to cope with all the emotional upheaval, it helps to know what is happening, and how to recognize it, in the same way that under-standing the physical changes at puberty helps you to deal with those. We have already looked at ways that you can help yourself feel physically fit and look good. Being fit and well can certainly help you feel good about yourself, so take a look at Chapter 3, **Caring for Your Body**, and Chapter 4, **Making Healthy Choices**, for some ideas.

However, you can do all of this – keep thoroughly clean, eat well and enjoy enough exercise – yet still have days when you feel low-spirited and insecure about yourself. This is perfectly normal, and happens to everyone during adolescence. You may worry about exactly who you are and what will become of you in the future. Another area of concern for a lot of young people is the way they look – their body image – and many are worried about how to deal with the strong emotions and stress they experience from time to time.

Remember, you are not the only one with worries and concerns, although it might feel like that sometimes – but you are the only you. If you can find ways to appreciate your unique body and personality, you will be well on the way to feeling good about yourself.

Self-identity

Adolescence is a time when most young people ask themselves the question: 'Who am I?' This may sound silly, because of course you know who you are! But this is about more than just knowing your name. It is about developing a clear idea of who you are as a person, how you define yourself. It's also about understanding how others see you, and what sort of impact you have on the world. This is called your *self-identity*, and it can take a while for you to become clear about it. It's hard to be sure about yourself and what you will become, since you can't see into the future. But although you may feel a long way from being settled or grown up, you *can* start to identify characteristics within yourself that help to define who you are. After all, there are many aspects of you that make you quite different to your classmates, or brothers and sisters.

Recognizing your personal attributes

Identify and make a list of some of the good, interesting characteristics you have; for example, you may be very kind, smart, thoughtful, funny, strong, imaginative…the list goes on. Think about how you can use these positive characteristics every day, at home and at school.

Recognize what you enjoy and what you are good at. These are your strengths, and help to define the sort of person you are. You could nurture some of these strengths so that you become even more capable.

Here are a few examples. See whether any of these are right for you, and what you could add to this list:

- If you are particularly good with animals, you could offer to walk neighbourhood dogs for owners who don't get enough time; or you could do voluntary work at the local animal shelter at the weekend. Perhaps there are riding stables nearby, where you could help out sometimes.

- If music or maths (or any other subject) is your strength, you may be able to help classmates or younger children with their study. As you get older, you might be able to take on tutoring jobs.

- You may have excellent computer skills. Lots of older people don't – so maybe you could use your skills to help someone you know develop basic computer literacy.

- You may be accomplished in the kitchen, and have a natural flair for cooking. Nurture this talent, and cook the evening meal on a regular basis. Perhaps you could teach a younger brother or sister to cook.

- Drawing and art may be your talent. This is a great one to have, because so many other people appreciate it. You may get a reputation in your class or among your friends for being a good artist. Perhaps you could contribute to a class publication, or the school magazine. You could make greetings cards for your family and friends, or help design and draw posters to advertise events for your school or your youth group.

The possibilities are endless. Sit down with a parent or carer, and together come up with a list of things you enjoy and are good at. Work out how you might use your talents and interests.

All of this will help you to recognize the sort of person you are, and what you might become in the future. This helps you to gain a good sense of your identity, which, in turn, can help you feel good about yourself.

Body image

The way you look changes a lot at puberty, as we read in Chapter 2, **Puberty**, and it is normal to take a while to get used to your changing face and body. There will be days when you look in the mirror and feel quite satisfied with the image you see. Then there will be other times when you feel thoroughly discontented with some aspect of your looks. The way you feel about how you look has a great deal to do with your mental image of how you think you *should* look, and whether you match up to this image. Where do we get these ideas about how we think we ought to look?

Influences are all around us. Popular culture, such as films, television programmes and magazines contain thousands of images of so-called 'perfect' people. Our families and our friends also have their own ideas about what is 'good looking', and their attitudes and comments can influence our expectations and the way we feel about ourselves.

The 'perfect face' or the 'perfect body' don't really exist, although fashion magazines and Hollywood would have you believe they do. They are as changeable as any other fashion, such as styles of clothing, interior design or the shape of cars. Most film stars, fashion models and pop stars spend most of the time that they aren't acting, modelling or performing in the pursuit of the so-called 'perfect' image. They work out for hours at the gym, usually with the help of a personal trainer; they follow rigorous and unrealistic diets; they have help with their make-up and hair; and on top of all this, the photographic images we see of them have been enhanced by computers. And yet we allow ourselves to be 'brainwashed' by these images, believing them to represent the ideal way to look.

Although 'thin' (for women), and 'muscular' (for men) are the height of fashion at the moment, this hasn't always been the case – and isn't the case today in some cultures. There are many places in the world where thin represents poverty, while fat represents wealth, and is therefore desirable! Going back one or two hundred years (and more) the 'ideal' woman's body, as painted by artists, was well-rounded. Even in the middle of last century, film stars such as Marilyn Monroe, whose figure was quite curvy, represented a very different ideal to the one we have today.

The fact is there are as many variations in body shape and facial features as there are people, and it is simply impossible, and silly, to try to achieve some sort of fashionable ideal, or be exactly like someone else. All that happens, when we pursue an impossible ideal, is that we become discontented and unhappy. Many of today's film stars, models and even sportsmen and women are very unhappy with their bodies, and often struggle with eating disorders, because there is so much pressure on them to look a particular way.

Some ways to feel good about how you look

- Accept that the way you look is determined to a great extent by heredity. Take a look at your family – the chances are that you have many similar features, both facially and in your body shape.

- Be aware of how much fashion influences what is thought to be the perfect look. It changes from one year to the next – there is no one 'perfect' look.

- Be sceptical of the images you see in magazines. A range of techniques are used to enhance pictures of models and actors, so that their skin can be made to look blemish-free, their legs longer and thinner, their breasts bigger and their eyes a brighter colour. Seeing should *not* be believing!

- 'Put down' comments by other people about your looks tell you more about those people than they do about you. People who feel the need to be critical of your looks probably feel quite insecure about themselves. They may be trying to impress others around them.

- Some people are naturally thin, and are perfectly healthy. Equally, other people are naturally fatter, and are also perfectly healthy. Once you have stopped growing, your body will settle into the shape it is supposed to be. You can help it to achieve its own ideal by eating a healthy, balanced diet and enjoying the right amount of exercise (see Chapter 4, **Making Healthy Choices**).

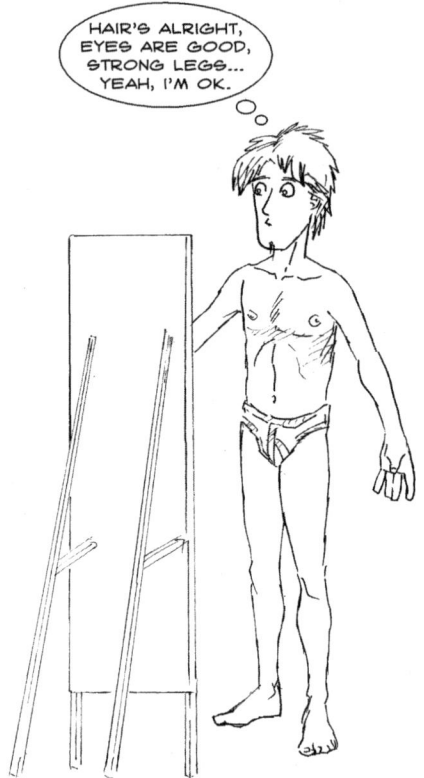

- Stand in front of a mirror and take a long look at yourself. Instead of dwelling on the features that you don't like, look at some of the things you *do* like about yourself (and there are sure to be some). Make a mental list of all these good features, and try to recall these when you are feeling insecure about your body.

- You have probably heard the saying 'Beauty is in the eye of the beholder'. This means that each one of us tends to see the world a little differently, and we each have our own idea of what is beautiful. You may not always feel that you look as attractive as you would like to be, but rest assured you will look just perfect to someone else!

Remember, you are unique. You will look good if you are healthy – that means eating a nutritious diet, doing some exercise that you enjoy and getting enough sleep. And there is nothing more attractive than a friendly smile!

Mood swings

Mood swings are those sudden, unexpected changes in mood, from happy to sad, relaxed to anxious, calm to angry, and back again, that you will almost certainly experience as you go through puberty. First, it is important to remind yourself that these sudden fluctuations in your mood are caused by hormones, and are very much a part of adolescence. You are absolutely normal, and not going mad! And they do pass. By the time most young people are through adolescence, their moods have stabilized, and life seems a lot smoother again. But in the meantime, it is a good idea to have some ways of coping with mood swings, particularly those that make you feel very sad or angry.

Handy hints for managing bad moods

- Explain to your friends or family that you are in a bad mood; remind them that it is temporary, and while it lasts you would prefer not to have to talk or join in. If you do this, they will be able to understand if you seem a bit irritable or unfriendly, and may be able to help you feel better.

- Do something quiet you enjoy, such as reading, drawing, listening to music, watching television, playing on the computer, or just daydreaming.

- Sometimes really energetic activities can get rid of a bad mood more quickly. Go for a brisk walk or a run, jump on the trampoline, take the dog for a walk, go for a swim – in fact, anything that is vigorous and that you really enjoy.

- Spend time with, or talk to, your pet. Animals can be very soothing when you are in a bad mood. They listen to you without making any judgement, and are nearly always pleased to see you. There is research that shows that when you stroke your pet, certain hormones are released that make you feel content.

- If you really feel you must thump or punch something, just make sure that it's something you can't damage (and that can't hurt you). For example, thump a punch bag, or your mattress or pillow – not the wall or a door, and *never, ever* another person.

Managing stress

Your body has a very effective way of dealing with an emergency. You get a rush of a hormone called *adrenalin* (sometimes known as the 'fight or flight' hormone), which causes your heart to beat faster. This pumps the blood more quickly to where it is needed: to your brain, so that you are more alert and can think quickly, and to your muscles, so that they are stronger and can move faster. When the danger has passed, your body can relax and return to normal.

This is a terrific response to protect you from danger. However, our bodies tend to respond this way to any unsettling situation that makes us anxious – even having a disagreement with a friend, taking an exam or going to the dentist. You will recognize those signs of nervousness that everyone experiences from time to time – a faster beating heart, sweaty palms, perhaps sweating under the arms, and shallow breathing. These symptoms generally disappear once the anxious situation is over.

If, however, you are the sort of person who becomes anxious very easily, or if there is something happening in your life that makes you feel anxious all the time (e.g. being picked on or bullied every day, or arguments at home) then your body can start to show signs of stress.

See if you recognize any of the following signs:

- continual feelings of nervousness or anxiety

- problems getting to sleep or staying asleep

- stomach pains, headaches or nausea (feeling sick)

- aches and pains in your muscles

- constipation or diarrhoea

- tiredness

- feelings of anger or sadness

- difficulty with concentration.

If you experience these sorts of symptoms day after day, it isn't good for your health in the long run, and you can end up becoming ill.

It is important to recognize when you may need help. If something worrying is happening in your life, and you are experiencing the symptoms of anxiety listed above *all the time*, you should talk to a trusted adult about it. Bullying, for example, should always be reported to your teacher, as the only way it will stop is if it becomes common knowledge (see Chapter 6, **Friendships**, for more about how to deal with bullies). You may need to talk to a counsellor or psychologist about your concerns, whatever they are. Remember, sharing your worries is a smart way to ease the burden, and is the first step in bringing about change.

As well as talking to someone about the things that are worrying you, there are some simple strategies that can help you deal with your reaction to some stressful situations – especially the more temporary ones – so that you don't experience the sort of build-up of symptoms that can lead to you becoming ill.

Winding down

Any number of activities can help you wind down and feel good. These might include things such as playing on the computer or games console, bouncing on the trampoline, or any other vigorous exercise that you enjoy; spending time engaged in an interest that you love; spending time with your pet; reading, drawing or listening to music; or watching your favourite television programme or film – the same sort of activities you might use to help overcome a mood swing, in fact.

Sometimes even just thinking about your favourite wind-down activity can be helpful. For example, if you are feeling stressed by your day, perhaps worn out by the effort of trying to understand other people, or be understood, you can mentally give yourself a treat. Imagine the fun activity you can reward yourself with once you get home. This positive thought can help you get through the difficult parts of your day.

Thinking positively

As well as thinking about a good-fun activity to reward yourself with at the end of the day, you can also use your thoughts to overcome your feelings of self-doubt.

- You are good at lots of things. Remind yourself of some of these *every day*. For example, say to yourself, 'I am really good at such and such' or, 'I know loads of stuff about such and such'. These regular reminders to yourself of your talents and knowledge will help you feel more like the capable, worthwhile person you really are.

- Try to put things in perspective. You may be very worried about a particular situation or event, which, if you think about it sensibly, is not going to be the end of the world. Say to yourself, 'Honestly, is the sky *really* going to come crashing down if such and such happens?'

- You have been successful plenty of times in your life. If you are anxious about something you have to do (e.g. a test; a talk to the class; attend a social gathering you're not keen on), remind yourself of some of the things you have done successfully in the past. If you could do it then, you can certainly do it again – you have got what it takes!

- Try picturing yourself in a positive, successful situation. Even better, keep a photo of yourself in such a situation, in your wallet. When you look at it, it will remind you that you *are* successful, and you can be just as confident as this again.

These positive thoughts can help you feel more capable and confident, and when you feel more confident, you look it and act it.

Relaxation

It can be very helpful to know some simple relaxation techniques for times when you feel especially tense and anxious.

These first techniques can be applied anywhere, even if you are sitting at your desk, in the playground or on the school bus.

- *Slow your breathing down*: take deep breaths and, with each breath, imagine pulling the air from your feet all the way up to the top of your head.

- *Deep breathing*: breathe in deeply through your nose, so that the air fills your lungs. Breathe in right down to your stomach. Then let the air out really slowly, by breathing out through your mouth, and while you do this, concentrate on letting your muscles all over your body relax.

The next two techniques require that you have a bit more space and can move your body freely. This one could be done while sitting or standing. You wouldn't necessarily have to be in a private place, but you would need to be sure that anyone around you wouldn't mind (the classroom or public transport probably aren't suitable places!):

- *Stretching*: stretch out your muscles, by reaching your arms above your head, and stretching out your legs and your feet as far as you can. Then relax. Stretch and relax whichever part of your body needs it.

The last technique is easier to do if you are lying down, and is a very good method to use at night to prepare your body for sleep:

- Tighten and relax your muscles in order, holding the tension for about ten seconds. Start with your toes, and gradually work up your body, each muscle group at a time. You can get relaxation CDs to help you learn this technique. It takes practice, but is particularly helpful.

Consider other activities that may be effective in helping you relax:

- Yoga, t'ai chi and some martial arts (e.g. tae kwon do) can be very relaxing, strengthening and excellent for your mood. Check out what is available in your local area.

- Any exercise you really enjoy will help you relax and feel good.

- Playing music and singing can be very good ways to relax. If you have abilities in these areas, check out what youth choirs, orchestras or bands exist in your area – you may be able to engage regularly in making music with like-minded people.

A balanced lifestyle

A balanced lifestyle is just as important as a balanced diet. No single type of food on its own can provide your body with all the nutrients it needs for good health (see Chapter 4, **Making Healthy Choices**).

Likewise, if you put all your energy into just one or two aspects of your life, to the exclusion of other things, you will fail to meet all your emotional needs. When your life is unbalanced, it's much more likely that you will feel tense, tired and low-spirited, and be less able to deal with some of those stressful situations.

It is important to have a wide variety of activities and interests in your life, not just school or work, or one special interest. Try balancing your time between school (or work), hobbies and interests, physical activities and socializing with friends or family. And don't forget, you need plenty of rest and sleep, too.

So how can you fit all these things into your life? Time management may not be your greatest skill – very few people are good at this while they are going through puberty. Perhaps you could get an adult to help you make a list of all the things you do – or should be doing – in your life. Together you can come up with some sort of weekly plan, to include both work (school), and 'play'; that is, all the fun activities that you enjoy.

In this way, you should be able to find a balance, which is really very helpful in enabling you to cope with any stress there may be in your life.

Managing anger

It is perfectly normal to feel angry sometimes – everybody does. There's no doubt that most young people go through a stage when they seem to be angry a lot of the time.

However, there are different ways to be angry, and they're not all healthy. If you show your anger in an aggressive way by 'exploding', hurting yourself or other people, and damaging property, or if you break the law because of your anger, then quite obviously this isn't healthy or safe. You may, on the other hand, turn your anger inwards, and look and act in a surly, hostile way all the time. You might want to keep to yourself, and refuse to talk properly to your parents, teachers and even your friends, always answering their questions with just single words and grunts. This isn't healthy either, as you are not really expressing what is wrong.

The healthy way to be angry is to express your feelings clearly to the appropriate person, without using physical or emotional violence, and be able to reach some sort of resolution without either you or the other person coming to any harm. This is easier said than done, and can take quite a bit of practice.

The first step is to recognize *signs of anger* in yourself:

- your heart beats faster, and your breathing becomes faster

- your body may start to shake

- you may feel like shouting, screaming, crying, hurting yourself or someone else, and hitting out at a person or an object

- your body becomes tense, and you might clench your fists

- your face may change colour – some people turn red with anger, while others go very pale.

If you know that you are becoming very angry, the next stage is to learn how to deal with it. Remember, when you are very angry you do not think clearly (some experts say that your IQ drops by 30 points when you are angry), so the smart thing to do is to find a way that works for you of reducing your anger before you lose your temper and do something you regret.

Coping with your anger

- If possible, remove yourself from the situation, or at least take a step back (literally).

- Breathe deeply, and concentrate on gradually steadying your breathing until it feels calm. You might accompany this by squeezing a stress ball or something similar.

- If the situation allows, scream and shout really loudly. If you are in your room, you can scream into your pillow to muffle the sound. To gradually achieve a sense of calm, count backwards slowly from ten (or fast from 100), reducing the volume as you go so that you end up whispering 'one'.

- Do something active and physical, such as walking fast or going for a run, hitting a ball against a wall with a racquet, punching a punch bag or your pillow, doing sit-ups, bouncing on the trampoline...all sorts of vigorous activities work really well. However, *don't* do anything that requires judgement, such as bike riding, as your judgement is impaired until you have calmed down.

- Do something both vigorous *and* useful, such as sorting out a cupboard or tidying your room. If your household is into recycling, crushing cans and cartons can be very satisfying.

Once you are calmer, then you can begin to deal with the situation; for example, you might be able to sort out the problem that is frustrating you, or discuss the issue with the other person. You may need a bit more time to work out exactly what you want to say to the other person. Here are some ideas as to how you might do this.

Sorting out what you want to say

- Type your thoughts on the computer. Sometimes when you are working at the computer you have more time to think and compose your words properly. You could even get someone else to check what you have written, to ensure that you are 'on track', before you go ahead and say any of it to the person you are upset with. You may decide *not* to say any of it. Sometimes simply writing it all down can 'get it out of your system', and be all that you need.

- If your mobile telephone has a voice-record function, you could record what you think, verbally. Listen to what you have said. This can be a very good way of reflecting about your feelings, putting them in perspective, and helping you to calm down. You can then decide whether to voice your feelings to anyone else.

- 'Role-play' with a trusted adult or good friend what you would like to say to the other person. In this way you can practise getting it just right.

Managing aggression

You may find that you often express your anger or frustration by being aggressive. Some people are aggressive most of the time, both in the way they talk and in the way they behave towards others. It might be that this is their defence against a world that they see as unjust, don't understand or can't control – it's as though they think that life is going to be a battle anyway, so they may as well approach every situation as though it's a fight. The trouble is, once you start thinking like this, it *does* become a fight. Sometimes aggressive behaviour can become a bit of a habit.

You don't do yourself any favours if you behave aggressively. Even though you may appear to get what you want by acting this way, in the end you will find that you drive other people away with your actions and your words. People will be afraid of you, and will probably become angry or resentful towards you. An aggressive attitude and aggressive behaviour always get other people 'off-side', so that they are much less inclined to be helpful towards you or treat you with respect. In the long run, they won't want to be your friend.

If aggression is your standard response when you feel angry, read the previous section about managing anger. There are much more productive ways to respond to situations that annoy you, and it is possible to express your thoughts and feelings without becoming aggressive.

If aggressive behaviour has become something of a habit for you, then you need to learn ways to behave differently, so that you don't get everyone off-side and spoil opportunities to make friends.

Dealing with aggression

- It's very important to understand the perspective of other people before you 'fly off the handle'. The situation might not be quite as you thought, and there may be no need to get angry. Try not to always assume that everything is 'someone else's fault', or was deliberate. It may be nobody's fault, or it might have been an accident.

- If you find that you often misunderstand situations, which results in you being aggressive much of the time, it might be a very good idea to have the help of a social mentor or a trusted adult (see Chapter 6, **Friendships**). This person can help you to understand what is going on, and suggest better ways of managing these situations.

- Practise some self-talk techniques, such as 'By getting what I want in this way, is this person going to like me?' or 'I might have misunderstood this situation. I'll breathe slowly, count to ten to calm myself, and then assess the situation.'

- If you have been aggressive and made someone afraid of you, learn to apologize. Being able to say sorry is a very important skill, and one that can get you out of all sorts of difficulties.

- Try to be friends with someone who is socially competent – they can help you through many difficulties and teach you how to keep your cool, or help you to calm down if you are starting to get upset.

- Social skills and emotion management groups can be very helpful. They teach you ways to behave, and give you opportunities to practise different techniques.

When you may need professional help

If you have a lot of difficulty managing your anger and aggression, so that you are getting into trouble at school and at home because of your explosive reactions to people and situations, then you may need professional help. It's really good to learn some anger management strategies while you are still young, and before you get into any serious trouble. Learning how to stay calmer in the face of frustration will help you enormously as you grow up, both in sorting out and solving your problems, and in communicating effectively with other people.

Friendships

The friendships you have as a child are a bit different to those you will have as an adult. Childhood friendships are about having fun together with someone who likes the same things that you do. Of course, having fun and sharing interests are important qualities of friendship at any age, but as you go through adolescence and become more grown up, other factors become important. Adult friendships are more about emotional support and sharing thoughts and feelings. Have you noticed how adults get together with each other and happily spend hours just talking? Children get together and spend hours *doing* all sorts of different things – usually with others of the same sex. They talk to each other, of course, but usually about the game they are playing – they would find it very boring to do nothing *but* talk.

Puberty is the time when this change in the quality of friendship starts to happen. Boys and girls start to socialize with each other. They become more interested in how their friends are *feeling*, and often support each other by listening to each other's problems. When they have disagreements, they prefer to resolve these by discussing the problem with each other, rather than having an argument or a physical fight. Many teenagers love to talk to each other all day (usually driving their teachers mad in class), message each other the moment they start walking out of school and get straight on to the computer as soon as they get home, to continue the conversation.

But as with all aspects of puberty, this transition to a different style of friendship happens at a different time for everybody. While one person may be interested in talking at length about their feelings, and what is going on in their life, their good friend may just want to play the games and do the sorts of activities that they have always done together. This means that two people who were close childhood friends may find themselves drifting apart because their needs and interests are different. Starting at secondary school can be a big upheaval in lots of ways, including a major reshuffle of friendships for lots of young people.

All this can be very unsettling, especially if you find friendships and the way people interact with each other confusing at the best of times. This chapter is about understanding friendships – why they are important for everybody, how to go about making friends and keeping them, and how to withstand some of the pressure you may experience from your friends and classmates from time to time. We will also look at the issue of bullying, which can be so distressing for many young people at this time of life.

There are whole books devoted to the topic of friendships because there is a lot to know. Even though we can only deal with it in a small way in this chapter, there are some important points that can be covered to give you some ideas.

The importance of friends

There are many reasons why friends are important. Friends are people you have fun with, and whose company you enjoy. You may share similar interests with them, and have a similar outlook on life. By negotiating friendship you learn about sharing, about being loyal and trustworthy, how not to hurt someone's feelings, and how to resolve conflict. Friends give each other compliments, and can help each other out when things get difficult. When you do things with friends you are often more daring and adventurous than you might be by yourself. Friends can give you confidence, and help you to feel good about yourself. Having at least one or two friends at school helps to pass the time and make break-times (recess) more interesting – and if you're with someone you are less likely to be bullied. And (looking to the future) you will only be ready for a sexual relationship once you know how to have successful friendships.

How many friends do you need?

That depends on you. Each one of us has an individual capacity for friendship, with some people needing lots of friends in order to feel good, while others may be quite content with just one or two good friends. Think of it rather like a bucket – some people find their 'social bucket' is very easily filled, because it's only small – more the size of a mug; they only need one or two friends who they see just occasionally. Other people have enormous social buckets (like water tanks), which are only filled by having lots of friends and frequent social contact.

You may be a person who is happy to spend time by yourself – lots of people enjoy their own company much of the time. Don't feel you have to have lots of friends just to please other people, and don't force yourself to socialize in situations that you find really uncomfortable. Certainly you must never do things that go against your nature or better judgement just to try to have friends or be popular (see the later section on peer pressure). Equally, don't try to 'buy' friends by doing things such as giving away your lunch money or buying little gifts for people all the time. Obviously, these are nice, friendly things to do sometimes, but if you're doing them all the time, and getting nothing back in return, it could be that people are simply taking advantage of you, and aren't your real friends at all.

Even if you're a person who needs very few friends, it's probably smart to have more than one if possible, simply because it's good not to become too dependent, and you can't always rely on just one person. You might have a disagreement with each other, or he or she may be ill, or have to go away sometimes, leaving you with no one at all for a while.

If friends do seem a little 'thin on the ground' from time to time, remember that family members can be very supportive and good fun, and can take the place of friends, at least for a while. And don't forget pets! Lots of people get a great deal of pleasure and emotional support from their pet, because pets often love you unconditionally, never judge you and are nearly always pleased to see you.

Making friends

Who can help?

If you are someone who finds the whole area of friendship quite bewildering, one of the very best ideas is to have a 'social guide' or 'social mentor'. This can be anyone, such as one of your parents, a brother or sister, another relative or family friend, or a good friend. It doesn't matter, just as long as it is someone you trust, possibly a bit older than you, who is good at understanding the social world. Your social mentor can help you work through difficulties and make sense of some of the social situations you find yourself in. They can be your 'interpreter' when things are feeling a bit foreign.

Another way you can learn about friendships is to observe what other people do, especially those people who seem to be very successful at making friends. Watch what they do, discuss some of these techniques with your social mentor, and try them out for yourself.

Perhaps you could get involved in drama classes or social skills groups. These can be lots of fun and a really good way to learn and practise some important friendship skills.

But for now, let's look at some of the basic information you need if you want to 'crack the code' of friendship and be able to make friends, especially as you move into adolescence.

How to be the sort of person others want to be friends with

Very few people are going to rush to be friends with someone who looks miserable and rejects every offer of friendship. Nor are they necessarily going to try to make friends with someone who looks particularly weird or different. People are far more likely to approach someone who looks clean, presentable and friendly. The following information may give you a few ideas about how to present yourself, and how to behave, in order to give yourself the best chance when it comes to making friends.

PRESENTING AN ACCEPTABLE IMAGE

It is a fact of life that people judge each other to begin with by the way they look. It is also a fact that if you choose to fit in with the majority in terms of what you wear, your hairstyle and the way you care for yourself, you open yourself up to more possibilities for friendship. If you choose to dress in an unusual way, or don't see the point of looking after your personal hygiene, it's possible that fewer people will want to get to know you (and, in fact, you may be more likely to become a target of bullying – see later section). This may seem superficial – after all, it is the 'person inside' that counts – but it *is* a fact of life. Getting to know someone happens bit by bit. The first stage is to like the look of a person. After that, you get to know them in more depth, and their appearance becomes less important.

So your image is important. It is the way people see you initially, before they get to know you. Chat with your social mentor, or a trusted adult, about the image you present to the world.

But don't lose sight of who you are, and don't make yourself feel uncomfortable just in order to fit in. It may just be a matter of compromising a little (such as getting a few fashionable items of clothing, or having a shower every day, even when you think you don't need one) so that you give yourself the very best opportunity to fit in and make friends.

FEELING GOOD ABOUT YOURSELF

When you feel good about yourself, you are more likely to look cheerful, friendly and approachable. A person who is sullen and miserable doesn't look like the sort of person that most people want to be friends with, or like the sort of person who even *wants* friends. So what can you do to help yourself feel good?

First, it's important to accept yourself for who you are. Try reminding yourself regularly of all your good points. You have an interesting, unique combination of talents and abilities that you must learn to appreciate. Pursue interests that make use of these – this enhances your abilities and allows other people to appreciate them.

Look after your physical and emotional health. When you are clean, eat well and get the right amount of sleep and exercise, you are far more likely to feel good about yourself (see Chapter 3, **Caring for your Body**, Chapter 4, **Making Healthy Choices**, and Chapter 5, **Understanding Emotions**).

Even if you don't always feel it, try to *look confident*. Here's how... (to begin with, you might have to be a bit of an actor):

- smile at people, especially when they have smiled at you

- look at people's faces and make eye contact when you talk to them (if making the right amount of eye contact is something you find difficult, practise getting this right with your social mentor)

- keep your head up, and stand up straight.

This doesn't sound like much, but these small adjustments can make a world of difference. When you look cheerful and confident, other people will find it much easier to approach you.

BEING WELL-LIKED

Other people are more inclined to like and accept you when you:

- are as friendly as you can be; smile at people, ask how they are, and respond politely to people who talk to you

- are the first to say hello sometimes – don't always wait for someone to talk to you before you can have a conversation

- are kind and helpful to others

- are careful with your hygiene: clean hair and teeth and a nice-smelling body are always attractive

- are willing to share your things – and your friends

- speak clearly so that other people can easily understand you; avoid talking in a threatening or aggressive way

- listen to other people, and take care not to *always* talk about yourself or your special interest (see later section on conversation skills); try not to be too opinionated about things, and take care not to insult or criticize people

- are moderate in terms of your actions and behaviour; too much fooling around or hyperactivity tends to put other people off

- aren't too quick to react, or overly suspicious of others – an elbow in the ribs or a foot stuck out from the desk may be accidental and aren't necessarily deliberate actions to hurt you (if this sort of thing happens a lot, and you feel it may be deliberate, there are ways to respond; see the later section on teasing and bullying)

- know how to join a group of people without being pushy or dominating (see later section)

- show your appreciation of your friends, and know what to do to keep them (see later section)

- are light-hearted and see the funny side of things sometimes; in other words, use your sense of humour when you can – other people appreciate someone who isn't too serious all the time.

All these things help to create a good first impression and establish friendships more smoothly. Once friendships are firmly established, you can sometimes get away with being less 'well behaved'. But be careful. Too much anti-social behaviour will drive away even good friends eventually.

Understanding how friendships work
LEVELS OF FRIENDSHIPS

It's obvious that among all the people you know, you have a more friendly relationship with some than others. You may have one or two people you consider to be your closest friends, who you know really well, and with whom you feel completely comfortable. Then you may have a few friends for different occasions, who you may not be quite so close to, but who may share some of your interests and are fun to be around. There are probably several other people who you know a little, perhaps just to talk to occasionally (acquaintances); and then there will be a lot more who you recognize by face but not necessarily by name. And everyone else is a stranger.

It is important that you recognize these 'levels' of friendship, since they determine the way you behave towards someone. When you know someone well, you can be more relaxed around them – you can 'be yourself'. Conversation may be easier, you can be silly if you want, honest about how you are feeling, and you can talk about more personal topics. The less well you know someone, the more 'formal' your behaviour has to be, otherwise it can seem inappropriate. It's not okay, for example, to discuss your feelings or talk at length about your special interest to someone who is just a casual friend or an acquaintance – this could be viewed as a bit weird or boring.

Talk with your social mentor about the various people in your life. Work out what level of friendship they belong to, and discuss what type of behaviour is most appropriate at this level (e.g. How open can you be about yourself? What sort of things should you be able to talk about? How often should you be in contact, if at all?).

CHANGING LEVELS OF FRIENDSHIP

The people in your life can move back and forth through these levels of friendship. Someone who was a very good friend at primary (elementary) school can become more like an acquaintance at secondary (high) school, while someone you hardly knew can become a very good friend. And of course, new people come into your life all the time.

Friendships can change for many reasons.

- You lose contact with each other – perhaps one of you moves away, or you go to different schools, where you meet new people.

- Gradually you find your interests changing. You may find yourself drifting apart from one friend, but becoming closer to someone else.

- Other people come onto the scene. This doesn't necessarily change friendships, but it can.

- You have a disagreement about something, which damages the friendship. It's very important to note, however, that a disagreement doesn't *have* to break up a friendship. Arguments often happen between friends, yet the friendship can be repaired (see later section 'Keeping friends).

GROUPS AND HIERARCHIES

If you go to quite a big school, there is another aspect of friendship that you will need to understand, especially if you are to have any success with making friends at school. You may already be aware that most people at school belong to a group of one sort or another. The names of these will vary from school to school, but may include groups such as 'band', 'theatre', 'nerds', 'techies', 'trendies', 'popular kids' and so on. The bigger the school, the more of these there will be, and they are particularly strong in the early teenage years. While some people are loners and don't associate with any group in particular, most teenagers belong to at least one group, and some fit into two or three, or even drift between several. When someone belongs to a group they are able to identify with their friends, which helps them to feel good about themselves.

Some of the groups are considered to be more desirable than others, so that there is a hierarchy (or 'pecking order') of groups. The most elite are the 'popular' groups, usually made up of confident, fashionable people who are socially able, and often sporty. Most people, however, fit into the 'mainstream' groups, and are neither especially popular nor unpopular, but they are reasonably well-respected and liked. They tend to just blend in with each other. A few people stand out as being a bit different from everyone else, and the groups they belong to may be more unusual in some way. These groups may be viewed as 'unpopular', and sometimes the people who belong to them are the targets of teasing or bullying (although belonging to a group can protect them from this to some extent – it is usually the loners who are the targets of the worst bullying).

Although this may all sound a bit complicated, it's important to recognize this social hierarchy at school, whether you agree with it or not. It has a strong influence on the way people behave, and on how friendships are made. For example, people in the more popular groups tend to make friends with each other, and are very unlikely to make friends with anyone in a less well-respected group. If they do choose to do so, however, the move towards friendship usually comes from them, not from the person in the less popular group. If someone in a less well-respected group attempts to befriend a 'popular' person, they may well be rejected, because they will be breaking the social code, and this is viewed as unacceptable.

You may need some help to 'decode' these complicated rules and social levels, and to work out where you fit in all of this, but once you do have some understanding, it makes it easier to work out who is likely to be a potential friend and who isn't.

These groups and hierarchies are very much a feature of early teenage years, and teenagers decide for themselves who is 'popular' and who isn't. It is very important that you understand that, in reality, someone who belongs to a popular group is no better a person than someone who belongs to a less popular group, or someone who is a bit of a loner. You are not a 'good' or a 'bad' person because of the people you identify with. It is the way you behave and the way you treat other people that define what sort of a person you are.

As people grow up and become more mature, these social groups become less well-defined and much less important. Adults tend not to be so judgemental about each other, and are more accepting of people who are different. Once you leave school, you will probably find you have much more scope in terms of who you can choose to be friends with.

Where to meet friends

You can meet friends anywhere at all, and it is possible for a friendship to develop from a chance, brief meeting. This is unusual, however, and it's far more likely that you will make friends with people that you encounter on a regular basis, in situations where you are sharing experiences and getting to know each other gradually.

The sort of places you may meet friends are:

- school
- work
- church

- youth groups or support groups
- evening classes
- sport and recreational activities or camp
- drama or theatre
- hobby groups, such as modellers, chess clubs and so on.

Since one of the fundamental features of friendship is sharing a common interest, a good way to make friends is to join a group that does something you are interested in. These may be clubs or activities outside of school, or that run at lunch-times at school. By doing something you enjoy, you will be more relaxed and confident, and when you are in this frame of mind, it's much easier to make friends.

FRIENDS OF DIFFERENT AGES

You may find that you relate better to people who are slightly younger or older than you. That's fine – there are no rules about who you can and can't be friends with, just so long as you can be open about and proud of your friendship, you both treat each other with respect, and abide by the law.

How to recognize a potential friend

Even when you are surrounded by people who share your interests, they can't all be your best friends. How do you recognize which of the people you meet can be a friend?

First, although there's no doubt we do form an initial opinion about someone just from the way they look, it's important not to be too quick to jump to conclusions. The way someone talks or dresses, and where they live may give us a bit of an idea about them, but it is never the whole story. Don't dismiss someone or judge someone until you have found out a bit more about them. Be friendly – or at least polite – to people, no matter what they look like or where they come from – they could be potential friends.

If you are going to be friends with someone, they need to be as interested in you as you are in them. But how would you know? There are ways you can tell whether someone is interested in being your friend.

SIGNS THAT SOMEONE IS INTERESTED

The person:

- looks pleased to see you; they may smile, make eye contact, stand and wait for you to join them, or invite you to join their group

- looks at you when you are talking; they don't constantly look around them as if they are looking out for someone else

- is interested in what you have to say; they listen to you, ask relevant questions, and appear to share some of your interests

- seems relaxed with you; they are able to laugh and use their sense of humour

- shows an interest in swapping phone numbers or email addresses, and follows through on arrangements that you make together.

And, of course, this is how *you* must behave if you want to make it clear to someone that you are interested in them.

AND IF SOMEONE ISN'T INTERESTED...

If someone isn't interested in you, they:

- may ignore you as you approach them

- don't return your phone calls or respond to your emails or messages

- may treat you rudely by excluding you from gatherings

- may even tell you to your face to go away.

If any of this happens, *don't persist* after the first two or three attempts at friendship. This only makes life difficult for them and for you. There are plenty of other people who are probably much better-suited to you, anyway.

Ways to develop a friendship

Once you have established that someone is a potential friend, you need to be able to develop the friendship.

SLOW AND STEADY

It's always best to move gradually, taking care not to overwhelm the person with your enthusiasm. You may make opportunities to work alongside each other, or talk more together. You might suggest things you could do or places you might go that build on a shared interest. You may be introduced to each other's friends and included in a new group. You may spend time at each other's houses, and meet each other's families. Bit by bit, as long as you continue to enjoy each other's company, you can spend more time together and gradually get to know one another better.

As you get to know someone better, you are constantly discovering more about them, learning to trust them, finding out whether you share interests, values, humour and a general outlook on life. The more similar these are, and the more relaxed you are able to be with this person, the firmer and closer your friendship will become. Not everyone can be your best friend, and that's okay. The main thing is that you develop a friendship slowly and steadily so that it reaches a level that is comfortable for you both.

Becoming part of a group

You will find, when you start at a new school, or join a club or organization, that people tend to gather in small groups of friends. If you want to become part of one of these, you need to know how to do this in an acceptable way. There are a few definite 'dos' and 'don'ts' that you should be aware of when trying to become part of any existing group.

Do:

- Watch closely in order to get an idea of what is going on. If you are going to be part of the group, you will need to understand the social rules and the way people behave, so that you can behave in the same way.

- Listen to what people are saying. This helps you to work out how the people in the group are relating to one another, who is 'in charge' (if anyone), what is important and so on. In this way, you will be aware of the sort of things you can say.

- Move closer to the group. By doing this, you are showing that you are interested, and are more likely to be noticed by someone.

- If you catch someone's eye (in other words, they look at you and acknowledge you are there), smile at them, and say something like, 'May I join you?'.

- Ease into the group, taking care to fit in with existing rules, ways of behaving and conversation. If you are friendly and co-operative, you are far more likely to be welcomed into a group than if you behave in a surly, critical or argumentative way.

Don't:

- Barge straight into the group without any introduction and disrupt what is happening. This is viewed as *butting in*, and is unacceptable social behaviour.

- Feel it is your place to offer advice or put right something that was going on (unless someone in the group has asked you to do this). Other people will see you as a 'know-it-all', and be more inclined to reject you.

- Try to split up the group by taking aside one or two people who are already involved in it.

If you follow these guidelines you are more likely to be included in the group you wish to join. Once you are sure of the protocol, and people accept you, you will be able to contribute by giving your opinion, offering suggestions and so on.

Keeping friends

It's important that you know how to make friends – that's a good start. But it's just as important to know how to keep the ones you've got. Friendships don't maintain themselves, unfortunately – they take a bit of effort; and of course, this should be a two-way process. If one person makes all the effort, that isn't really fair. A good friendship is a bit like a game of tennis, with the ball going back and forth between the two players. If one person keeps serving the 'friendship ball' over the net, but the other one keeps failing to return it, you would have to wonder how much they really care about being friends. Each of the friends should take it in turns with aspects such as contacting each other, making suggestions for what to do, giving each other compliments or gifts – even with conversation (see the later section on conversation skills), so that the friendship is equal and balanced.

THE 'FRIENDSHIP' BALL

Skills for maintaining a friendship

These factors are important if you are to keep your friendships healthy and flourishing. This list may look a bit daunting, but you may find you're doing most of this anyway, without thinking too hard about it.

- *Regular contact*: of one sort or another is one of the most important ways to maintain any friendship. This may be face to face, letters or email, telephone calls, text messages – whatever you want. But how often should you be in contact? This depends on the circumstances and your level of friendship. One way to get it right is to use the 'game of tennis' idea, where you try to match the frequency or type of contact that your friend is giving you. If you do this, you won't appear overly keen by getting in touch more than would be expected, and equally you won't appear to lack interest or not care by being too slow to respond. By doing your best to be sensitive to your friend's level of interest, the friendship can progress steadily, or be maintained at a reasonable level.

- *Make suggestions:* for interesting things to do. In a good friendship you are both responsible for this (it's that game of tennis again). If the friendship seems to be getting a little stale, and you always do the same things, try suggesting something different. This can give life and energy to a friendship.

- *Don't be a pushover:* it's good to be a flexible friend, and agreeable to your friend's suggestions, but at the same time make sure you don't give in to things you really don't feel comfortable with (this can be a form of peer pressure – see later section). Your friend will respect you more if you show some character and stand up for yourself – as long as you aren't aggressive about it.

- *Give each other freedom:* it's perfectly okay – in fact, really healthy – to both have other friends, and to do things apart from each other. This brings more depth and interest to your friendship. If you are possessive and clingy, you will exhaust your friend and drive them away. If the only reason they are still your friend is because you won't let them go, they are with you for the wrong reasons. They will resent you for 'smothering' them, and this is not the basis of a good friendship.

- *Different opinions:* and different interests are okay. You and your friend don't have to like all the same things, and in fact some differences make your friendship healthy and interesting. Learn to respect and value your differences.

- *Help your friend:* you almost certainly have different skills and abilities, and you can use these to help each other out in all sorts of situations.

- *Be reliable:* stick to arrangements if you can, and try to follow through on anything you have promised to do. If anything has to change, or you are unable to do something you promised, be sure to let your friend know.

- *Be thoughtful:* you can show your friend that you are thinking about them in all sorts of ways, such as giving small gifts, lending each other items of interest and remembering to ask them about things that are important in their life. Remember important dates, such as birthdays and Christmas. Tell your friend from time to time how much you enjoy the friendship, and compliment your friend when they do something well or look good.

- *Be loyal*: good friends support each other. It's very important that you don't gossip or make unkind comments about your friend to other people. Respect your friend's privacy – if they tell you something in confidence, it's vital that you keep this to yourself.

- *Be honest*: this is a tricky one. Mostly, honesty in a friendship is very important. For example, you should be able to be honest about yourself, what you like and don't like, what you believe in, and so on. It's very difficult to live comfortably with untruths; continual lies put a barrier between you and your friend. However, there is a place for 'white lies' in some circumstances. Read about these, and why they are important, in the next section, 'Conversation skills'.

- *Be flexible*: sometimes plans have to change, so there's no point going into a sulk or giving your friend a hard time just because an arrangement doesn't quite go according to plan, or even falls through altogether. Be open to suggestions and remain as good-natured as you can.

- *Learn to negotiate and compromise*: a difference of opinion does not have to turn into an argument. You can negotiate with your friend so that you reach an agreement that suits you both. This may mean one or both of you having to change your original ideas – but that's okay. You haven't 'lost' anything by compromising, but you may have avoided unnecessary hard feelings and gained your friend's respect.

- *Learn how to resolve conflict*: it takes practice and a certain amount of maturity to sort out disagreements without using your fists or harsh words to hurt each other – but it is possible! All friends have disagreements from time to time – it's an indication that you are two lively people with your own opinions. The sign of a good friendship is that you can sort out these differences without holding grudges. When you have a disagreement, try listening to your friend's point of view. You may agree to differ – or you may be won over by a good argument. And (sometimes even more difficult) you may need to apologize, or graciously accept an apology. Whatever happens, if you value your friendship, you will be able to get past disagreements, and your friendship will be stronger because of it.

An awareness of these friendship skills will help you do the right thing in terms of how to treat your friends. It will also help you to understand why friendships sometimes fail. When you find yourself drifting apart from a friend, you may find it useful to check some of the points above, to see if you can gain some insight into what is going wrong. Sometimes there is no point rescuing a friendship – you may just have to acknowledge that it is over. On the other hand, it might be very important to you, and you may find that, by addressing the particular aspects that have gone wrong, you are able to rescue your friendship.

Conversation skills

We've already mentioned that teenagers love to communicate with each other, and tend to do so, in various ways, just about all day and half the night. Conversation of one sort or another is at the very heart of adolescence. But what if you're not very good at it? It's very easy to be left out or become a victim of teasing or bullying if you find aspects of conversation difficult. While you may find it easier to communicate with someone online or by email (and these are often really valid alternatives), there's no escaping the fact that face-to-face conversation is an essential part of life.

The ability to communicate well is something that most people develop gradually, and it does take a certain amount of effort and practice. We are going to look at some of the most basic, but essential, conversation skills that you need to develop if you are to communicate well and have successful relationships. Discuss some of these points with your social mentor, decide which are the areas you need to pay most attention to, and then get plenty of practice. Remember, practice makes perfect!

But first, something you need to be aware of…

TEENAGERS BREAK THE RULES

Unfortunately, when it comes to communication, teenagers break rules and follow fashion just as much as they do in any other aspect of life. Each group of teenagers will have their own unwritten 'codes of conduct' that can be very difficult to decipher, and these rules will vary from country to country, school to school – even from group to group within a school. This makes it very difficult for someone who is new to the group to fit in and be accepted, and even more difficult for someone who finds the subtle details of communication a challenge.

Luke Jackson, a teenager who has written an excellent book about adolescence (see the **Recommended Reading** at the end of this book), points out that when you watch any group of teenagers in conversation with each other, you will notice that they seem to be breaking every one of the rules for appropriate behaviour – rules you are sure to be aware of, such as:

- look at the person who is talking to you, but don't stare at people generally
- don't make personal comments, especially about someone's body or the way they look
- don't stand too close to someone when you talk to them
- don't touch someone unless you know them well and you both agree that this is okay
- don't be too loud or opinionated. Be careful not to make offensive remarks or use obscene language.

With what seems to be complete disregard for these rules, teenagers talk loudly, swear, push and jostle each other, point out each other's faults, and comment on the way others look, all as part of their everyday communication with each other. The risk is, though, if you attempt to join in this so-called 'normal' teenage behaviour, you are likely to be looked at with scorn, and you will realize you didn't get it right somehow.

You may have a close friend of your own age who can lead you through this 'minefield' of teenage communication and, bit by bit, you may be able to negotiate it yourself. If you are relying on an older social mentor, however, the wisest thing may be for you to be polite (as above) and stick to the general rules for communication, which we are about to explore. This may make you seem overly polite and a bit old-fashioned, but ultimately these are the guidelines you need for life beyond teenage years, and it's probably better to be seen as pleasant and polite than rude and difficult.

GUIDELINES FOR MAKING GOOD CONVERSATION

Again, this is a long list, but don't let that put you off. You may do a lot of these things quite naturally, without even realizing it. But if you *are* having some problems in conversation, check through the list, perhaps with your social mentor, and see what you may need to do to 'polish' your skills a little.

- Stand or sit an appropriate distance from the person you are talking to. You shouldn't be too close, or too far away – about an arm's length is just right. You may need to practise this with your social mentor.

- Learn how to begin a conversation. You should never just 'launch' straight into the topic you want to discuss. Rather, you should begin with what are known as 'pleasantries'; that is, you may ask the person how they are or what they have been doing, or ask about something relevant to that person that you happen to know is important to them. Practise a few conversation starters with your social mentor.

- Talk at the right volume. In a quiet place, you need to talk more quietly, while in a noisy situation you will need to increase your volume. If you're not sure whether you are talking too loudly or too quietly, try to match the volume level of the other person, and check with them that your volume is okay.

- Make frequent eye contact. Look at the other person for a few seconds, which shows you are genuinely interested – but don't stare too much. Look away briefly every few seconds. Practise getting eye contact just right with your social mentor.

- Take turns in conversation. Remember that game of tennis we have referred to? The 'conversation ball' should go back and forth between the two of you, so that what you say should roughly match what the other person says in terms of length. That means *no monologues!* Always leave spaces, so that the other person can have their turn, and don't talk over the top of someone else.

- Don't always talk about yourself. By all means answer questions about yourself that the other person asks. But take turns – ask the other person's opinion, and get them to tell you a bit about themselves – and really *listen* to the answers.

- Learn to listen carefully to what the other person is saying. In this way, you will be better able to work out what you should say next. Keep your comment relevant to what they were talking about, so that the conversation 'flows', rather than jumping from one topic to a completely different, unrelated one.

- Go with the flow of conversation. If you are joining a group conversation, listen to what is going on rather than interrupting. Keep any comments that you make relevant to the topic. Sometimes in conversation with a group of people, you may think of something to say, but before you've had a chance to say it the conversation moves on, and your point is no longer relevant. If this happens, *leave it*. Going back to it is tedious, and breaks the rules of good conversation.

- Don't tell very long or personal stories to anyone but a good friend. If you tell stories that are too detailed or that give too much personal information for the level of friendship, you risk being seen as a bit weird or boring. Keep communication short, interesting and relevant.

- Learn to watch carefully for the other person's level of interest. If they are giving signs of being bored, cut short what you were saying, and give them a chance to speak. If, on the other hand, they appear to be genuinely interested, you can say a little more but continue to leave spaces so they can have their say.

- If you have an area of special interest, you will know that not everyone feels as enthusiastic about it as you do. It's probably best to talk only to good friends about your special interests, and, even then, you must watch carefully to gauge their level of interest in what you are saying (see previous point).

- If you have raised a laugh by something you said, or you have told a joke that was received well by everyone, *don't say it again.* Remember, a joke is only funny the first time. Also, carefully consider your audience before you tell a joke. What you are about to say may be inappropriate in certain circumstances (e.g. a rude sexual joke may go down well with other teenagers, but not at all well at the family dinner table).

- Learn how to exit a conversation politely. You can say something like, 'It's been great talking to you, but I really have to go.' Practise a variety of 'exit' phrases with your social mentor.

WHEN HONESTY IS NOT THE BEST POLICY

It may seem strange, but there are times when it is better not to be completely honest. These are those occasions when to speak the truth would hurt the other person's feelings. Here are two examples.

- On your birthday, someone gives you a present and watches with anticipation as you open it. You discover that it's something you really don't like. The person asks you if you like it, so you smile and say, 'It's great! Thank you very much.'

- Your good friend is excited because she has just bought some new jeans. She studies herself in the mirror, suddenly looks worried and asks, 'Do these make my bum look big?' You were thinking to yourself that perhaps they did. But you say, 'No, not at all! You look really good in them.'

These are examples of 'white lies', which are an important part of social interaction. It may not be easy for you to be dishonest in this way, but in such situations *you don't always have to tell the truth*. A white lie spares another person's feelings and helps to avoid an awkward situation. White lies are harmless, and help to keep a situation positive, or a person happy, while telling the truth in these circumstances would only succeed in ruining someone's confidence or creating a bad atmosphere.

Talk with your social mentor about situations where people have told white lies. Discuss what might have happened and how people might have felt if the whole truth had been told.

Peer pressure

You may feel that one way of keeping your friends and fitting in is to join in with everything they do. To a certain extent, this isn't a bad idea – it's good to be an agreeable friend who joins in, and it does help you to feel as though you belong. But, although it's good to join in with healthy, fun activities, it's not such a great idea to do things that will get you into trouble, are dangerous or even illegal.

You need to be able to recognize when you are being persuaded to do things that you don't feel comfortable with, and to learn some ways of coping with this pressure.

Who are your peers?

They are people of your own age or status. For example, in a workplace, your peers are the people who do a similar job to you; at school, your peers are your friends and classmates.

What is peer pressure?

This is the feeling you have that you *must* do something in order to be accepted by a friend, or fit in with the group. Sometimes others may try to persuade you with words ('Come on, give it a try', 'Don't be a baby', 'Are you weird or something?'). Sometimes you just feel that you have to act or look a certain way in order not to be teased.

Pressure such as this can happen to anyone, at any time of life – people often do uncharacteristic things to fit in with friends – but it is especially likely to happen during puberty and adolescence. This is because you are busy trying to establish your own identity, become independent from your parents and fit in with other young people. You are still trying to work out what you do and don't like. At the same time, you may not have enough self-confidence to stand up to your friends.

It isn't always obvious that you are making decisions because of peer pressure. And you may not always be aware that you are being unkindly set up or manipulated to do things by people who know how important it is to you to fit in.

When peer pressure is a good thing

Peer pressure isn't always bad. Your friends may influence you in such a way that you try out new things and discover abilities and talents you never knew you had. For example, because you may not want to be accused of being faint-hearted or a baby, you may try slightly more daring activities with a group of friends than you would if you were by yourself. You may be encouraged to work harder at school, join in helpful community activities or charity work, or join groups where you are able to develop skills you might not otherwise have considered. And it may be because of the influence of your friends that you choose *not* to smoke, drink alcohol or take drugs. All of this can be very good for your self-esteem and your sense of identity.

When peer pressure is a problem

Peer pressure becomes a problem when you make choices that you know aren't right. You may find yourself joining in activities that are bad for your health, harmful to others, dangerous, or even illegal.

Your friends can influence you in many ways, but here are some of the most typical.

- *Pressure to follow fashion*: you may be influenced by your friends to wear a particular style of clothing, wear make-up, get body piercings or tattoos, have your hair done a certain way, listen to a particular type of music or even talk in a certain way. It's not unusual to want to follow fashion, but it does become a problem if, for example, it results in arguments with your parents or your school, or leads to you stealing items that you couldn't otherwise afford, or you do things to your body that you later regret.

- *Pressure to smoke, drink alcohol or take drugs*: you might be influenced to try these in order to look grown up or 'cool'. But as we saw in Chapter 4, **Making Healthy Choices**, these can be particularly risky activities, and are not good for your health whatever age you are. They are especially dangerous, and illegal, if you are very young.

- *Pressure to have a 'good body'*: We discussed in Chapter 5, **Understanding Emotions**, the current fashion for girls to be very thin and boys to be muscular. Comments by your friends can greatly influence the way you feel about your body. You may be pressured to follow strenuous exercise routines or strict diets that are not appropriate for you as you are growing, and will almost certainly be bad for your health.

- *Pressure to be involved in sexual activity*: many teenagers start to experiment with sexual activity because their hormones are active, and they are experiencing strong sexual feelings for the first time in their lives. Some interest in sexual activity is normal and can be healthy, just so long as it is what you want and feel ready for. But it is vitally important that you are aware of, and abide by, the rules about sex (see Chapter 7, **Sex**). It is not okay to feel pressured into having any sexual activity, and you must never feel that by doing something sexual you will be popular. It is far more likely to earn you a bad reputation and loss of respect.

- *Pressure to bully or hurt others*: it can be easy to get caught up in this sort of behaviour, but it is never okay. It is very important to think about how the person who is the target of the bullying must feel (see the later section on teasing and bullying).

- *Pressure to join in shoplifting, stealing or vandalism*: sometimes your friends may do this to prove to each other how 'brave' or tough they are, or they might suggest to you that you can only be part of their group if you 'prove yourself' by stealing or damaging something. It is *never* okay to steal from shops or from individuals, or to vandalise property; it will only get you into serious trouble eventually.

- *Pressure to skip school*: sneaking out of school to hang around with friends is never a good idea. Ultimately it leads to trouble with your parents, the school authorities and sometimes even the police. If you are skipping school because you are very unhappy, this is a different issue, and one that you must discuss with your parents and teachers in order to find a solution.

How to cope with peer pressure

There is no single way to deal with peer pressure, because everyone's personality and situation is different. One of the best things you can do is talk with a trusted adult about the situation you are in. By doing this, you may be helped to see it from a different perspective. Obviously, you need to be able to resist the pressure, and say 'no'. This sounds easier than it really is, of course. You have to feel strong in yourself in order to be able to say 'no'. Let's look at some things you may be able to do to help you say 'no' to unwanted peer pressure.

- Be well-informed about issues that are important, such as health, sexuality and drugs and alcohol. In this way, you will know what is right and what is good for you, and you will feel more confident about saying 'no' if you want to.

- Do good-fun, healthy things that make you feel good about yourself and help to give you confidence and develop your identity (see Chapter 5, **Understanding Emotions**). This will enable you to resist doing unhealthy, dangerous or illegal things in order to try to feel good.

- Try hanging around with different people. You will find that not everyone is doing the things you're feeling pressured to do, and that there are plenty of people who feel more like you do.

- Think about why other people may be pressuring you. Are they doing it to have a laugh at your expense? Are they doing it to make themselves feel good? When you have worked out what may be in it for the other people or person, you will put the problem in perspective, and be better able to resist.

- Think about what *you* actually get out of being pressured. Is it helping you be the person you want to be? Are you really more respected by the group because of it? When you stand back (not literally) and look at the situation, you may find that it doesn't really benefit you in any way. If this is the case, you may feel more confident about saying 'no'.

- Practise ways of saying 'no' with your social mentor.

- Remember, you can sometimes simply walk away from a situation. If you aren't actually there, no one can make you do anything!

Teasing and bullying

Just about everyone is teased from time to time, and although it can make you feel bad, it is mostly fairly harmless. Bullying, on the other hand, is a more persistent form of teasing, and is much more serious. It can have lasting effects on your confidence and self-esteem. Since teasing and bullying are different from each other, it's important to be able to recognize the difference, and also to learn how to respond in both situations.

What is teasing?

Teasing is an attempt by someone to make another person feel humiliated or ashamed, which sounds very unkind, but quite often (though not always) it is intended in a good-natured way. The problem is you may not always be in the mood for it. When you are going through puberty, you tend to be hypersensitive about what others think about you, and any sort of teasing can be very hurtful.

There are a few reasons why someone might choose to tease you. They may be annoyed with you, or envious of you, and by picking on something you are sensitive about they can demonstrate their dominance over you. Sometimes the person who is teasing you is keen to show off in front of his or her friends, and perhaps raise a laugh at your expense. You have probably noticed that some people are habitual teasers, and seem to communicate all the time by constantly joking and putting others down. Teasing can be 'currency' between friends, where it is not intended to hurt, and is enjoyed by both the people concerned. Then there is the sort of teasing that someone might do because they actually find the other person attractive; but because they are rather self-conscious about liking someone, they cover it up by teasing them.

How to deal with teasing

If you are being teased, try the following:

- If possible, act as though you don't care; it can be best not to give the teaser the satisfaction of knowing you're upset by what they have said or done.

- Humour can defuse the situation really quickly. Laugh along with the teaser and shrug it off.

- Perhaps agree with what the teaser has said – this 'takes the wind out of their sails' and tends to stop the teaser in their tracks.

- Try confronting the teaser – verbally, never physically. Tell them how you feel in a serious and determined way. But don't whine or sound pleading – this only tends to make things worse.

Occasional teasing is an inevitable part of adolescence. If it happens all the time, however, and is making you feel scared or depressed, then it has become bullying, and needs to be taken more seriously.

What is bullying?

If you are being singled out for regular and persistent tormenting, this is no longer teasing – it is bullying. Unfortunately, it isn't always obvious, even to you, and because of this it can go on for a lot longer than it should before anything is done about it.

So it's very important to recognize what bullying actually is. It can include any of the following, when they are done *repeatedly* and *relentlessly*, and nearly always *out of sight of authority*:

- any sort of physical tormenting (pushing, kicking, pulling hair, poking and prodding and so on)

- stealing or damaging your possessions

- name-calling
- spreading rumours about you
- photographing you on mobile phones
- adding unkind photos of you on their website
- sending you threatening text messages
- ignoring or laughing at you
- excluding you from gatherings, and deliberately leaving you out of teams and games
- ridiculing you because of your looks, behaviour or abilities
- sexual tormenting – either inappropriate touching, or 'leading you on' to say or do something inappropriate.

When someone is subjected to any or all of these things every day – sometimes many times a day – they may be frightened, will probably become very anxious and low-spirited, and eventually will become depressed.

Why are some people bullied?

First and foremost, they are people who are alone, and who are not 'rescued' by their friends. People who have at least one supportive friend, or even better, several people they can rely on, are less likely to be the targets of bullying.

Second, they may respond to bullying by cowering and showing their discomfort, which only serves to encourage the bully. It is even worse if they react by being explosive, and subsequently get into trouble for it. Lots of bullies really enjoy this.

The person who is targeted as a 'victim' of bullying nearly always has some sort of weak spot or vulnerability. This may be something obvious, such as being fatter or thinner than average, or shortsighted so that they need to wear thick glasses. They may have a slight physical disability, or talk with a different accent...the list is endless, but can include all sorts of physical differences. It can also be because the victim dresses differently, or has poor personal hygiene. It can be that they behave a little differently, are very shy, or talk incessantly about one thing. Sometimes the reason can be very difficult to determine. For example, even people who appear to be bright, confident and friendly can be the targets of bullying.

The point is, the bully discovers a 'weak spot', and mercilessly torments the victim because of it.

You can see that this is unfair and cruel behaviour, but it happens a lot, to many people. It can happen even among young children, and among adults in the workplace, but it tends to be at its very worst in the teenage years. Teenagers can be some of the cruellest people on earth – they have strict 'codes of behaviour', and are very intolerant of anyone who doesn't understand these, or is different in any way.

Understanding the bully

Strangely enough, bullies aren't always aggressive people, and they don't necessarily feel any anger towards their victim. They are heartless, though. They don't feel sorry about what they are doing, and usually have no idea about how much their behaviour is affecting their victim. They usually carry out the bullying in front of at least one other person, and sometimes in front of a whole group, because they enjoy having an audience while they wield their power. To them, bullying is an enjoyable social event.

Understanding the victim

People who become the target of bullying do not deserve it in any way. They do not 'bring it on themselves' and they are definitely not 'asking for it'. Nobody would ever choose to be on the receiving end of bullying. Victims are not even necessarily helpless or physically or psychologically weak. They are, however, vulnerable in some way that the bully has spotted.

Victims may be reluctant to report what is happening, partly because they may not be entirely sure that it is bullying. They may also fear that by reporting it the bullying will get worse. But while it continues, the bullying will be having an effect on their self-esteem, and, unless something is done to stop it happening, it can have a lasting effect on their confidence.

Dealing with bullying

If you are ever the victim of bullying, try the following:

- *Don't hide away*: being completely alone will make you much more vulnerable. Stay visible, and stay around other people.

- *If possible (and this is much easier said than done), act as though you don't care*: certainly *don't* fight back physically. Be firm, speak clearly and loudly, but don't lose your cool and act in a crazy, frantic way. This only gives the bully what they want – the enjoyment of seeing you get really angry and lose control.

- *Tell someone what is happening*: it's very important that you don't try to deal with this by yourself. And remember, if other people have no idea what is happening, they can't help you. To begin with, tell a trusted adult. This person can help you understand what is happening, and together you can work out a way to bring an end to the bullying. There may be some quite logical and simple solutions, such as hanging around with different people; organizing a 'buddy' to accompany you into the playground at break-times, or sit with you on the school bus; going somewhere 'safe' at break times, such as the library; joining lunchtime clubs; travelling to school a different way and so on. The main thing is to ensure that you are not alone and therefore an easy target for bullies.

- *If you have tried everything you can think of, then there needs to be more serious intervention*: report the bullying to the school authorities. They have a responsibility to ensure the safety of every student. They will work out what has to be done to bring the bullying to an end, and make sure you are safe. Just be careful that any reporting is done without the bullies knowing, as this could temporarily make things much worse. In the most serious cases, people may decide to change schools. This can work very well; but be aware that sometimes things go wrong again – it isn't always the answer.

The important thing for you to understand is that bullying *can* be stopped. It needs to be made public, and the bullies need to be confronted with what they are doing. As we said, it may be 'sport' for them,

but it could be ruining your confidence and self-esteem, and affecting your mental health.

When you are the bully

We talked in the section on peer pressure about the fact that you may be encouraged by others to join in bullying behaviour towards another person. It can also happen that you are bullying someone without realizing how much you are upsetting them. It doesn't matter whether it is face to face, or via email, mobile phone or the internet, it is not okay to mock or insult people, or intimidate them in any way. If you tease someone in what you consider to be a friendly way, make sure that they are okay with it. You must really try to think about how another person feels about the way you are treating them – and also about how other people might view your behaviour. If in doubt, just don't tease anyone.

The fact is it is not socially acceptable to behave like a bully. Eventually, bullies are rejected by other people because of their behaviour, and will end up being lonely.

It isn't always bullying

It can be difficult sometimes to work out somebody's intentions. Some people use joking and teasing as their natural way of communicating. The trouble is, if you are feeling particularly vulnerable, you might mis-interpret something that was intended as quite harmless, and believe it was meant to hurt or offend you.

The main thing is to resist 'flying off the handle'. Stay calm and explain to the person, if you can, that you're not always very good at telling when someone is joking, and that you would prefer that they don't treat you this way. If they are a reasonable and kind person, they will respect this. If this approach doesn't work, you may need to get a trusted adult or your social mentor to intervene on your behalf.

But perhaps if you can recognize that teasing and joking are not always malicious, you will be able to relax and accept it as just another way that people communicate.

Sex

It's important to have good information about sex, even when you are still going through puberty. Because it is such a personal topic, it isn't always easy to ask questions and get the answers you need. This chapter aims to give you interesting, detailed information about sex that you may not feel able to ask an adult. Once you have read the chapter, and are better-informed, you may feel more comfortable with the topic. Remember, sex is a normal, natural part of life, and just because it is private doesn't mean it must never be mentioned.

It's good to be able to talk openly, but appropriately, about sex, as this is a very valuable skill in a sexual relationship. Also, being well-informed and being able to ask questions will help you to be better prepared, and more able to make wise choices, if and when the time comes for you to have a sexual relationship.

So what is sex all about, and where do we begin?

Sexual feelings

The best place to start is by recognizing that all of us are sexual people, capable of sexual feelings. Even very young children can enjoy the feeling of touching their own genitals. Of course, they have to be taught that this is something they must do in private, not in front of everyone. The warm, tingly sensation they experience when they touch themselves like this is called a *sexual feeling*.

Sexual feelings can become especially strong at puberty, as the sex hormones start being produced. However, everyone is different, and some people don't experience very strong sexual feelings until they are quite a bit older. Some people never have strong sexual feelings. And sometimes we simply don't recognize what a sexual feeling is when it happens.

What are sexual feelings?

Sexual feelings are quite difficult to describe, as everyone experiences them in their own way. They could be described as 'tingly', 'squirmy' feelings, a sort of throbbing, warm feeling low down in the abdomen and around the genitals. They make your heart beat faster, and give you an all-over feeling of excitement. Increased sex hormones cause a flow of blood to the genital area, and this is what causes these tingly sensations. In the male, the penis responds by becoming firm and erect, and in the female, the clitoris enlarges slightly and becomes firmer and more sensitive. Glands in the vagina produce a fluid that makes the vagina moist, and the female may be aware of a slight 'wetness' at the entrance to her vagina.

When people experience sexual feelings, we say they are 'feeling sexy'. Other phrases that are commonly used (especially by teenagers and in popular culture) are 'turned on', 'hot' or 'horny'.

When do sexual feelings happen?

During puberty, these feelings can occur 'out of the blue', as we talked about in Chapter 2, **Puberty**, and boys may experience unexpected, or 'spontaneous', erections. During sleep, both boys and girls can have dreams that make them feel sexy; boys may wake up and find they have had a wet dream (see Chapter 2, **Puberty**), and girls may also have strong sexual feelings, and sometimes experience an orgasm (see the section on masturbation for an explanation of orgasms).

Sometimes, sexual feelings can happen in response to certain physical situations, such as travelling in a bumpy car or bus, or riding a horse. They may also happen when people are reading books or watching films that they find romantic or sexy.

Gradually, both boys and girls may become aware that they sometimes experience sexual feelings when they are around someone they like, or even if they just think about someone they really like. They may develop a 'crush' on this person, and may even believe they are in love with him or her (you can read more about crushes during adolescence in Chapter 2, **Puberty**). They may even imagine sexual situations with this person – these are called *sexual fantasies* (see later section).

Sexual feelings, especially when they are very strong, can make someone want to be physically close to the person they are attracted to – almost like a magnetic attraction. It is these strong feelings of attraction that can motivate and encourage the two people to get to know each other, and perhaps begin a relationship (see Chapter 8, **Sexual Relationships**).

When people are in a sexual relationship, they will find that sexual feelings make them want to touch and kiss and cuddle the other person. It works the other way, too – kissing, cuddling and touching can make the sexual feelings stronger.

Is it okay to talk about sexual feelings?

Sexual feelings are private, and normally you would keep them to yourself. The only exceptions to this are if you are in a sexual relationship, when you can show your sexual feelings by touching and kissing your partner, and you might choose to talk to your partner, in private, about your feelings. The other time it can be okay to talk about your sexual feelings is if you have a very good, trusted friend (or family member) with whom you can talk very closely.

In Chapter 1, **Your Body**, we read about Emily, a young girl who was unclear about what information about her own body should be private, and what can be public. Emily needed to understand that it wasn't okay to talk about her own private body parts in a public setting. The same goes for sexual feelings. Because they are private, it's okay to talk about them in a general sort of way, but not okay to talk about your own.

Usually, if you experience sexual feelings in the sort of situations described at the beginning of the chapter, you don't need to tell anyone what you are feeling. Other people won't know just by looking at you that you are experiencing sexual feelings (as long as a boy is careful to conceal his erection – see section on spontaneous erections in Chapter 2, **Puberty**). It's important to understand that these feelings can disappear just as quickly as they arrive, and will go away without you having to do anything about them.

Masturbation

Masturbation (sometimes called 'touching yourself', 'playing with yourself' or 'wanking' among many other terms) (see Chapter 11, **Sexual Language**), is when a person rubs or touches his or her own genitals in a way that gives sexual pleasure. Masturbation can also involve touching the genital area of a sexual partner to give sexual pleasure. When two people touch each other's genital areas at the same time, this is known as *mutual masturbation.*

A male may masturbate by holding his penis in his hand and moving his hand rhythmically up and down; a female may use her fingers to rub gently and rhythmically on or around her clitoris. While they do this, the feelings build up and can become quite exciting and intense, and may result in the person having an *orgasm.* This is where the muscles in the genital area, around the base of the penis, and surrounding the vagina, squeeze rhythmically for a few seconds. It is usually at this point that the male ejaculates semen from the end of his penis. An orgasm relieves the sexual tension and gives the person a warm, relaxed feeling that spreads right through their body.

Masturbation doesn't necessarily lead to orgasm. Quite often people just enjoy the pleasurable feelings they experience while they masturbate, without it resulting in an orgasm, and this is okay. And not everyone wants to masturbate – some people never do it, and that's okay, too.

As long as masturbation is *always* done in a private place (see Chapter 1, **Your Body**), and is never used as a way to shock or upset someone else, it is a healthy, safe and uncomplicated way for a person to experience sexual pleasure and release his or her sexual feelings.

Sexual fantasies

A fantasy is an image or thought inside your head – an imaginary situation. People often fantasize about all sorts of things. If you're having a boring day at school or work, you might fantasize about something fun you're going to do once you get home. This thought can keep you cheerful all day.

Sexual fantasies are similar. They are imaginary situations where something sexual is happening, perhaps including you or someone you know. The sexual images in a fantasy can make you feel very sexy. People will often fantasize during masturbation, or while having sex with their partner.

The important thing to understand is that, no matter what sort of unusual or unlikely images you may have, sexual fantasies are harmless because they're in your imagination, and are not real. They are a great way to help you feel sexy, and to imagine all sorts of things that might not be okay in real life. Sometimes people might share their fantasies with a sexual partner, but mostly you don't need to tell anyone what you are thinking about.

Sexual feelings in relationships

As you go through adolescence and your sexual feelings become stronger (due to hormones), you may find yourself becoming a lot more interested in people in a sexual way; that is, finding them attractive, and being fascinated by their bodies and the way they look. Of course, this sexual interest happens at different times for different people, and for some people this may be in their late teens or early twenties. For a lot of other people, though, it begins to happen during puberty.

We have to learn gradually about relationships, and none of us gets it all right to start with. To begin with, girls and boys who are attracted to each other tend to tease each other in a friendly way, and get silly and show off in front of each other. Two young teenagers might say they are 'going out' together, even though it might not mean that they actually *go* anywhere – in fact, they might not even talk to each other very much. Gradually, though, people become more confident, and really do go out with the person they are sexually attracted to. In a good relationship, they love to spend time with each other, doing interesting things, and talking and laughing together. Their strong sexual feelings mean that they want to touch each other. To start with, they link arms, put their arms around each other's shoulders or waists, and hold hands. Soon, they might choose to hug and kiss each other.

When people are more mature, their sexual relationships may involve more intimate touching. People explore each other's bodies, and touch and kiss what are known as the *erogenous zones*; that is, the parts of the body that make a person feel especially sexy when they are touched, such as the breasts, thighs and genitals. While not everybody experiences good feelings when these parts of the body are touched, a lot of people do. This kind of touching can be very pleasurable, and can easily lead to a desire to go even further; that is, to have sexual intercourse.

Having sex

Sexual intercourse

When a man and a woman have sexual intercourse, it usually follows the sort of touching that was described above, where the couple kiss and cuddle, and touch each other's bodies. This stage of lovemaking is often referred to as *foreplay*, and can last anything from a few minutes to hours,

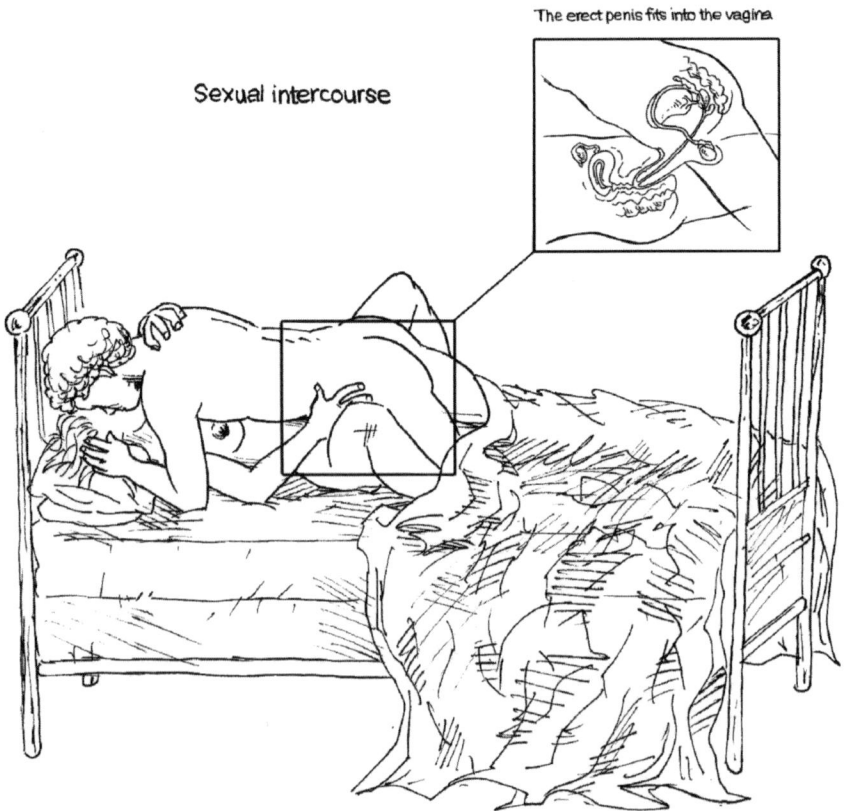

The erect penis fits into the vagina

Sexual intercourse

if they want it to. During this time, the man's penis becomes erect and the woman's clitoris hardens and enlarges slightly, and her vagina produces a lubricating fluid, making it moist and slippery. This makes it easier for the next stage to happen, where the man fits his penis into the woman's vagina. They move together so that his penis slides in and out of her vagina, causing them both to experience good feelings. They may continue to kiss and fondle each other while they have intercourse, and the sexual feelings become even stronger.

After a little while, these good feelings may become quite intense and result in an orgasm for one or other, or both, of them. At this point, the man may ejaculate semen, containing sperm, from the end of his penis. It is thought that the woman's orgasm, which involves contractions of the vagina and uterus, helps the sperm to travel up into her reproductive tract. However, it is important to understand that sperm can make their way up into the uterus and along the Fallopian tubes even if the woman *doesn't* have an orgasm (you can read more about the journey of the sperm in Chapter 10, **Fertilization, Pregnancy and Birth**).

During an orgasm, both men and women experience intense pleasure and excitement, followed by an all-over feeling of warmth and contentment, and sometimes sleepiness. Sometimes the man and the woman have their orgasms at the same time, but they may not, and this doesn't matter. Sometimes one or other of them doesn't have an orgasm at all, and this is okay, too.

Other ways to have sex

When a couple have sex, it may not always involve the man putting his penis in the woman's vagina. Sometimes, couples choose to explore each other's bodies all over using their hands and their fingers. They can use their mouths, too. *Oral sex* is when a person uses his or her mouth on the genital area of the other person. If the man puts his penis into his partner's anus (back passage) this is known as *anal sex*.

People can be in any position for sex, too. You will probably notice that in movies and on TV, couples that are 'having sex' (don't forget, they're only acting) are nearly always under the sheets, with the man on top. This is so they are more discreet and less likely to offend the viewer. But in reality, people don't have to be covered up when they have sex if they don't want to be. And sex with the man on top is not the only way

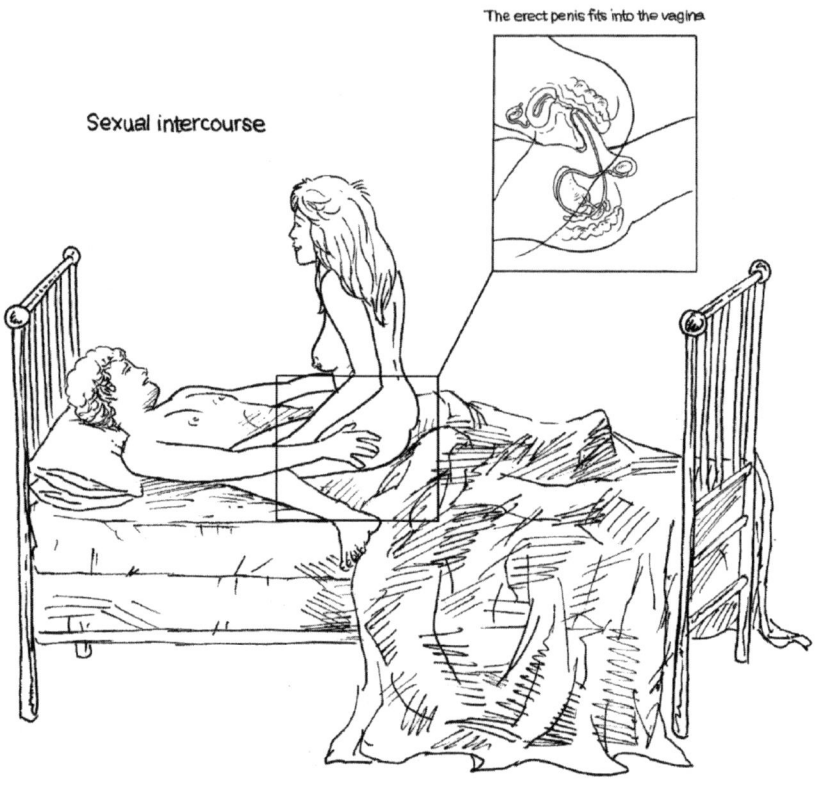

The erect penis fits into the vagina

Sexual intercourse

for people to have sex: they may choose for the woman to go on top, or they may lie side by side. In fact, as long as they are in private, comfortable and both enjoying themselves, they can choose any position and be as imaginative as they like.

Is sex just for fun, or to make babies?

Sex can be lots of fun! It is also a very special way for two people to express their deep love for and commitment to each other.

But for sex to be a good experience, both people must *want* to be doing it – neither one of them should be feeling pressured to have sex, or uncomfortable about it. A good sexual relationship always involves lots of communication – the couple need to be able to talk to each other and tell each other what they enjoy and how they feel. If something is wrong, they need to be able to talk about that, too (see Chapter 8, **Sexual Relationships**).

Of course, sexual intercourse can result in pregnancy, so sex is about making babies, too. But not all couples want to have babies, and some can't have babies. This doesn't mean that they can't have sex, though – they will still do this as a special way to show their love for each other. And the same goes for couples that do have children; sex doesn't stop just because they already have their family. Sex doesn't have to stop at a particular age, either – people can go on enjoying sex right into old age if they want to, as long as they are fit and well enough.

How often do people have sex?

There is no 'normal' frequency for sex, as everyone is different. Some people have a stronger sexual desire than others, and may want to have sex often (every day, for example). Other people don't have such a strong desire, and may be quite content to have sex less frequently – once a week, once every two weeks or even less often. Some people aren't interested in having sex at all. Sometimes people might want to have sex more often, but can't because their lives are so busy, or they are apart from their partner for various reasons. And each person will find that their interest in sex will vary from day to day and from year to year, for all sorts of reasons. The main thing is that couples talk to each other about how they feel, and work out for themselves what suits them best, and how often they would like to have sex.

What if someone doesn't want sex at all?
CELIBACY

When someone decides not to have any sexual activity, for whatever reason, this is known as *celibacy*. Celibacy may be a temporary decision for someone. For example, a person may decide they aren't ready for, or even interested in having, sexual relationships. Sometimes someone who has been sexually active decides to become celibate for various reasons – perhaps they didn't enjoy it, or had a bad experience, or perhaps they want to put their energies into something else, such as travel, work or study, for the time being.

Celibacy can be a choice someone makes for life. This is the case in certain religions, where priests, monks and nuns take a vow of chastity, and promise not to become involved in sexual relationships, but to dedicate themselves to their religion instead.

ABSTINENCE

Some people may be in a sexual relationship, in that they kiss, cuddle and touch each other's bodies, but choose not to have sexual intercourse for various reasons. They may feel they are too young, or perhaps don't know each other well enough yet. Some people have strong convictions, or maybe a firm religious belief, that sex is only okay within marriage. Whatever the reason, they decide to *abstain* from sexual intercourse until they feel the time is right.

Sex for the first time

VIRGINITY

A person (male or female) who has never had sexual intercourse is usually referred to as a *virgin*. When someone has sex for the first time, they are said to be *losing their virginity* (in some cultures this is referred to as *making their sexual debut*).

Around the world, there are many different beliefs about the right time to have sex for the first time, depending on someone's culture or religion. For many people, these deep-seated beliefs and customs will influence their decision. But for lots of young people, particularly in Western culture, there is strong peer pressure to lose their virginity: some people are led to believe they aren't really grown up until they've had sex. But obviously this doesn't make sense – simply having sex doesn't make you an adult! And if you are already an adult, but have never had sex, being a virgin doesn't mean that you aren't grown up! The decision to have sex for the first time should be a positive one, made for the right reasons, and not one that you make because of peer pressure, or to prove anything to yourself or anyone else.

DOES IT HURT?

First-time sex can sometimes be a little uncomfortable for a female, especially if her hymen is still intact (see Chapter 1, **Your Body**). This can cause not only discomfort, but a small amount of bleeding. In the past, and sometimes still today in some cultures, this was seen as a good thing, since it proved that the girl was a virgin. These days, however, girls tend to be quite physically active, and many use tampons during their period, so the hymen tends to tear quite naturally long before she has sexual intercourse, and there may be no bleeding the first time.

But first-time sex can still be a bit uncomfortable, especially if the couple are nervous. When a female is nervous, she may not produce enough lubrication in her vagina; and a male who is nervous and inexperienced may push his penis in a little too quickly, and too hard. First-time sex is more comfortable if the couple takes it slowly and gently, and they may choose to use extra lubricant (such as K-Y Jelly) to help. But best of all, they should communicate with each other, and tell each other how they are feeling, which will make first-time sex much more relaxed, comfortable and enjoyable.

Heterosexuality and homosexuality

You have almost certainly heard the expressions 'gay', 'lesbian' and 'straight'. These are the more commonly used terms for *homosexual* and *heterosexual*. Homosexual men, often referred to as *gay*, are attracted to and prefer to have sex with other men, while homosexual women, or *lesbians*, are attracted to and prefer to have sex with other women.

People who are attracted to and prefer to have sex with someone of the opposite sex are heterosexual, which is often referred to as being *straight*.

Just a few people don't fall strictly into either of these categories, and enjoy sex with both men and women. These people are *bisexual*, often referred to simply as 'bi'.

Whether a person is gay, straight or bi, it is part of *who they are*, and not something they can change about themselves, any more than they can change being male or female, or left- or right-handed.

How does someone become homosexual?

It isn't really known for sure what causes someone to be homosexual. Some people believe that a person is born that way. Other people think that perhaps certain events during childhood may be the cause. It's quite possible that it is a combination of both of these factors.

What we do know is that it is a normal way for a minority of people to express their sexuality, and that homosexual people exist in every society.

How does someone know they are homosexual?

It can be very difficult for a person to know for sure whether they are homosexual or heterosexual while they are still growing up. Lots of children have sexual experiences with other children of the same sex, during childhood games such as 'doctors and nurses'. Young people going through puberty may experiment with their friends, kissing or touching each other's bodies; they may have sexual fantasies or dreams about a friend, or have a crush on someone of the same sex. But all this is just part of growing up, and is no indication of whether the person will be homosexual or heterosexual when they become an adult.

For most gays and lesbians, it's not until they are in their late teens or early adulthood that they are able to be more certain about their sexuality.

COMING OUT

Coming out is the term that is used to describe the process where a person gradually becomes aware of his or her homosexuality, and chooses to tell other people about it. Coming out isn't always an easy process, however, because not everyone is accepting of homosexuality. This means that the person will have to consider very carefully who exactly they tell in terms of family members, friends and workmates. If it is going to prove too difficult or confronting, some people choose not to tell people about their homosexuality. They may choose to seek counselling first, to help them decide what to do, and to assist them in the process of coming out.

If homosexuality is normal, why is it an insult to call someone 'gay'?

Some people are critical of homosexuals because they consider they are 'different' and that homosexuality is wrong. These views may be part of their religious beliefs, or the views held by their family or their culture. Sometimes people hold these views because they are not well-informed, and they may be afraid of something they don't understand. If a person has learned to dislike anyone who is homosexual, they will probably consider it an insult to call someone 'gay'.

When this term is used in school as an insult, it will almost always be by someone who knows very little about what homosexuality really is.

How do homosexual people have sex?

As you know from what you have already read in this chapter, two people in a sexual relationship don't just have sexual intercourse. They are often each other's best friends, and enjoy spending time together just having fun and relaxing. When they are having sex, they kiss and cuddle and may use their hands, fingers and mouths on each other's bodies. This is exactly the same, whether the people are gay, lesbian or straight. In addition to kissing, cuddling and touching, lesbian couples may choose to have oral sex, and straight couples and gay (male) couples may choose to have both oral and anal sex.

Can you tell when someone is homosexual?

The short answer is 'no'! There is nothing in the way they look or behave that distinguishes homosexual people from heterosexual people. You may hear people say that you can tell homosexual people by the way they walk, talk, dress or wear their hair, or by the jobs that they do, but none of this is true. These ideas may come from the stereotyped images that are sometimes portrayed on television or in films, usually to try to raise a laugh, and have little to do with reality.

Homosexual people go about their daily lives in exactly the same way as heterosexual people, looking after their homes, going to work, shopping, exercising, going out and so on. Some homosexual couples are parents, and raise their families in the same way that heterosexual couples do.

The important thing is that you don't make assumptions or judgements about people's sexuality based on the way they look or the way they live their lives.

Rules about sex

A sexual relationship can be a very important part of someone's life. Ideally, sex should make both people feel good and strengthen their relationship. But in the wrong circumstances, sex can be inappropriate and damaging to the way a person feels about him- or herself. In order to ensure that sex is a positive, appropriate and enjoyable experience, there are some very clear rules and guidelines. These help people to make wise choices and stay safe. The most important of these are:

- a person must be old enough to have sex
- sex must take place in private
- sex must never be forced
- sex between family members is *not* okay.

Let's look at these in more detail.

Being old enough to have sex

Sex is not for children. In fact, in most countries people have to be at least 16 years old before they can have sex. This is known as the *age of consent* – in other words, the age at which someone can 'give permission' for another person to have sex with them. Until they have reached this age (usually 16, though it varies slightly from place to place), they are too young to give consent, and it is illegal for them to have sex.

This makes sense when you think about it. For one thing, sex can result in pregnancy. Not very many young people below the age of 16 really want to be parents, or even make very good parents without a great deal of help from their families. If they don't want to get pregnant, they must use contraception (see Chapter 9, **Looking After Your Sexual Health**), which means a visit to the clinic or doctor, but very few young people below the age of 16 are ready to be this responsible.

Also – and this is very important – sex is emotional as well as physical, and most young people below the age of 16 are not mature enough to handle the strong emotions that go with sex.

It is worth noting here that the rules for anal intercourse, in particular concerning the age of consent, are even more variable than those for vaginal intercourse. In some countries and states, anal intercourse is illegal.

THE RIGHT AGE FOR SEX

So is there a 'right age' for sex? The simple answer is 'no'. Obviously, as we have just discussed, there is an age below which it is illegal, usually about 16. But just because someone has turned 16, it doesn't mean they are ready for sex. Lots of people don't feel ready for sex until they're much older, because there are some very important considerations.

For example, some people believe very strongly that sex should only ever happen once the couple is married (in some countries this is the law). In contrast, some other people don't think this is important at all. These conflicting views can be confusing. A person needs to be very clear in their own mind what they believe, and be able to talk about this with their partner. They must also respect each other's feelings and opinions. When it comes to something as personal as sex, it does help if the two people share similar values and beliefs.

Another thing people need to consider before they start having sex is how they are going to protect themselves from sexually transmitted infections and pregnancy (see Chapter 9, **Looking After Your Sexual Health**). They will need to visit the doctor or the sexual health clinic to have a check up and organize contraception.

And, most important, they need to be very clear how they feel about their partner. Just because two people are attracted to each other, and have strong sexual feelings doesn't automatically mean they should have sex. A mature relationship that involves sex must also include trust and respect. These qualities take time to develop (see Chapter 8, **Sexual Relationships**).

The main thing is, if a person feels unsure in any way, then it is probably a good idea to wait before deciding to have sex.

As you can see, these factors are not so much to do with an exact age, but more to do with confidence, experience and maturity. There are people who will be mature enough by the time they are 16, but many more people will be in their late teens or early twenties, or even older, before they meet the right person and choose to have sex.

DO SEXUAL PARTNERS HAVE TO BE ABOUT THE SAME AGE?

Often people in a sexual relationship are about the same age as each other, within a couple of years, but there is no law that says they have to be. Very often a person will fall in love with someone of a similar age simply because they have similar interests and life experiences, and feel comfortable with each for these reasons. However, it is perfectly possible for two people who are very different ages to find each other very attractive, feel relaxed in each other's company and have lots to share. As long as they are both older than 16 (or whatever the age of consent happens to be in their country), there is no legal reason why two people who are many years apart in age can't have a successful sexual relationship.

Sex must be in private

The law, everywhere in the world, is quite clear about this – sexual intercourse is a private act and should never occur in a public place.

Other sexual acts, such as touching another person's body in a sexual way, and masturbation, must also take place in private. In most (but not all) countries, people can show affection for each other in public by holding hands, putting their arms around each other, hugging and even kissing. However, people don't generally want to watch a couple engaged in a passionate kiss that goes on and on for several minutes, and although this sort of kissing may not be against the law in a public place, it is usually considered to be private.

Sex must never be forced

Even when two people are legally old enough to have sex, it should never, ever take place unless both of them want it to. Sex should *never* be forced. When one person forces another to have sex, it is a crime known as *rape*. In fact, any sort of sexual activity – whether it is kissing, hugging or touching in a sexual way – that is done against someone's will is a crime known as *sexual assault*. All sexual activity should only ever take place when *both* people have consented to it.

'NO' MEANS 'NO'

This is a simple phrase, but a very important one when it comes to sexual relationships. Whatever the sexual activity – it could be kissing, hugging, touching each other or even sexual intercourse – if one of the people decides they want to stop, then the activity must not continue, no matter how aroused the other person may be. The person who wants to stop might indicate how they feel by turning away, pushing away their partner's hand or body, or saying 'no', 'stop' or something similar. It doesn't matter how they show it – if they have made it clear that they want to stop, then the sexual activity *must stop*.

You may sometimes hear people say things like, 'When she says "no", she really means "yes" – it's all part of the game'. This is nonsense. Even if a girl has learnt somewhere that it *is* some sort of game, and that she is supposed to 'play hard to get', her partner must always listen to 'no' and respond accordingly. If, in fact, she really *does* mean 'yes', then it is up to her to say so clearly, and not involve her partner in guessing games.

You may also have heard that once a boy is sexually aroused and has an erection then he must continue with the sexual activity until he ejaculates – that once he starts, he can't stop, and that if he doesn't ejaculate, his testicles will explode. Quite obviously, this is nonsense, too. As you know from Chapter 1, **Your Body**, sperm are microscopic, and can't possibly cause testicles to explode – and a person certainly doesn't have to have sex just because they happen to have strong sexual feelings. Erections and sexual feelings can go away by themselves. Everyone is capable of stopping if the situation isn't right – and it isn't right if one of the people involved is uncomfortable with what is happening.

A good sexual relationship involves good communication, and this means being very clear and straightforward about what you do and don't like. It also means listening to your partner, and respecting their wishes.

SEXUAL ABUSE

Sexual abuse is any sexual situation where one person uses another person for his or her own sexual pleasure, without that person's permission.

We talked in the previous section about rape, which is when someone forces another person to have sex. Rape is one – very forceful and violent – type of sexual abuse. And the other activities we talked about, such as kissing, cuddling and touching, should never be forced upon someone. When they are, it's called *sexual assault*, and is another type of sexual abuse.

But sexual abuse is more than all of this. It involves an abuse of trust and power by one person over another, and can include all sorts of activities. Sexual abuse is any sort of sexual activity that someone displays towards you that you *don't want*, and that *makes you feel uncomfortable*. Here are some examples.

- Having any part of your body rubbed, stroked or touched in a sexual way when you don't want it.

- Any inappropriate kissing, on the mouth or any other part of your body.

- Being asked by someone to touch parts of their body when you don't want to, or to watch them masturbate or touch their own body in a sexual way.

- Being asked to watch a sexy film or look at sexy pictures that you know are inappropriate.

- Being watched by someone while you are showering, bathing or getting dressed such that it makes you feel uncomfortable.

- Someone making unwanted or inappropriate sexual comments to you, even over the phone, by email or text message.

These things can happen at school, at work, anywhere at all – even at home.

There are some very important things to remember.

- Sexual abuse is *never* your fault, whatever the other person says. It is an abuse of power, and the other person is the one who is breaking the law.

- The only way abuse will ever stop is for it to be reported. First, you must tell someone you trust (this may be someone at home, but it doesn't have to be. Sometimes people prefer to tell a trusted teacher, the school principal, or a trusted adult outside of the family).

- If the first person you tell doesn't believe you, find someone else to tell. Go on telling people you trust until someone does something to help you.

- If you can, tell the person who is abusing you to stop it. The simple formula to remember is:

  - *No*: tell them that you don't like it, and that you want them to stop.

  - *Go*: remove yourself from the situation as soon as you can.

  - *Tell*: report what has been happening to a trusted adult (see the points above).

- It isn't always easy to tell someone what is happening, and you may not be able to for some time. Don't blame yourself – you can only do your best.

- Your body may appear to respond to what is happening by becoming sexually aroused, even if you are frightened. This is just a physical reaction, and doesn't mean that you are enjoying it.

- It doesn't matter how much the person may try to scare you, or threaten that they will harm you or your family – what they are doing is *wrong*, and they are *breaking the law*.

The reason it is so important to stop sexual abuse is that it can have a lasting effect on a person. It can make them anxious and depressed, and can spoil their chances of forming loving, trusting relationships later in their life. Nobody deserves to have his or her life spoilt like this. It is possible to recover from sexual abuse, but only with the appropriate help, and this is why it should be reported as soon as possible.

THE DIFFERENCE BETWEEN SEXUAL TOUCHES AND LOVING OR FRIENDLY TOUCHES

Touching doesn't have to be sexual. It is normal for people to touch each other in a friendly way for lots of reasons. People who don't know each other very well may shake hands as a greeting, while friends may greet each other with a hug or a kiss on the cheek. They may put their arm around the other one's shoulders to comfort them, or to demonstrate friendliness.

Not everyone enjoys being touched. Some people only enjoy it sometimes, when they are in the mood. Other people really enjoy touch, and find it reassuring and soothing. We're all different. In some families, for example, people hardly ever touch each other, while in other families, people touch each other often, by hugging and kissing each other, holding hands, and giving each other back rubs, head massages and so on.

These touches between family members or close friends are ways of showing love and caring for each other. They are not sexual touches, because neither of the people involved is doing it to get sexual pleasure. Sexual touches give one or both of the people tingly, sexual feelings. A non-sexual, loving touch simply makes them feel comfortable and relaxed.

Sex between family members is not okay

In most societies, sex with family members (known as *incest*) is against the law. Parents must not have sex with their children, grandparents must not have sex with their grandchildren, uncles and aunts must not have sex with their nephews and nieces, and brothers and sisters must not have sex with each other. In some societies, sex between first cousins is allowed, while in others it is against the law. Every society has its own guidelines regarding which particular family members may or may not have sex with each other, but without fail, in every society on earth, people are taught that sexual relationships between certain family members is unacceptable, or 'taboo'.

One possible biological reason is to do with healthy genetics (see Chapter 10, **Fertilization, Pregnancy and Birth**, for a brief explanation of genetics). People within the same family share the same genetics – all the children will have inherited half their genes from their father and half from their mother. Because genes occur in pairs, it is possible for one gene in the pair to be defective, but not to show up as an abnormality in the person. If, however, two people with this same defective gene have a baby, there is a much greater risk of the baby having the abnormality. It is much healthier, therefore, from a genetic point of view, that when people reproduce they do not come from the same family.

The other reason why sex between, for example, a parent and a child, or a grandparent and grandchild, is frowned upon in most societies is a bit more difficult to understand, but very important. In a healthy, mature sexual relationship, the two people involved should be equal and free to make their own decisions. If sex were to take place between a parent (or step-parent, uncle, aunt or grandparent) and their young relative, the two people aren't really equal, because the older relative is in a position of authority and trust. This trust is betrayed when they have a sexual relationship with the young person, which can have a lasting and damaging effect on that young person's life.

There are other situations that involve trust where sex is not allowed; this is between people in authority, such as teachers, lecturers, doctors, nurses and therapists, and their students or patients. It is for the same reason as above, and that is the betrayal of trust between a person in authority and someone they should be caring for.

Getting information about sex

Where can you get information about sex? We are surrounded by sexual messages and information in our everyday lives, from television, books, newspapers and magazines, the internet, music videos, advertisements and jokes. But it can be difficult to work out how much of this is reliable – some of it certainly isn't. Let's look at ways you can get reliable, accurate information about sex.

Parents and carers

The adults in your life can be a great source of information, just as long as they feel comfortable talking about sex. Not all adults do, even though they would probably like to be able to; but the fact is, most people get better at it with practice. If you would really like to talk to your parents or carers, but recognize that they are a bit embarrassed, just keep quietly persisting with your questions. This shows them that you are genuinely interested, and that you need some answers. However, be careful not to ask important questions about sexuality in a public setting (such as the shopping centre, church, family outings with friends or even the dinner table). And even when you are sure the situation is private, you will still need to choose your moment. Conversations about sex are much more successful if your parent or carer is not too busy or distracted. Wait until there is a quiet time together and you have their complete attention. You could even book an 'appointment' by saying something like, 'Mum, I really need to talk to you about something. When would be a good time?' And finally, don't feel that, if you are a girl, you *have* to talk to a female, or if you are a boy, you must talk to a male, although this may often be the case. It's more important that you talk to the person you feel most comfortable with, regardless of their sex.

Brothers and sisters

Trustworthy older brothers and sisters, if you are lucky enough to have any, can be excellent to talk to about sexual matters. Lots of young people get good information and help this way. Sometimes it is less embarrassing to talk to someone who is closer to you in age, and whose information you may feel is more 'up to date'.

Friends and people at school

People your own age are not always the most reliable sources of information. You can be lucky, and have a very reliable, trustworthy friend who is well-informed. But often, other young people your own age can be prone to exaggerating their own experiences, believing nonsense that they may have read in a magazine or on the internet, and teasing you by telling you things about sex that aren't true – so be careful. It's always best to check out with a trusted adult the truth of any information you get from friends or classmates.

Health classes at school

Information you get this way is most likely to be true, so if you are lucky enough to get good sex education at school, go along and listen and learn. Sometimes it can be a bit embarrassing, with all your classmates there too, but a good teacher will help the class to get past this embarrassment. Lessons like this can be an excellent forum for asking the sorts of questions you might not want to ask someone in the family – just remember that, unless you are speaking privately to the teacher, your questions should be general, rather than personal.

The media: magazines, the internet, television and films

Some of the articles and 'agony aunt' letters in teenage magazines can be really informative. They should be well-researched and accurate (though there is no guarantee of this). The main problem is that you may be reading information that isn't really aimed at your age group, so that it may be a bit too detailed and perhaps rather confusing. Even though most of the magazines are written for girls, there is no reason why boys can't read them too, as a lot of the information can be just as relevant for them.

Certainly, accuracy and appropriateness can't be guaranteed on the internet – it depends on who has written the information, and often there is no way of knowing this. At the end of this book are the addresses of some genuine, helpful websites that offer reliable, appropriate information.

Although television shows and films can be very entertaining, and may give you all sorts of ideas about sex, you must be careful to recognize that this *is* just entertainment, and not necessarily accurate. Often, sexual relationships are simplified, mainly to fit into the time slot of the television show or film; and aspects of sex may be exaggerated to make them funny. You might be led to believe that 'everyone is doing it', while of course this isn't true. Watch out, too, for any stereotyping that might be occurring (e.g. men depicted as strong and in control, and only interested in sex without emotional commitment; and women depicted as passive, overemotional and intent on getting married), since this is not necessarily the way people really are – it is very limiting and unhelpful in your understanding of sexuality.

The best way to make sense of any information you get from the media, whether you have read it in a magazine or on the internet, or seen it on the television or in films, is to discuss it with a trusted adult.

Pornography

Pornography is any material (photos, drawings, film or writing) that is designed to make people feel sexy. Unfortunately this is often done in ways that are demeaning to people. Pornographic images are quite different to factual pictures, which you may see in the context of sex education. Pornography is aimed at adults, not children, and is inappropriate for people below the age of 18.

If ever you do get to see any pornographic material, it is very important that you understand its purpose is to help adults fantasize about sex. The scenes you may see are probably staged, and don't represent normal, healthy sexual relationships or real situations. Stories and letters that you may read in some magazines are almost certainly made up, and are definitely *not* the way relationships really work. Pornographic images, in particular on the internet, are very often degrading and sometimes quite violent. It is thought that such images can influence a person to believe that this sort of violence is acceptable, whereas, of course, in a healthy relationship it certainly is *not*.

It is also really important to recognize that the pictures you see are not necessarily real. These days, photos can be manipulated on the computer to remove blemishes, whiten teeth, change the colour of skin and other features, and even change and enhance the size and shape of bodies (including penises and breasts). Don't think that by seeing a naked man or woman in a pornographic picture you really know what a naked body looks like.

Another thing to be aware of is that it is *never* okay for an adult to show you pornography. If this ever happens to you, it is very important that you report this to a trusted adult.

Graffiti and jokes

Things you see written on toilet walls and jokes you hear around the schoolyard may be funny, but definitely aren't the best way to learn about sex. Jokes usually rely on exaggeration and shock tactics in order to be funny, so be cautious about any information you get this way. Again, it is a really good idea to check out anything you didn't understand with an older person you trust, who may be able to explain what the joke was about (if you didn't get it), and also put the information in perspective. And because most sexual jokes are quite offensive, it's important that you take care not to repeat them unless you are very sure your audience would find them funny.

Books about sexuality

There are numerous books available (see the **Recommended Reading** at the back of this book), and they all vary a bit in their style and the amount of information they give. Some are humorous, some are more 'medical' – but all should be accurate. It's a matter of finding one that you find interesting and easy to read, so you can refer to it at any time that you need some information about sexuality.

8

Sexual Relationships

What happens when two people are involved in a sexual relationship? You may think, 'Sex – obviously!' but you might be surprised to know this isn't necessarily the case. A sexual relationship is any relationship in which the two people experience the feelings of sexual attraction described in the last chapter. These tingly feelings of attraction act rather like a magnet, drawing the two people together and encouraging them to find out more about each other. If they like what they find, and the sexual feelings are still strong, they will spend time getting to know each other better. They will have a desire to touch one another: this usually begins with holding hands and hugging, may lead on to kissing and

closer cuddling, and maybe even to touching each other's bodies in a sexual way. Eventually, when they are very comfortable with each other, they may decide to have sexual intercourse.

But, as you know, teenagers going through puberty shouldn't have sex, should they? As you read in the last chapter, it doesn't matter how strong someone's sexual feelings are, sex is against the law if they are younger than 16, and the strong emotions that tend to accompany sex are often too overwhelming for a very young teenager. Usually, then, when two young people are attracted to one another and go out together, they probably just hold hands and perhaps kiss each other. It's only as people get older, more experienced and more confident that they gradually explore more sexual activities, including sexual intercourse.

Everyone is different. While some people may feel ready for a relationship when they are in their early teens, many others wait until their late teens, early twenties or even older. This is okay. It isn't some sort of competition, and you must never feel that you have to have a relationship in order to prove anything to yourself or to anyone else.

People choose to have relationships for many reasons, and, of course, having a boyfriend or girlfriend can be lots of fun. But because emotions are involved, relationships can also be confusing and complicated. In this chapter we will explore relationships in a logical way, to try to simplify some of this confusion. We will look at some of the factors that will help you to make smart decisions, so that you are able to have happy, healthy relationships when the time comes.

Healthy sexual relationships

A healthy sexual relationship is one in which both people have fun and feel good about themselves and each other most of the time. Obviously, it would be unrealistic to expect that people would never argue with or criticize their partner: all relationships have their ups and downs. But a relationship that makes someone feel used or abused, exhausted and unhappy most of the time is *not* healthy. While it doesn't make sense that someone would stay in a situation like this, it can unfortunately happen quite easily, especially if a person is unclear about the sorts of things that are really important in a relationship. The following list includes the vital ingredients of a healthy sexual relationship; that is, one where both people feel cared for, respected, safe and happy.

Characteristics of a healthy relationship

- *You both really want to be in the relationship*: a relationship should be fun, and both people should feel good about themselves when they are together. You should be in it because *you* want to be – not because you are feeling pressured in any way, either by the other person or by your friends.

- *You feel relaxed in each other's company and are able to be yourselves, without having to pretend or 'act' a part*: obviously, none of us can be completely relaxed in a new relationship – mostly we're too nervous and self-conscious to begin with. But as time goes on, and you get to know the other person better, each one of you will gain confidence, and should feel able to be natural, to '*be yourself*' – in other words, you accept each other for who you are.

- *You are able to trust one another*: when you trust a person, you are able to have confidence that, in any situation, they want the best for you, will do their best to be loyal to and support you, and will never hurt you. By spending time together, and seeing each other in many different situations, you will gradually learn to trust one another.

- *You are honest with each other*: being honest with someone means you are able to tell the truth and say what you really think. It's important not to lie to someone; but if you are to be completely honest about how you feel, you need to be able to trust the other person to respect your feelings. Honesty and trust in a relationship, therefore, tend to go hand in hand.

- *You listen to and respect each other's points of view*: you might not agree with everything the other person says or believes, but it is important in any friendship or relationship that you can acknowledge that they have a right to think the way they do. When you really listen to and respect each other, you will understand each other better, and resolve or accept your differences without feeling resentful.

- *Neither of you ever pressures the other to do anything, sexual or otherwise, that he or she doesn't want to do*: this is important at every stage of your relationship, no matter how long you have known each other. You must listen carefully to each other, and if one of you is uncomfortable with something, the other one must respect this. You must not insist that the activity continues, no matter what it is. You both have a right to feel safe.

- *You both understand and behave according to the rules about sex*: the rules about sex exist to protect people, and keep them safe. As you may remember from the last chapter, these rules were: that both people in a relationship must be old enough, if they are going to have sex; their sexual activity must take place in private; no sexual activity should ever be forced; and sexual activity between family members is against the law. You must abide by the rules about sex if your relationship is to be healthy.

It is when one or more of these important qualities is missing that a relationship feels as though it is not okay. When you feel too uncomfortable, unhappy or guilty in a relationship, or you feel it's going nowhere, you may choose to end it – sometimes the issue is just too difficult to fix. But sometimes a relationship *is* worth rescuing. If you work together to identify the problem, you may be able to sort it out, and help your relationship become happy and healthy.

Taking it slowly

The healthiest relationships are those that are based on friendship, and friendships usually develop bit by bit. Even when sexual attraction is involved, the process is the same. Just because your sexual feelings may be strong, and you might really like the look of someone (you might think they are the sexiest, most beautiful person you have ever seen and you can hardly take your eyes off them), it doesn't mean you can walk straight up to them and just ask them out, or put your arm around their waist, or, even worse, give them a passionate kiss the very first time you are introduced to them. All these things break the rules, and the person would probably be very surprised, if not angry. They could even accuse you of assault.

When people start a relationship slowly and take it gradually, they can learn and gain confidence as they go along, only moving on to the next stage when both they and their partner feel ready and comfortable. It's rather like dipping your toe in the water to test it. You check that the temperature is comfortable and that the water is safe before you

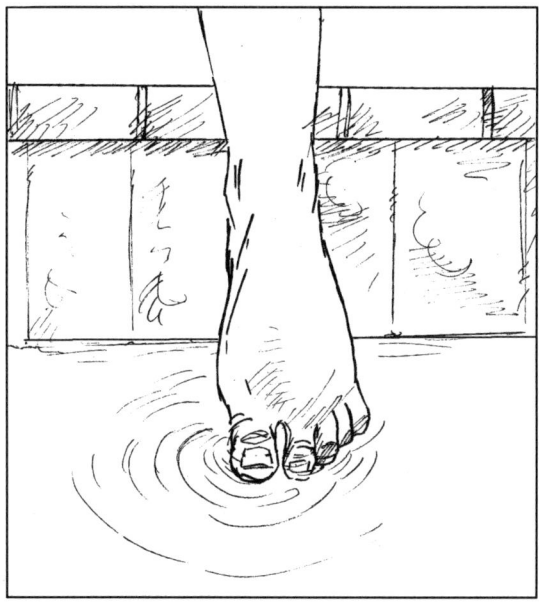

gradually go in deeper and deeper to the point that you can swim. If you 'take the plunge' and dive straight in without checking first, it can be risky. While you *might* be okay, you might equally find that the water is uncomfortably cold, too shallow or concealing hidden obstacles. You could end up in real trouble.

The 'diving straight in' approach to relationships doesn't really work because it doesn't give you a chance to get to know the person properly, or to work out what you do and don't like. You might find that you don't enjoy the sexual contact as much as you'd hoped, and you may soon discover that the person isn't as nice as you thought they were. Close physical contact, including kissing, is always much more enjoyable if you really know and like the person first.

Of course, in real life people do take chances, and sometimes this works out well. There are times in most relationships where one or other of the partners 'takes the plunge', and this element of risk can be part of the fun, and what moves the relationship on to the next stage. Relationships would probably never get anywhere if everyone was too cautious. However, it makes sense to know the person a little bit before you try to begin a relationship, so that you do at least have something to talk about.

The stages of a relationship

Every relationship is different, simply because of the way two unique individuals interact with each other, but there are some similarities in the way most relationships progress. As you read at the start of this chapter, a sexual relationship tends to move through certain stages, becoming closer and more physical as it goes on.

A very easy, visual, way to understand this is to represent the different stages as a continuum: that is, on a line, beginning at one end with the very first stage of a relationship (meeting someone and finding them attractive), and moving through all the stages that follow, leading to the closest physical contact of all – sexual intercourse – at the other end of the line.

RIGHT AT THE START ('WOW! I LIKE THE LOOK OF YOU!')

This is the very start of a relationship. The two people recognize that they are attracted to each other. They might be meeting for the very first time, or they might have known each other for a while (e.g. at work or school, or in a social group) and it starts to dawn on them that they find each other attractive. In both cases, whenever they are around each other they experience those sexual feelings that were described in the last chapter. It's quite normal to feel nervous, too, and not know what to say. They may blush easily, have sweaty palms and notice that their heart is beating faster and their breathing is quick and shallow. As they get to know each other better, and the relationship progresses, these nervous feelings will disappear.

GETTING TO KNOW YOU/MAINTAINING THE RELATIONSHIP ('YOU'RE SPECIAL. I CARE ABOUT YOU')

This is a very important stage of both new *and* established relationships. When a relationship is just beginning, these behaviours help people to get to know each other. In relationships that have lasted months or even years, these same behaviours are what keep the romance in the relationship. They help to keep it alive and healthy.

- *Flirting*: this is the playful behaviour that often goes on between two people when they are attracted to each other, and may include all sorts of things from simply smiling at each other a lot, to sharing jokes, sitting or standing very close to each other so

Sexual Behaviours

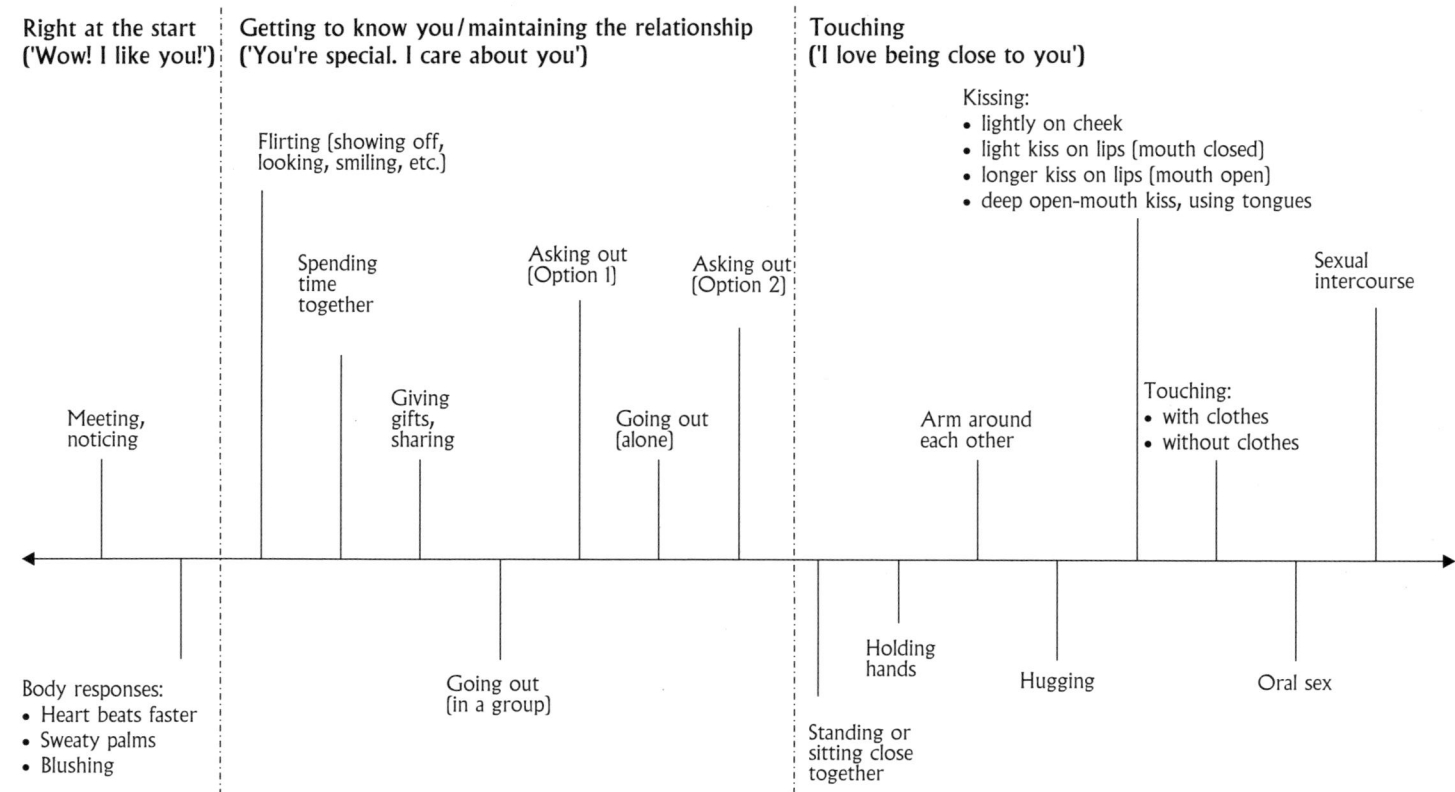

Right at the start
('Wow! I like you!')

Getting to know you / maintaining the relationship
('You're special. I care about you')

Touching
('I love being close to you')

Flirting (showing off,
looking, smiling, etc.)

Kissing:
- lightly on cheek
- light kiss on lips (mouth closed)
- longer kiss on lips (mouth open)
- deep open-mouth kiss, using tongues

Spending
time
together

Asking out
(Option 1)

Asking out
(Option 2)

Sexual
intercourse

Meeting,
noticing

Giving
gifts,
sharing

Going out
(alone)

Arm around
each other

Touching:
- with clothes
- without clothes

Body responses:
- Heart beats faster
- Sweaty palms
- Blushing

Going out
(in a group)

Holding
hands

Hugging

Oral sex

Standing or
sitting close
together

that their bodies touch lightly, showing off, good-natured teasing and gentle pushing and shoving. As well as being a way of getting to know each other better, flirting is a way for two people to pay attention to each other, and to indicate that they are attracted to one another – and a way to enjoy touching one another.

- *Spending time together:* two people can only get to know each other by spending time together, and communicating with each other. This can be in a work situation (at work or at school) where they may get a chance to work alongside each other. Or it could be in a social situation – break-times at work or school, or while involved in a recreational activity. There may not always be enough time to talk to each other properly, if they find they like each other's company, so they might swap email addresses or phone numbers to continue the contact. Emailing and text messaging can be less confronting, too, if they are a bit shy. In school people may send each other notes or text messages. Each time they communicate, the two people are getting to know a little bit more about one another. They are finding out about each other's likes and dislikes in a whole range of things (favourite hobbies and interests, television programmes, music, food and so on), and also about each other's personalities, attitudes and beliefs. Accepting and liking these things about another person are vital if the relationship is going to go any further. When a relationship is already established, it is healthy for the couple to spend time together, sharing ideas and showing an interest in each other.

- *Sharing and giving gifts:* most people enjoy giving gifts to the person they are attracted to, as a way of demonstrating that they are thinking about each other. The traditional things you have probably heard of are chocolates and flowers, but of course it doesn't have to be these. It can involve lending each other music, computer games, books and so on that they may share an interest in. Sometimes people enjoy 'sharing' their time, such as helping with homework, treating each other to a coffee or a meal, or walking each other home.

- *Going out together (in a group)*: at first, it is much easier to go out in a group, or go to parties with a few other people. The couple can still spend time together if they want to, but it does mean that, if they are a bit shy with each other, there are always other people around to talk to, so conversation doesn't get too awkward. Once a relationship is established, it is very important to go out from time to time with friends and have fun.

- *Asking out (Option 1)*: it may be around this point that one or other of the people summons up the courage to ask the other one out – in other words, become an 'official' couple. Even when they are a couple, and the relationship is established, it's still important to ask each other out on dates (see next point).

- *Going out alone*: alternatively, before they officially become a 'couple', people may choose to go on dates alone together. Young people will probably choose places that are free, or at least aren't too expensive, such as each other's houses, the movies, fast-food restaurants, walks in the park, swimming, skating and so on. Older couples usually have more choices, because they have more money and freedom, and often their own transport. If a relationship has lasted for months or years, it's still very important that the couple go on dates to keep the romance going, and to stop things getting too routine or boring.

- *Asking out (Option 2)*: sometimes people wait until they have had a few dates together before they ask each other out officially. This way they can feel more certain that they really do like each other.

TOUCHING ('I LOVE BEING CLOSE TO YOU')

When people have strong sexual feelings for each other, any touch can feel exciting and sexy. To begin with, they might touch each other briefly while they are flirting, and people often touch each other on the arm when they talk to each other. If they are out together, or working alongside each other, they may stand or sit close to each other so that their bodies touch lightly. Touching tends to happen in a sequence, too, beginning with the couple side by side (holding hands, putting arms around each other's waists or shoulders). It progresses to touching where they face each other (hugging), and then to much closer physical contact (kissing, touching the sexual parts of each other's bodies). This sequence is important – it's back to 'dipping the toe in the water' again. By taking it gradually, people are able to find out how comfortable they are with what's happening, and decide whether they *want* to go further. Even when people have been in a relationship for many months or years, touch is still very important. When they hold hands, hug and kiss, they are demonstrating affection for each other, and reassuring each other of their love. And of course, cuddling, kissing and touching each other's bodies sexually are the usual ways people lead up to having sexual intercourse – these activities are often known as 'foreplay'.

- *Holding hands:* people often find an excuse to hold hands in the particular activity they choose to do together. Sports such as ice-skating are good fun, and a great excuse to hold hands! Couples may enjoy holding each other's hands while they are walking around together, or sitting at the movies or watching television.

- *Arms around each other:* if they enjoy being close, they may put an arm around the other's waist or shoulders as they are walking along, or sitting beside each other.

- *Hugging:* when people hug each other, they face each other and hold each other close. To begin with, hugs may be short and quick, but as the couple get to know and like each other better, their hugs will be longer and closer. When a hug is closer, lasts longer and is more affectionate, it is usually known as a *cuddle.*

- *Kissing:* kissing is even closer than hugging, because the couple's faces touch. Just like touching, kissing happens in stages, so that people have an opportunity to get used to it and work out what they like:

  ○ a light kiss on the cheek (this is the sort of kiss that is quite okay with friends or family)

  ○ a light kiss on the lips, with mouth closed

  ○ a kiss that lasts longer, on the lips, with mouth slightly open

  ○ a deep, open-mouth kiss, using tongues (often known as 'French' kissing – see Chapter 11, **Sexual Language**).

Lots of young people believe, probably because of what they see in films and on television, that French kissing is the normal thing to do, and what kissing is all about. This isn't true! In fact, French kissing is only appropriate when a couple is very passionate. Certainly, very few people would enjoy a kiss like this for their first kiss. It's much better, and more romantic, to take it slowly. You will gradually gain confidence with the technique, and with each other. When it comes to kissing, lips are more sensitive than tongues, in any case.

- *Touching bodies*: couples will touch each other's bodies while cuddling and kissing – this is sometimes referred to as 'petting'. To begin with, the touching happens through the clothes. They touch the parts of the body that are known as the 'erogenous zones' (that is, the parts that feel particularly sexy) – the breasts, thighs, buttocks, vulva, penis and testicles ('light petting'). Soon they will move on to touch these body parts directly, underneath the clothes ('heavy petting'). This may eventually lead to them wanting to remove their clothes and be naked together.

- *Using mouths on each other's bodies*: when the couple is confident about seeing each other naked and touching each other's bodies with their hands, they may move on to touching each other's bodies with their mouths, and kiss each other all over their bodies. This may lead to using their mouths on their partner's genitals – *oral sex*. If a couple doesn't enjoy or feel comfortable with the idea of oral sex, they may miss this stage out, or introduce it *after* they are experienced with sexual intercourse.

- *Sexual intercourse*: eventually, following all the other sexual activity, sexual intercourse may occur. You can read about sexual intercourse in Chapter 7, **Sex**. If couples choose not to have oral sex, they may move straight to this stage from heavy petting.

Understanding sexual relationships

Many aspects of relationships can be confusing, and may leave you feeling quite bewildered. This is because relationships involve strong emotions – and when people are emotional, they can be illogical, and often don't think clearly. Very few people get relationships right every time, and most of us go on learning about them all our lives.

The continuum is a helpful way to explore relationships, because it is visual and simple. You can apply its logic to any relationship, whether the people involved are older or younger, gay or straight. Obviously, most relationships are more complicated than this simple linear representation, but the continuum is still a useful guide.

In this section, we are going to explore lots of relationship issues, and, with the help of the continuum, answer some of the many questions you may have. If you have questions that aren't raised here, try applying the logic of the continuum, perhaps with the help of a good friend or your social mentor, and see what solutions you can come up with.

What is the point of relationships when you're young, if you know they're not going to last?

Every relationship is worthwhile, because it teaches you something about yourself, and about other people. Early relationships are usually short-lived (very few people end up spending the rest of their life with their eighth-grade boyfriend or girlfriend), and this is okay. People learn about what they do and don't like, and how to respond and express themselves sexually. They also have fun. For lots of people, these short-term, 'practice' relationships are an important part of growing up and self-discovery.

Do people always do things in the order that is indicated on the continuum?

The simple answer is 'No, they don't!' But there is an advantage in them doing things in *approximately* this order, and that is that they get to know each other well, and gradually.

One situation in which sexual behaviours happen 'out of order' is when young teenagers experiment with kissing and sexual touching because they are curious. This may happen at parties and dances, with people they may or may not know very well, and have no intention of going out with. Some young people really enjoy this, and appreciate being able to satisfy their curiosity. But not everyone enjoys it – some people find it embarrassing and unpleasant. It's important to understand that you don't have to join in this sort of behaviour if you don't want to – no one has to do something they don't like. However, as long as no one is getting hurt or exploited, it is usually harmless and mostly just for fun. Just remember, though, it very rarely leads to meaningful relationships.

Similarly, especially in the more intense atmosphere of parties or clubs, more mature couples can meet for the first time and in no time at all be kissing and touching each other's bodies. Sometimes people simply enjoy this sexual contact with 'no strings attached' (i.e. no commitment). But the reality is, they don't know anything about each other, and they have to accept that this encounter may not lead to anything. If they do get together later, in a different situation, they may find that they have very little in common, and the relationship may come to nothing.

However, if people take things stage by stage, they have a chance to work out how much they really like the other person, and whether they want to move on to the next stage. Physical contact happens in a sequence such that the two people's bodies are gradually getting closer, and, again, this gives them a chance to work out how much closeness feels good, and whether they feel ready for the next stage.

Some very important relationship qualities are developing and strengthening gradually as the two people progress from one stage to the next. These are *friendship, trust, respect* and *intimacy*. These are all vital ingredients of a successful, healthy sexual relationship.

How long does all this take?

There is no set time for this whole sequence of events to occur. The continuum is not a 'time line', just an 'order line'. It may depend how experienced the two people are – that is, whether they have had lots of relationships in the past – in which case it might all happen quite quickly (days or weeks). Sometimes older, more experienced couples can get to the point of being physical with each other very quickly; but if the relationship is going to be successful, they will still need to spend time getting to know each other socially as time goes on.

Mostly, though, it will probably take several weeks, even months, for a couple to reach the point of having sexual intercourse. And remember, lots of relationships don't ever reach this point! (See next question.)

Should all relationships lead to sex?

Definitely not! Each couple will progress just as far as they are ready to go. It will depend on their age, experience, the strength of their sexual feelings and how comfortable they feel. Young people in the seventh or eighth grade who are just starting out in relationships may get no further than flirting with each other. Older teenagers may reach a point where they touch each other's bodies. There are no hard and fast rules, other than both the people trying to be very aware of what feels right, and *never* putting any pressure on each other to do something they don't feel ready for. It is never okay to do anything sexual just because you think 'everyone else is doing it'. First, that is never true (everyone else is *not* doing it); and, second, we are all individuals – what is right for one couple may not be right for another.

The couple must also take into account the rules about sex, of course, no matter how strong their feelings for each other. Therefore, they must abide by the law and be old enough for sex. They are also more likely to feel good about their relationship if they behave according to their own values, religion or beliefs, which may or may not allow them to engage in certain sexual activities.

Many couples are perfectly happy to wait to have sexual intercourse, if they believe, for example, that they are still too young, or that sex should only happen once they are married. There are lots of other fun sexual activities they can do to show their love for, and attraction to, each other and satisfy their sexual feelings.

Can sex 'just happen'?

When a sexual relationship becomes physical, especially when the behaviours include some of those at the far end of the continuum (such as touching each other's bodies with or without clothes), it is *very* easy for a couple to find themselves desperately wanting intercourse. Heavy petting (touching without clothes) often leads to intercourse – in fact, this type of sexual activity, often known as 'foreplay', tends to excite the couple to the point that intercourse becomes almost irresistible. When sexual feelings are strong, one sexual activity can very easily lead to another further along the continuum.

It is important to recognize that this can be a very normal, natural response. If sex does 'just happen', one or both of the partners may find themselves feeling very ashamed, guilty or angry with themselves afterwards. They may be very concerned, not just about the possibility of pregnancy or infection if they didn't use protection (see Chapter 9, **Looking After Your Sexual Health**), but also about their reputation.

It is much easier to resist getting 'carried away' if both of them are very clear in their own minds what they want and believe in. It's important to understand how easily intimate touching can lead to intercourse. They may choose to avoid the kind of sexual activity that can lead to them getting so sexually aroused that intercourse feels inevitable. Ideally, they should have discussed this with each other, and can support each other in their decision. Good communication, especially about really important things such as this, is a vital part of a healthy relationship.

In the movies, people meet and in no time at all are having sex. Is this okay?

First, it's important to remember that this is just fiction. Characters in movies and on television meet, fall in love and have wonderful sex all in the space of 90 minutes. If you use these fictional relationships as your guide to real relationships, you will be disappointed. Real-life relationships can't be like this, because love and good sex both take time to develop.

Some people *do* choose to have sex within a very short time of meeting each other. When they do, they are missing out on the important stages of making friends with each other, and finding out about each other's likes and dislikes, beliefs, sense of humour and so on. If they're lucky, they might find these out later and discover that they *can* become good friends. But, equally, they might find there is nothing more than strong sexual attraction between them. When this happens, the relationship isn't very happy or successful, and probably won't last very long.

It's very rare in movies to see couples talking about safe sex (i.e. protecting each other from pregnancy or infection. You can read more about this in Chapter 9, **Looking After Your Sexual Health**), yet sex with a virtual stranger, without protection, is risky behaviour, and not the basis of a healthy relationship.

Remember, in a healthy sexual relationship, the couple trust and respect each other, and are good friends. Building up trust, respect, friendship and love takes time.

'Consent' is one of the rules of sex; at what stage in a relationship is it important to get the other person's consent?

At every stage! Persisting in any one of the activities on the continuum when the other person does not welcome it can get you into trouble, ranging from being accused of harassment, to sexual assault or rape. Here's why...

HARASSMENT

If you were to persist in flirting, giving gifts to someone or asking them out when they are trying to make it obvious to you that they aren't interested, your behaviour could be viewed as very irritating, and you could be accused of *harassment*, a crime that is punishable by law.

Sometimes people are quite straightforward. They may say 'No thank you' when you try to give them something, or 'Leave me alone' if you try to flirt. This is easy to understand – so take note of their response and *don't persist* with what you were doing.

It's harder to understand, however, if they aren't clear. Often, it is a person's body language that gives them away, but if you aren't good at reading body language this can be very difficult. Try to notice if the other person seems pleased with what is happening; for example, they might smile and look you in the eyes, or move slightly closer to you. If they seem relaxed and happy with what is happening, then you can carry on.

If, however, they avoid looking at you, appear to be trying to move away, and don't smile or look welcoming, there's a fair chance they aren't comfortable with what is happening. If this is the case, then don't persist with what you were doing.

You might need to engage the help of a good friend to help you interpret this sort of thing. It would be awful to be accused of harassment simply because you misunderstood a person's body language.

SEXUAL ASSAULT

All sexual touching, from holding hands to oral sex, requires consent. If you touch someone in any way that is sexual without their permission, you can be accused of *sexual assault* (a more serious crime than harassment).

Often, people don't ask someone if they can hold their hand, or put their arm around their shoulders. Mostly during sexual activity, one thing leads naturally to another. People have to be sensitive to each other: they must listen to each other (remember, 'no' always means 'no'), and recognize from each other's body language (see previous section) whether they both feel okay about what is happening. If you feel you aren't reading the signals very well, the best thing, *always*, is to ask the person directly whether or not you can hold their hand, or touch them in whatever way you are wanting to. It might sound a little formal to say, 'Would you like to hold hands?' but communicating about sexual activity, no matter what it is, is a mature and healthy thing to do, and far better than being accused of sexual assault.

RAPE

Rape is the most serious of the sexual crimes. If a person forces another person to have intercourse (anal or vaginal), *even if they are already a couple* – in fact, even if they are married – it is never okay, and they can be accused of rape. The trouble is, sometimes people do lose their self-control when they are involved in sexual activity, and feel that they have reached a point where intercourse is the next most obvious stage. They may feel that the situation was automatically leading to sex ('She led me on'), or they may feel that the person 'owes' them sex ('We had a really nice dinner and she invited me back to her place. What did she expect?'). Some people believe that when a male is stimulated to a certain point he can't stop. All of these are mistaken ideas. Men *can* stop, no matter how much they have been 'led on', and there's no such thing as 'owing sex'.

It is absolutely vital in a healthy sexual relationship that people talk about how they feel and how far they want to go with sexual activity. They must listen to each other and respect each other's wishes. Forcing someone to have sex is *always* a crime.

Where does love fit on the continuum?

Love is the most difficult of emotions to describe, and can mean so many different things to different people.

The word 'love' is widely used, and doesn't always mean very much. When people say they 'love' chocolate, or they sign off a text message with 'luv u', it doesn't really mean love in the sense of deep, committed, two-way love (which we will talk about in a moment), but is an indication that they like this thing or this person. In the case of chocolate, they may like it very much indeed; in the case of the text message (or letter or email), it may simply be the conventional way to sign off.

However, when it comes to sexual relationships, the feelings of love can be quite confusing. When two people are very attracted to each other, right at the beginning of their relationship, they experience all those nervous body sensations – a strongly beating heart, sweaty palms, blushing and so on – and a general feeling of excitement. They want to be near to the person they are attracted to, they may think about them all the time, and find it hard to concentrate on anything else. It's almost like an obsession. This is when people may say they are 'falling in love' with each other.

Really, however, this infatuation with another person, accompanied by strong sexual feelings, is not love, but *lust*. The two are often confused, but they are definitely not the same thing. Lust is very powerful and strong, but doesn't usually last very long. It is the 'driving force' at the beginning of a sexual relationship. When people are 'in lust', everything seems wonderful. While this is a good thing in that it tends to keep them together while they get to know each other better, it also means that they may not be very realistic about the situation, and often don't see their partner's faults. For this reason, it is much better if they don't make any major decisions too early in the relationship (such as deciding too quickly to have sex, or even to get married or have a baby).

As a relationship develops, the feelings normally change. The exhausting, obsessive sort of love is gradually replaced by something deeper and more settled. This is mature love, and it is about deep, caring friendship, respect for each other, trust, thoughtfulness, a shared sense of humour, and a sense that you care more about the other person's well-being than you do about your own.

This sort of love is a sign of a mature, healthy relationship. It is the sort of love that makes the two people feel energized by their relationship. They will be happy most of the time, and appear to the rest of the world to be generous and kind. Their love makes them nice people to be with.

Sometimes, however, the relationship doesn't develop in such a healthy way. Their love continues to be obsessive and immature, and, although the two people may believe they love each other, there may be a lack of trust in the relationship. They may both feel unhappy, exhausted and unable to get on properly with their lives. This sort of immature love makes people selfish. They will often be inconsiderate or even mean towards other people, whom they have very little time for, because they are so obsessed with their own emotions. Immature love is not the basis of a good relationship.

Love can happen at any point on the continuum, but there is a greater chance of it becoming mature love, which is the basis of a lasting, healthy relationship, if the two people learn to trust and respect each other, and take their time to really get to know each other properly.

Where does marriage come on the continuum?

Some people believe that it is right to wait until after marriage to have sex, while others feel that it is okay to have sex before marriage. Some people don't think marriage is important at all, and remain unmarried in long-term sexual relationships. Yet other people are in arranged marriages, where the whole process of getting to know one another, followed by all the sexual behaviours, takes place *after* marriage.

So you can see that marriage isn't, in fact, a sexual behaviour, but what we call a 'social construct'. It can fit anywhere on the continuum, depending on a person's culture, values or beliefs.

Do people sometimes want different things from a relationship?

It is certainly possible for two people to have completely different expectations in their relationship. This can happen whatever age they are, or at any point in the relationship. One young teenager might be keen to start kissing, while the other prefers just holding hands. Sometimes one of the people is genuinely in love, while the other one is 'in lust'. Sometimes one person is keen to progress quickly through all the sexual behaviours, while the other is happy to stay at a particular stage for a bit longer. There may be differences of opinion about whether they should have sex before or after marriage, or whether marriage is something they want at all.

Whenever there are different expectations, there will be conflict and difficulties until the two people communicate properly about the problem. Sometimes they may be able to 'meet each other halfway'; that is, to compromise. Sometimes one of them may feel okay about agreeing to do what the other one wants. But sometimes the differences can't be resolved, and the only solution may be to end the relationship.

What is wrong with casual sex, if that's what people want?

We have already talked about the fact that if people choose to have sex without leading up to it gradually through all the stages, then they are missing out on the opportunity to get to know more about each other, and become good friends. Being good friends as well as sexual partners is a lot more emotionally satisfying. People who choose to have casual sex may convince themselves that they are perfectly satisfied, and that they are getting their sexual needs met without the complication of a relationship. They may even believe that they *are* finding love with each sexual encounter. Sadly, this isn't the case. Without a real friendship and a level of commitment between the two people, neither of them will be getting their emotional needs met, and in the long term this will leave them feeling empty and dissatisfied.

The other problem is that the more often someone has casual sex, the greater the likelihood that they will eventually encounter someone who has a sexually transmitted infection (see Chapter 9, **Looking After Your Sexual Health**). They have to be careful, therefore, to use protection (e.g. condoms) *every single time* they have sex.

They may also need to think about what sort of reputation they are gaining. Do they really want to lose the respect of everyone they know by becoming known as a 'stud' or a 'slut' (that is, someone who is prepared to have sex indiscriminately with just anyone)?

What happens if you are attracted to someone who isn't attracted to you?

Sadly, you can't force someone to be attracted to you. Sexual attraction is such a difficult thing to explain, and can be quite illogical at times. What you can do is be as friendly as possible towards the person you are attracted to. Don't make the mistake of jumping straight in and asking them out. Instead, try to organize times when you can be together as friends, not necessarily on a date but at gatherings with other people. If you do make suggestions for meetings and times to get together, try to notice how keen the person is. If they seem happy to come along and spend time with you, maybe their interest in you could be sparked. You may eventually be able to ask them out on a date – but when you do, watch carefully to see how keen they seem to be.

If they don't seem keen when you suggest getting together, or they make excuses not to come, don't push it for too long. Ask no more than three times (see next section). After this, *give up*. If someone gives in to your repeated requests to go out simply because you wore them down, they won't appreciate you for it. In fact, they are more likely to feel resentful towards you, and that isn't a good start to a relationship. There's no point making them angry – and you certainly don't want to be accused of harassment.

How do you ask someone out?

First of all, remember it is always best to know the person, even just a little bit. Don't ask someone out the very first time you set eyes on them! Once you have established that you like them as a person (not just for their good looks), then it is usually best to ask them along to something that involves a group of people, such as a party, a school dance, youth group, a group outing to the movies or other similar events. This makes it a lot less threatening, and is a good way to start. From then on you can try to judge how interested you both are in each other. Perhaps you could get a good, trustworthy friend to help you with this judgement.

It can be very difficult to ask someone out. But if you've spent some time getting to know each other, then summon up your courage, and take the plunge! If they want to go out with you, then you can work out together where you would like to go, and what you would like to do.

However, there is also the risk that you may be turned down, and this can be very hard to accept. But don't forget, it can also be hard to turn someone down, and not everyone is very good at being honest about their reasons for refusing. Often people will make up excuses to 'let you down gently'. When this happens, their meaning may not be clear. If they say something like, 'Sorry, I have to visit my grandma tonight', this can lead to you being unsure whether they meant 'no' altogether, or just 'no' on this occasion, so you might respond by saying something like, 'Well, that's okay – how about we go out tomorrow night instead?'

If you keep asking, however, and the person *keeps* offering excuses why they can't, it is likely they just don't want to go out with you. So follow this rule: Ask three times only. If they have an excuse every time, then you may need to be more direct. Say something like, 'I would really like to go out with you, but I'm not sure whether you are interested. Would you like to go out with me?' They may say yes, and explain that they really did have genuine reasons for turning you down initially. If this is the case, work out with them when would be a good time, and make a date.

If, however, they say no, they really don't want to go out, *you must accept this*. It isn't easy to accept rejection, but you can't force someone. In fact, if you keep on asking them out in spite of the fact that they keep refusing, you will be making a nuisance of yourself, and could be accused of harassment. As long as you are good-natured about it, you may be able to become or remain good friends with them instead.

BEING ASKED OUT

What if someone asks you out? If you want to go out with them, that's easy. You will almost certainly look pleased, and accept. Good luck!

If you don't want to go out, then it's okay to refuse. But do it nicely – remember, they probably had to summon up their courage to ask you, and it's not fair to make it worse for them by being unkind or rude. Be as truthful and straightforward as you can, without being hurtful. For example, if you know that they are attracted to you, but you aren't attracted to them, say something like 'Thank you for asking me, but I would prefer just to be friends.' If the idea of a relationship scares you, you might say 'Thank you, but I don't really feel ready to go out with anyone just yet.' If you make an excuse, such as 'I can't tonight – I've got to go to my grandma's for dinner' (which may or may not be true), the other person won't know that you don't *want* to go out, so they will just keep asking you, and you will have to keep on making up excuses. You will have to be truthful in the end, so you may as well be straightforward right from the start.

Chat with someone you trust about good ways to ask someone out, and polite ways to refuse if someone asks you out and you don't want to go.

What happens if a date doesn't work out?

It isn't always going to go well. You may find that, once you spend a bit more time with the person, they aren't quite what you thought. You may find you don't have much in common after all, or they're not as easy to get along with as you had hoped. Don't worry too much about this – the best thing you can do is be polite, say goodbye nicely and try to remain friends with them. As the saying goes, 'You win some, you lose some'.

Ending a relationship

Unless you happen to be with the person you want to spend the rest of your life with, this has to happen sometimes. It's hardly ever easy to end a relationship, because more often than not one of the people involved still wants to be in it. This means that someone is going to feel hurt.

When you want to bring a relationship to an end, honesty is always the best policy. For example, you might explain that you are no longer happy, and that it isn't working out. It's very likely that the other person won't want to hear this, but in the end the relationship can only be successful if you are both happy.

If you are the one being 'dumped', *you have to accept it*, for the same reason. If you make such a fuss that the other person feels they can't end the relationship after all, it won't help in the long run, as they will simply feel resentful towards you.

The bravest and most respectful way to end a relationship is face to face. This isn't easy, though, and sometimes people do it over the phone, or by email or text message. These could be seen as rather cowardly ways to deal with a difficult situation – but the worst way of all is to get a friend to do it for you. Never do this if you have any respect at all for your girlfriend or boyfriend.

Do people sometimes have sex just to be popular?

Yes, they do – but girls or boys who do this are sadly mistaken. They may appear to be much 'in demand', especially by other young people who are keen to experiment, and who will be delighted to find someone so willing. However, this isn't the same as being popular – or at least, it's popular for the wrong reasons. The people who want to have sex with them are exploiting them, just using them for fun, and not caring about them as people.

If a young person is shy and other people tend not to notice them, it can be very flattering, and make them feel special, when all of a sudden everyone seems to be interested in them. The sad thing is, if other people are only interested in them because they are willing to have sex, not only are they putting themselves at risk of unwanted pregnancy or infection, but they will also lose the respect of the people they care about, and gain a reputation as a 'slut' – and this isn't a label anyone wants.

How do people make sure they are choosing wisely and will be safe in a relationship?

No one knows when they first meet someone they are attracted to that this person will be reliable, kind, good fun – all the features we might want in a boyfriend or girlfriend. It is really only with time, and plenty of opportunity to see the person in a variety of situations that any of us can make a judgement.

This is why it never makes sense to rush into a relationship, and especially not to rush into any of the sexual activities at the far end of the continuum. When a person chooses to have sex with someone, they need to be sure that they can trust the person not to hurt them in any way. It's impossible to be sure of this with a stranger.

So the answer to the question is to take a relationship slowly enough that sound judgements can be made. The two people should go through all the stages of a relationship gradually, so that they give themselves a chance to recognize each other's real qualities in all sorts of situations.

Not everyone is a good judge of character, unfortunately. If this is the case for you, it can be very helpful to have a good friend or family member as your 'social mentor'. Talk to this person about your friendship or relationship. They can help you to work out how trustworthy and genuine the person you are attracted to really is.

Do people have relationships on the internet? How does this fit into the stages of a relationship?

You do hear stories of people who have met online and go on to have successful real-life relationships with each other. This is great – but it's also very lucky.

Remember, even when you have been chatting online for a long time (maybe for many weeks or months) to someone you've never met, you are still communicating with a *stranger*. Although you may have swapped a lot of information about each other, and really enjoy your conversations, the fact is you don't really know the person. You are still at the stage of getting to know each other, right at the very beginning of the continuum. Even if there is a certain amount of flirting, it is only in writing – you can't see the person to judge how genuine they are by their body language or facial expression.

They may not even be who they say they are. Just as you can take on a nickname or a different identity online, so can everyone else. So you really don't know whether the person who has become your friend is for real. Maybe they *are* genuine. But equally, they could be pretending and just having some fun with you; or, even worse, they could be lying and being deliberately cruel to you. They may not be telling the truth about their age, their interests or even their sex. Unfortunately, there are too many instances of young people being befriended by, and then being persuaded to meet up with, someone whose only intention is to abuse that young person.

There's no doubt that internet friendships can be fun, just so long as you stick to the rules.

- Don't give out personal information (name, email address, phone number, street address, name of your school). You don't know where this will end up, what it will be used for, or who may contact you.

- When you are going into a chat area, you may be asked for your age, sex and location. Don't give all these – just use a nickname (be careful that this isn't a nickname that attracts the wrong kind of attention), and don't be specific about your location.

- If you don't like the way a conversation is going, stop the conversation and leave the chat room. If necessary, block the person who is making you uncomfortable, so that they can't contact you again. You may choose to change your screen name.

- If you are really concerned that a conversation has become inappropriate or even threatening, you might choose to save the conversation and show a trusted adult. You can report this type of conversation to the chat facility, your internet service provider, or even the police.

- Never respond to messages or bulletin board items that are sexually suggestive, obscene or threatening. People can take advantage of you online just as much as they can in reality. Report anything like this straight away to a trusted adult.

- It's best not to agree to meet up with someone you have met online. This can be dangerous. It is wiser to keep an internet friendship as just that.

- If for some reason you do choose to meet up, *always* take someone you trust with you – preferably an adult – and meet in daylight, in a safe, public place.

The internet can be a great way of communicating with people, especially if you are a bit shy, or find face-to-face relationships difficult. You may make some genuine friends this way. Just bear in mind, though, that you can't necessarily believe everything and everyone you come across on the internet – even people who appear to be genuinely friendly.

There are some very helpful websites that provide information and guidelines for safe use of the internet (see the **Useful Websites** at the back of this book for details).

While the internet can provide lots of entertainment and a 'social life' of sorts, it's important that you try to make time for real-life, face-to-face friendships as well, otherwise you can become very isolated. This can make it even easier for unscrupulous people to exploit you in an internet relationship. Stick to the rules and stay safe.

9

Looking After
Your Sexual Health

All of us can do things to make sure we are sexually healthy. You have made a start simply by reading this book. That's because sexual health concerns a lot of the things we have already talked about. When you are sexually healthy, you have a good understanding of your body and how it works. You understand the changes you are going through, and know how to take care of yourself. All this helps you to feel good about yourself.

Sexual health is also about having an understanding of friendships and relationships, and ensuring that you have people in your life who care about you, just as you care about them.

It is sexually healthy to have good information about sex, too, so that you don't need to feel confused, ashamed or guilty. It's important that you feel able to ask questions and discuss sexual matters appropriately with someone you trust. And it's healthy to understand the rules about sex, and to recognize what values are important to your family or culture, so that you know how you should behave.

These are all ways that you can be sexually healthy as you go through puberty. As you become an adult, there are other things to consider. For example, the health of your reproductive organs is vitally important, and there are special checks that should be done on a regular basis to avoid any problems. If and when you start to have sexual relationships, you will need to know what you have to do to avoid catching any of the sexually transmitted infections that people can pass on to each other during sexual contact. You may decide to have children one day, in which case you will need to know how to space out your pregnancies so that you and your babies are as healthy as possible. You will also need to know how to avoid an unplanned pregnancy.

Even though you may not be in a sexual relationship right now, this is the sort of knowledge that you need well ahead of time. There's a lot to know, and it's good to get a basic understanding when you are young. It's also really important that you are able to separate fact from fiction, as there are several myths and untruths surrounding sexual health. As time goes on you can build on the knowledge you have. If and when you do have a sexual relationship, you can apply this knowledge to keep yourself and your partner safe and healthy.

Staying healthy

Care of your reproductive organs becomes increasingly important as you grow up. Boys can suffer damage to the testicles during sports, and testicular cancer, although rare, can affect boys from around the age of 15 upwards. Young women need to be aware that once they become sexually active they are at risk of catching genital warts, which in some cases can eventually lead to cancer of the cervix. A very good way to make sure that it never gets to this point is to have regular check-ups, a test known as a *Pap smear*. Although young women hardly ever get breast cancer, it is still important that they become familiar with their breasts, and learn to recognize when something might have changed.

Reproductive health checks for boys and men

A boy's testicles are responsible for producing testosterone, which gives him his male features; they are also responsible for producing sperm. Care of his testicles is vitally important for a male's good reproductive health.

TORSION OF THE TESTICLES

Testicles can become twisted, cutting off their own blood supply. If this isn't dealt with as an emergency, it can lead to the death of the testicular tissue, which may require surgical removal of the testicle. This twisting, which causes excruciating pain, nausea and fainting, is known as *torsion* of the testicle, and can be caused by a severe knock or kick (although it can happen for no apparent reason). This is why boys should always be careful when they are wrestling and fighting, and should never kick another boy in the testicles. If they play contact sports, they should wear a protective cup, available from sports stores, over the testicles.

TESTICULAR CANCER

Testicular cancer is rare, but it is the most common cancer in young men between the ages of 15 and 35. It is a highly curable cancer, especially when it is caught early, and treated straight away. For this reason, it is recommended that young men over the age of 15 should check their own testicles regularly (about once a month), and go straight to the doctor if they find any of the following:

- a swelling or lump (usually painless) in the testicle

- feeling of heaviness in the scrotum

- change in size or shape of the testicle

- pain or ache in the lower abdomen (groin), the testicle or the scrotum.

These symptoms *don't necessarily* mean cancer – they can indicate cysts or an infection – but the only way to confirm this is to have a check-up.

Testicular cancer normally affects just one testicle. The usual treatment is to remove the affected testicle in a simple operation. Sometimes radiation treatment or chemotherapy is required as well. Although he then only has one testicle, a man can function normally – he has normal erections and sex drive, and produces enough sperm to be fertile.

TESTICULAR SELF-EXAMINATION

It is a good idea to become familiar with the way your testicles feel normally, so do this simple self-examination about once every month. The testicles hang lower, and are easier to feel properly, if the scrotum is relaxed, so the best time to do this examination is after a warm bath or shower.

- Examine each testicle with both hands. Place your index and middle fingers under the testicle, with the thumbs on top. Gently roll the testicle between the thumbs and fingers. The testicles should feel smooth, rubbery and egg-shaped. It is quite normal

Testicular self-examination

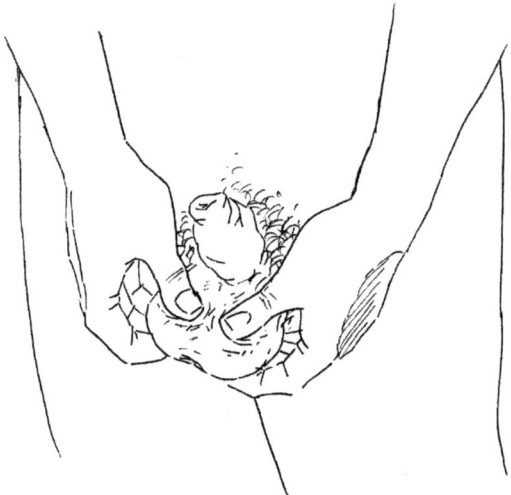

> for one testicle to be slightly larger, and for one (often the left one) to hang lower than the other.

- Feel the soft tube at the top and back of each testicle. This is the epididymis that stores and transports sperm. Don't confuse the epididymis with an abnormal lump.

- Feel for any lumps or bumps on the front or side of the testicles.

If you find a lump or anything else you think might be abnormal, contact your doctor immediately. It may well be an infection, not cancer – but whatever it is, the sooner it is treated, the better.

Reproductive health checks for girls and women

PAP SMEARS

A Pap smear is a test that is done to check for changes to the cervix (the opening to the uterus). Once a woman becomes sexually active, she may be exposed to genital warts (see later section). There are many strains of the wart virus, and some of these cause changes to the cells of the cervix that may eventually lead to cancer. It is only by checking the cervical cells on a regular basis that cervical cancer can be caught early and prevented.

It is recommended that a Pap smear should be done within two years of the first time a woman has sexual intercourse, and then every two to three years after that (the recommended interval varies slightly from one country to another). Women who have never had sex probably don't need to have Pap smears, but if a woman is unsure whether she should or not, it would be best for her to check with her doctor.

WHAT HAPPENS IN A PAP SMEAR?

The doctor or nurse who performs the Pap smear inserts a small instrument, called a *speculum*, into the woman's vagina while she is lying on her back. The speculum gently holds open the vagina so that the cervix is clearly visible. The doctor then takes a sample of the cells from the cervix using a tiny brush or spatula. These cells are smeared onto a laboratory slide and sent away for analysis.

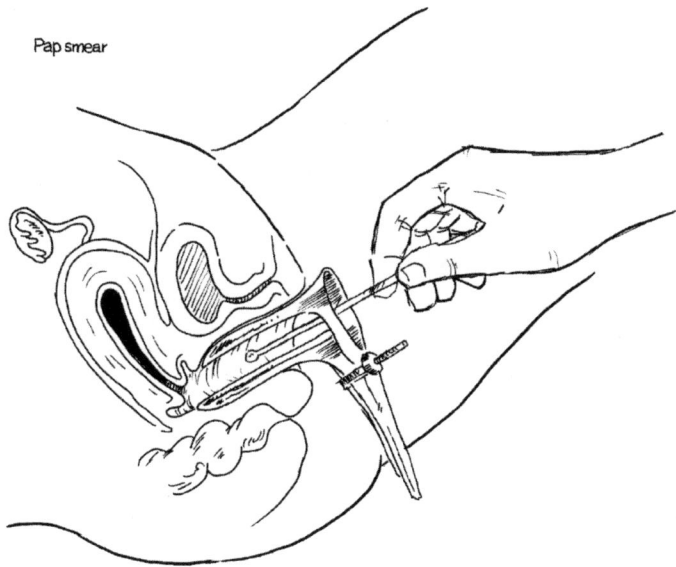

Pap smear

The procedure, although sometimes a little uncomfortable, is painless and quick, though some women don't like it because they feel embarrassed. Some women ask to be seen by a female doctor or nurse, as this helps them to feel more comfortable. Either way, the examination is over very quickly, and the doctor or nurse is always reassuring and professional, so there is nothing to be self-conscious about.

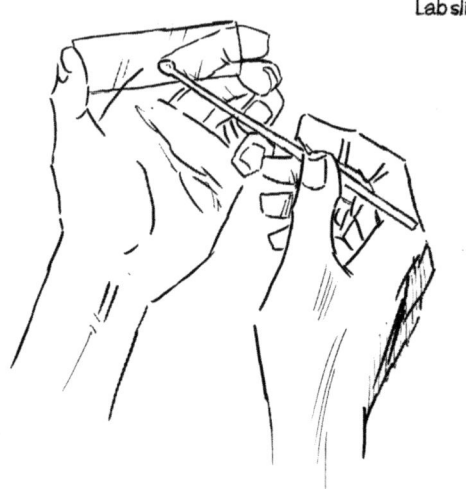

Lab slide

By having a test every two or three years, any changes that are detected can be treated well before cancer has a chance to develop.

VACCINATION FOR GENITAL WARTS

Many countries around the world now have a vaccination that protects against the particular strains of wart virus that may cause cervical cancer. It can be given to girls between the ages of 9 and 26 (and also to boys aged 9 to 15), and works best if administered before a person has become sexually active. Although it is very effective, it does not prevent all cases of cervical cancer, so even if a woman has been vaccinated, she will still need to have regular Pap smears.

BREAST HEALTH

You can read about the structure and function of the breasts in Chapter 1, **Your Body**, and how they develop at puberty in Chapter 2, **Puberty**.

Once you are an adult, but particularly as you become older, there is a slight risk of developing breast cancer. Since this has a much greater cure rate when it is detected and treated early, women are advised to check their breasts themselves, see their doctor regularly and have a special test called a *mammogram* every two years or so after the age of 40 (or sooner if there is a family history of breast cancer).

Breast cancer is very rare indeed in young women, and there really is no need to worry about it. However, it is recommended that you become familiar with your breasts so that you recognize when there are any changes.

Changes such as lumps, dimpling of the skin or swelling in the breast should always be checked by a doctor. There are two things for you to be aware of here:

- Your breasts will almost certainly be tender and lumpy as they are growing; and many women experience tenderness and thickening of breast tissue due to hormonal changes around the time of their period. *These changes are not cancer.* The important thing is that you are observant, and familiarize yourself with what is normal for you.

- Even in the case of older women, nine out of every ten lumps are not cancer – but they should still get anything unusual checked by the doctor.

Contraception

'Conception' is when a woman becomes pregnant. *Contra*ception, meaning 'against conception', is any method a couple may use to avoid a pregnancy when they have sexual intercourse. Other terms you may hear that mean the same thing are *birth control*, and *family planning*. By using contraception, people are able to choose how many (if any) children they have, and when they have these children. Once you start having sex, you must use contraception *every single time* you have intercourse, unless you want to become pregnant, or you want your partner to become pregnant.

All through history people have used many and varied methods to try to prevent pregnancy, often without much success. Today, our knowledge has increased, and the methods of birth control have improved. There are several methods of contraception now, some more effective than others, but all of them are well understood and researched. People are able to choose a method that suits the type of relationship they are in, their age, their personal preferences, their culture and their beliefs.

In a healthy sexual relationship, *both people* are responsible for contraception, and the choice of contraceptive method should be something that they discuss and decide together. They may need help to decide which method will work best for them, and many couples visit their family doctor or a special clinic (such as a family planning or sexual health clinic). Their consultation with the doctor or health professional will be confidential – that is, private – and, in some cases, free.

Methods of contraception

The only ways to be absolutely certain of not having an unplanned pregnancy are:

- to avoid having vaginal intercourse
- to be sure that ejaculation does not occur close to the opening of the vagina (see the section on myths about contraception later in this chapter for an explanation of this).

However, if people do want to have intercourse but at the same time avoid a pregnancy, then the most commonly used methods of contraception are:

- condoms (male and female)
- contraceptive pills ('the pill')
- emergency contraception
- contraceptive injections, implants and rings

Contraceptives

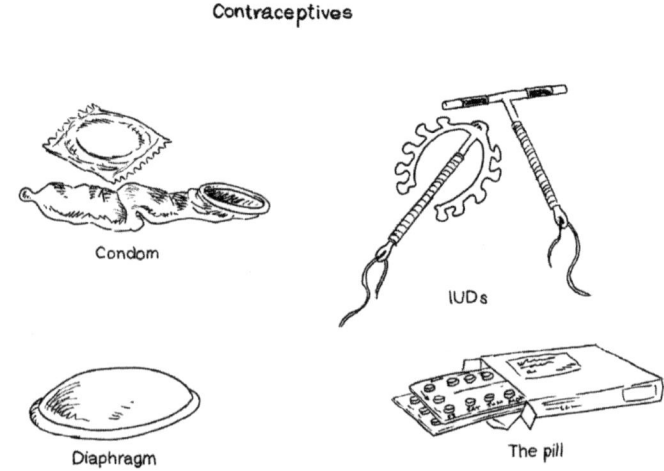

Condom

IUDs

Diaphragm

The pill

Female condom

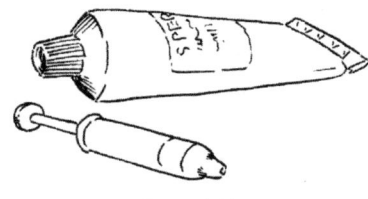

Spermicide

- diaphragms and caps
- intrauterine devices (IUDs)
- natural family planning
- sterilization.

The first thing to be really clear about is that contraception is a way of preventing pregnancy, *not* a way of preventing sexually transmitted infections (STIs). It just so happens that condoms *do* help to protect against STIs, but no other method of contraception has this dual function – certainly not the contraceptive pill, no matter what people might tell you.

CONDOMS

Male condoms

A male condom is a thin sheath, usually made of latex, but sometimes made of polyurethane. It is rolled onto the erect penis before the couple have any genital contact. It acts as a barrier so that the penis and the vagina do not come into direct contact with each other. When ejaculation occurs, the semen is collected in the tip of the condom, so that sperm are prevented from swimming up into the female reproductive tract. For these reasons (no skin-to-skin contact, and collection of the sperm in the tip of the condom), condoms are effective protection against both unplanned pregnancy *and* STIs.

All condoms are for one use only, so as soon as ejaculation has occurred the condom is carefully removed and disposed of in a rubbish bin – not down the toilet, since it can block the plumbing.

Condoms are impregnated with a little lubricant to make them easier to put on. Most people use additional water-based lubricant, such as *K-Y Jelly*, to make intercourse more comfortable and pleasurable.

All condoms come in packs, with easy-to-follow instructions about how to put them on, remove them and how to store unused ones correctly. If a condom isn't used or stored properly, it is possible that it may split during sex. For example, a condom that is kept for months in a wallet will almost certainly deteriorate due to excessive heat, and should not be used. If the condom does break, and the couple is worried about the possibility of pregnancy, they can use emergency contraception (see later section).

Condoms are available from family planning and sexual health clinics (sometimes at no cost), and can be bought from pharmacies and supermarkets. They are also available from vending machines in many public toilets, including those in night clubs, bars, service (gas) stations and so on.

They come in a few different sizes, and usually a man will only know what fits him best by trying different ones. They are also available in a variety of colours, and sometimes even flavours. This is to make them more fun and appealing so that people will want to use them, since they are such an important method of protection, particularly against STIs.

Female condoms

A female condom is a soft pouch-like sheath, made from polyurethane, which is inserted into the vagina before sexual intercourse. It lines the vagina, so that during sex there is no skin-to-skin contact with the penis. As with the male condom, when ejaculation occurs, the semen is collected in the end of the condom, and sperm are prevented from travelling up into the female reproductive tract.

The condom is carefully removed after sex so that the semen doesn't spill out of it. It can only be used once, and therefore must be disposed of into a rubbish bin rather than the toilet.

Female condoms are slightly more expensive than male condoms, and are not as widely available. Most couples have to practise in order to use them properly and safely; for example, it is very easy during intercourse for the condom to slip, and the penis to go up the side of it rather than inside it. However, with care and practice, couples will find that female condoms can make good alternatives to the male ones, and provide about the same level of protection against pregnancy and STIs.

CONTRACEPTIVE PILLS

The combined pill

This is a hormonal pill that contains a combination of the female hormones oestrogen and progesterone. The hormones act on the woman's body to prevent ova maturing and being released by the ovaries. In this way pregnancy is prevented. The pill is one of the most effective methods of birth control, but it does *not* protect against STIs.

The contraceptive pill is only available on prescription, so a woman must visit her doctor or clinic to be assessed. Some women can't take the pill for medical reasons, and a number of women do experience some mild side effects, such as headaches, tender breasts and slight weight gain. Mostly these settle down after two or three months. Once a woman has decided that the pill is the method of birth control she would like to use, she must be sure to follow the directions carefully, and to take a pill *every day* without fail.

One of the positive side effects of the pill that many women appreciate is its effect on periods. Irregular periods become regular and predictable, and heavy, painful periods become lighter, shorter and less painful. Some girls and women may go on to the pill for this reason, rather than for birth control.

Progesterone–only pill

This pill (sometimes also known as the 'mini-pill') is almost as effective as the combined pill, but only if it is taken at *exactly the same time* every day.

It works slightly differently to the combined pill, however. Rather than suppressing ovulation, its action is to thicken the secretions that are made by the cervix. This makes it more difficult for sperm to swim through into the uterus. Its other action is to change the lining of the uterus, so that even if an ovum were to become fertilized, it wouldn't be able to implant.

As with the combined pill, the progesterone-only pill is available only on prescription, so the woman will need to visit her doctor or clinic. Although it can cause a few side effects, such as irregular periods and tender breasts, it can be more suitable for some women than the combined pill. For example, some women may have medical reasons why they cannot take oestrogen; and the progesterone-only pill is ideal for women who want to breast-feed their baby. This is because while oestrogen in the combined pill affects the milk supply, the amount of progesterone that might pass through the breast milk from the progesterone-only pill is extremely low, harmless to the baby and will not affect the milk supply.

Again, as with the combined pill, the progesterone-only pill is no protection against STIs.

EMERGENCY CONTRACEPTION

If contraception fails or is not used for some reason, for example a condom breaks, the couple forget to use contraception or the woman is forced to have sex, there are two methods that can be used in an emergency.

The most common one is a pill, often referred to as the 'morning after' pill. It can actually be taken up to three days (72 hours) after unprotected intercourse, but is more effective the earlier it is taken after sex. It works by preventing ovulation and changing the lining of the uterus so that a fertilized ovum can't implant. It *doesn't* cause an abortion (see later section).

Emergency contraceptive pills are available from doctors, family planning and sexual health clinics, and pharmacies. In some countries and states a prescription is not required.

The emergency contraceptive pill is very effective, but should only be considered for occasional emergency use, and not relied on as a regular method of birth control. There are two reasons for this:

- The level of hormones in the emergency pill, while perfectly safe when taken occasionally, may not be okay for some women if taken on a regular basis. If a couple is having regular sex, it is important that they visit a clinic and consult with the doctor or nurse to establish which long-term method of contraception is best suited to them in their circumstances.

- If someone is having irregular sex, especially with different partners, there is a higher risk of them encountering someone with an STI, so condoms would be a much more suitable method than the emergency pill.

The other method of contraception that is sometimes used in an emergency is an intrauterine device (IUD), which can be inserted within five days of unprotected intercourse. You can read more about this method and how it works in a later section.

CONTRACEPTIVE INJECTIONS, IMPLANTS AND RINGS

Contraceptive injections, implants and rings are all methods that release hormone gradually into the woman's body, over a few weeks, months or even years. They are all very effective methods of contraception. Their action is to prevent ovulation, and to change the lining of the uterus to prevent a fertilized ovum from implanting. The advantage of all these methods is that the woman does not have to remember to take a pill every day, or use contraception at the time she has intercourse. None of these methods protect against sexually transmitted infections.

- *Injections*: can be given once every three months (progesterone-only) or every month (both oestrogen and progesterone). The slight disadvantage of these is that any side effects will last until the dose of hormone is all used up.

- An *implant* is a small plastic rod containing progesterone. It is fitted beneath the skin of the inside upper arm in a small surgical procedure, and can stay in place for up to three years. Should side effects become unpleasant for the woman, or she decides she doesn't want to use this method for whatever reason, she can have the rod removed easily.

- The *contraceptive ring* is a small, soft plastic ring containing both oestrogen and progesterone. It is inserted into the vagina and left in place for three weeks. When it is removed, the woman has her period. She puts in a new ring seven days after removing the original one. There are very few side effects, but even if there are, the ring can be removed easily.

DIAPHRAGMS AND CAPS

These are small, dome-shaped devices, made of latex or silicone, that fit over the cervix and act as a barrier to prevent sperm travelling up into the uterus. *Spermicide* (a substance that kills sperm) in the form of cream or gel may be used with these devices.

The woman fits the diaphragm or cap into her vagina before she has sexual intercourse. She leaves it in place for at least six hours afterwards, so that the spermicide has a chance to kill any sperm that may have made their way around the rim of the device. It can then be removed, washed, dried and stored until the next time she needs it.

Since all women are slightly different sizes and shapes inside as well as outside their bodies, the woman will need to be fitted for her diaphragm or cap at the clinic by a nurse or doctor. She will also be instructed how to insert it herself, and care for it. As long as it fits well, it will be comfortable, and neither the woman nor her partner will be able to feel it while they are having sex.

INTRAUTERINE DEVICES

An intrauterine device (IUD) is a small plastic and copper device that is inserted into the uterus by a doctor. There are various types and sizes available to suit different women. Depending on the type that is used, it can be left in place for three to ten years. It can be removed by the doctor at any time, if the woman decides she would like to become pregnant, or if she wants to use another method of contraception.

An IUD works by preventing sperm from meeting with an ovum, and also by changing the lining of the uterus so that a fertilized ovum is prevented from implanting. It is effective from the moment it is fitted, and, for this reason, it can also be used as a method of emergency contraception (see previous section).

IUDs do not protect against sexually transmitted infections.

NATURAL FAMILY PLANNING

Some people choose to use natural methods of birth control because of their personal preferences or religious beliefs.

Natural family planning (sometimes known as 'the rhythm method') means avoiding intercourse at the time that a woman is fertile. Successful use of this method depends upon the couple being very careful, and having a thorough understanding of the woman's menstrual cycle.

In a normal cycle, a woman ovulates (releases an ovum) around two weeks before the start of her next period. The ovum lives for about 24 hours in the Fallopian tube. Sperm, however, have a longer life. They can survive for up to seven days once they reach the Fallopian tubes.

Therefore, if a couple want to avoid a pregnancy, they must not have intercourse for around eight days before ovulation (to allow for the time that sperm might survive), and two days after ovulation (to allow for the time that the ovum might survive). The key, therefore, is to determine exactly when ovulation occurs, and this is not easy. Even for women who usually have regular menstrual cycles, the timing of ovulation can be affected by illness, stress and even long-distance travel. There are certain body signs that indicate the occurrence of ovulation, and these are the changes in the appearance of the cervical secretions (these vary in consistency throughout the menstrual cycle) and body temperature (which rises slightly just after ovulation). In order to recognize and make use of these indicators, a couple must be trained by a specialist natural family planning teacher.

Natural family planning is a high-risk method of birth control that is only suitable for use by mature couples who are prepared to dedicate time and attention to using it properly. It is rarely suitable for young people, and of course offers no protection against STIs.

STERILIZATION

This is a permanent method of contraception that can be used by couples who are absolutely sure they don't want any (or any more) children. It involves a simple operation for either the male or the female.

The male operation is called a *vasectomy*. A small piece of each of the vas deferens (the tubes that carry the sperm from the testicles to the urethra) is cut or tied. As a result, sperm are unable to swim along to mix with the semen. When the man ejaculates, the semen that he produces looks the same but contains no sperm.

The female operation is called a *tubal ligation* or *tubal occlusion*. In a ligation, a small piece of each of the Fallopian tubes is cut or clipped, whereas in an occlusion, a tiny coil is inserted into each of the tubes. During the next few weeks, tissue grows into the coils, permanently blocking the tubes. Following these operations, sperm and ova are no longer able to meet. The woman looks and feels normal, and continues to have her periods as usual.

Vasectomy and tubal ligation can sometimes be reversed, though reversal operations are frequently unsuccessful. Tubal occlusion is not considered to be reversible. It is important, therefore, that people are counselled before making their final decision about sterilization.

Myths about contraception

You will almost certainly hear some of the following untruths about contraception at some point. Often, couples in a relationship will try to convince each other that they are true, usually when they want to have sex, but haven't got around to organizing any contraception. The trouble with believing any of these myths (which can sound quite convincing until you read a bit more about them) is that couples put themselves at greater risk of having an unplanned pregnancy.

YOU CAN'T GET PREGNANT THE FIRST TIME YOU HAVE SEX

Yes, you can! As long as the female is releasing an ovum each month into the Fallopian tubes, she *can* get pregnant if the couple have sex around this time. Ovulation is difficult to detect, even for very experienced women (see section on natural family planning), so any time is risky to have sex without contraception if the couple don't want a pregnancy. And remember, the younger the woman, the more fertile (i.e. able to become pregnant) she is.

YOU CAN'T GET PREGNANT IF YOU HAVEN'T STARTED YOUR PERIODS YET

This sounds as though it ought to be true. After all, if you haven't started your period, then you haven't released an ovum yet. But the release of the ovum comes *before* the build up and then the loss of the lining of the uterus, which is the period (you can read more about the process of menstruation in Chapter 2, **Puberty**). So what if you *have* released an ovum for the very first time, and are just about to have your first-ever period? If you were to have sexual intercourse at this point, it would be possible for a sperm to unite with the very first ovum ever to be released. This would be very unlucky timing, but quite possible, and certainly not worth the risk. (And don't forget the law about the age of consent. In most countries it is illegal for a girl to have sexual intercourse if she is below the age of 16. See Chapter 7, **Sex**, for more details.)

YOU CAN'T GET PREGNANT WHILE THE GIRL IS HAVING HER PERIOD

You certainly can! Although some people don't like the idea of having sex during the woman's period, other people don't mind at all. As long as they are both comfortable with it, there is no problem. But it is *not* a method of birth control. Depending on the length of her menstrual cycle (the length of time between the start of one period and the start of the next), it is possible for a woman to release an ovum while she is still menstruating – this would be the case if she has a shorter than average menstrual cycle. Even though there may be some blood, sperm are still able to swim up through the cervix and the uterus, and into the Fallopian tubes. If there is an ovum in the Fallopian tubes, then fertilization can occur.

YOU CAN'T GET PREGNANT IF YOU STAND UP WHILE YOU ARE HAVING SEX

This myth is based on the assumption that sperm can't swim against gravity. But they can! They are helped on their journey into the female reproductive tract by the secretions of the cervix and the uterus. It doesn't matter what position the couple are in when they have sex – as long as sperm are deposited inside (or even just on the outside of) the vagina, they can make their way very quickly and efficiently through the cervix and up into the uterus and Fallopian tubes.

AS LONG AS THE MALE 'PULLS OUT' BEFORE HE EJACULATES, THEN PREGNANCY CAN'T HAPPEN

This is a method of contraception called *withdrawal*, and is widely used around the world. It is included here as a myth, rather than in the previous section as a valid method of contraception, because it fails so frequently. People who use this method tend to have lots of children. Although it sounds good in theory, in practice it doesn't work very well, for two reasons. The main one is that it relies on the good timing and willpower of the man. Unfortunately, when a man is approaching his orgasm and ejaculation, he doesn't necessarily have very strong willpower, and may not feel like pulling out at that point. Younger men who are more inexperienced may not recognize exactly when they are about to ejaculate, and therefore get the timing wrong. The second reason that the method may fail, even if a man has good timing and strength of will, is that there is a release of ejaculatory fluid (sometimes known as 'pre-cum') from the tip of the penis a few moments before ejaculation. This fluid may contain sperm.

THERE'S NO RISK OF PREGNANCY, JUST SO LONG AS THE MALE EJACULATES *OUTSIDE* THE VAGINA

Yes, there *is* a risk of pregnancy if he ejaculates close to the opening of his partner's vagina. A sexually aroused woman produces secretions from her vagina and cervix. It is the job of these secretions to help the sperm on their way into the female reproductive tract. If sperm come into contact with the secretions, even on the outside of the vagina, they may be helped to make their way into the vagina and up into the uterus and Fallopian tubes.

AS LONG AS THE FEMALE DOESN'T HAVE AN ORGASM, SHE WON'T GET PREGNANT

It is true that the rhythmic contractions of the uterus during the woman's orgasm may assist the sperm on their journey into the female reproductive tract. However, sperm can swim up into the uterus and Fallopian tubes without this assistance, and it makes no difference whether the woman has an orgasm or not. She doesn't even have to enjoy the sexual encounter – women have been known to become pregnant after being raped. Becoming pregnant is not to do with whether or not the woman enjoys sex, but with whether or not the man and woman are fertile.

IF THE WOMAN GOES TO THE TOILET STRAIGHT AFTER SEX, SHE WON'T GET PREGNANT

This is a myth for two reasons. The first is that sitting on the toilet and allowing the semen to 'drain out' will not get rid of the sperm – they can swim up and against gravity, and are already in the cervix within a few moments of ejaculation. The second is that the urinary tract is quite separate from the vagina, and passing urine will not 'flush out' the sperm.

USING A VAGINAL DOUCHE IMMEDIATELY AFTER SEX WILL PREVENT PREGNANCY

A *douche* is any liquid that is flushed into the vagina. Some people believe that this is a good way to keep the vagina clean, but as we discussed in Chapter 1, **Your Body**, and Chapter 2, **Puberty**, the vaginal secretions that occur naturally keep the vagina healthy and clean. The introduction of 'feminine cleansing products' or any other solutions can affect the delicate balance of the good bacteria that keep the vagina healthy, which can, in turn, lead to an infection. Therefore, from the point of view of vaginal health, douches are not a good idea. As far as contraception is concerned, they certainly don't work to flush out sperm after sex – as we have already discussed, sperm make their way very quickly through the cervix, and flushing out the vagina with a douche won't stop them.

Abortion

An *abortion* occurs when a pregnancy ends early, and the embryo or foetus passes out of the uterus, through the vagina. This can be a natural event, usually referred to as a *spontaneous abortion* or a *miscarriage*. Miscarriages tend to occur quite early in the pregnancy. Although the cause is often not known, it can be because the embryo or foetus is not developing normally. Most women who experience a miscarriage will go on to have one or more successful pregnancies later.

What we usually mean when we use the term 'abortion', however, is a surgical or medical procedure to bring the pregnancy to an end by removing the embryo or foetus, along with the lining of the uterus. Sometimes it is referred to as a 'termination of pregnancy'.

Women have abortions for many different reasons. It may be that there is something seriously wrong with the baby, or that the pregnancy or birth will put the woman's own life in danger. Mostly a woman makes the choice to have an abortion because the pregnancy was unplanned, and for any number of reasons she feels unable to cope with a child. She may feel she is too young to have a baby, or may no longer be in a relationship. She may be pregnant as a result of being raped. She may have several children already, and may feel that she can't afford to have, or cope with, any more. It could be that this is simply the wrong time in her life to be pregnant. Every woman's situation is unique, and each woman has to make a careful decision for herself.

Abortion is very rarely an easy choice. A woman may feel very emotional when faced with an unplanned pregnancy, and this can make it difficult to think clearly. In addition, there may be other people in her life who feel strongly about the situation and will try to influence her decision. It is important that she is able to make the decision to either continue with or terminate the pregnancy without being pressured by anyone else. For this reason, it is nearly always a good idea for her to seek professional counselling; in this way she should be able to make the most appropriate decision, and one that she won't later regret. Following an abortion, some women feel greatly relieved, others feel very sad, and many experience a mixture of emotions.

Surgical abortions are usually performed in the first two or three months of pregnancy; very occasionally they may be done a bit later than this. The procedure is carried out by a doctor in a hospital or special clinic, and takes no more than about ten minutes. The woman is given an anaesthetic, and the contents of the uterus, including the foetus, the placenta and the lining of the uterus, are suctioned out. The woman is usually able to go home the same day.

Medical abortions are also performed early in the pregnancy, and involve two visits to the clinic and the use of special drugs to cause the uterus to expel the pregnancy, much as it would in a naturally occurring miscarriage. Again, in most cases the woman is able to go home the same day.

As long as it is performed by a medical practitioner, abortion is a safe procedure, especially when done earlier in the pregnancy rather than later. It normally doesn't affect the woman's ability to have successful pregnancies later on.

The laws regarding abortion vary from one country to another. In some places they are illegal, in others they are readily available, and in many countries they are legal, but with several restrictions. Many people believe that abortions should be readily available, and that it should be a woman's right to choose whether or not to terminate an unplanned pregnancy. There are many other people who are strictly opposed to abortion owing to their personal or religious beliefs. A woman who feels unable to have an abortion because of her strong beliefs will make alternative choices, such as having the baby and making the best of her situation, or arranging for the baby to be adopted soon after birth.

Sexually transmitted infections

Sexually transmitted infections (STIs) are infections that are passed from one person to another during sexual contact. You may also hear them referred to as *sexually transmitted diseases* (STDs) and in the past they were known as *venereal disease* (VD). In spite of the name changes, the infections themselves haven't changed, and many of them have probably existed for as long as people have been having sex.

Sex is a normal, natural and healthy part of life, and not everyone who has sex will get an infection. If two uninfected people have sex together, they will remain uninfected – infections don't just come out of nowhere. But if one of them does happen to have an STI, it is very likely to be passed on to the other one during sexual contact, unless they use a condom for protection.

Ways to catch an STI

The most risky sort of sexual contact in terms of passing on an STI is sexual intercourse – vaginal or anal – without the protection of a condom (for more information about the different ways people can have sex, see Chapter 7, **Sex**). This is because with many of the STIs, the infection is carried in the semen or vaginal secretions and can pass into the body through the mucous membranes of the vagina or anus, or head of the penis. Any infectious sores or lesions around the genitals can also be passed on during the close body-to-body contact of intercourse. Some STIs can be spread from the genitals to the mouth and throat, and for this reason oral sex may also carry a certain amount of risk.

Some of the more serious infections, such as hepatitis or HIV, are carried in the bloodstream as well as in the semen and vaginal secretions (and, in the case of hepatitis, also in the saliva), and have to get into the bloodstream of the other person in order to infect them. So if the uninfected person has any breaks in their skin, or sores or lesions, contact with infected body fluid can be risky as the virus can find a way directly into their bloodstream. Again, this means that as well as vaginal and anal sex, oral sex can be risky, especially if the person has mouth ulcers or bleeding gums.

Because these infections are carried in the blood, non-sexual activities that involve blood (such as sharing needles for drug use, getting tattoos and so on) can also be very high risk. This is why it is very important that injecting drug users always use a clean needle every time, and all practitioners who use needles and do surgical procedures (doctors, dentists, tattoo artists, ear piercers and so on) should adhere strictly to safe practices. It is never a good idea to share other people's razors or toothbrushes, partly for reasons of good general hygiene, but also because of the risk of catching a serious infection such as hepatitis.

If someone has a parasitic infection (pubic lice or scabies), sharing towels and bed linen can also be risky, though the main way of catching these is close physical contact, including sexual contact.

ACTIVITIES THAT DO *NOT* PASS ON STIs

STIs are not passed on by regular everyday contact. The sort of contact you may have with family or friends, such as shaking hands, 'high fives', hugging and kissing are all safe activities, and will not transmit STIs. Neither will the sort of contact you may have when you play sport or go swimming or dancing. STIs are not spread in the same way that colds are spread, so you can't catch an STI because someone coughs or sneezes near you, or shares their food with you. Donating blood and getting vaccinations are also safe, because all equipment is sterilized, and new needles are always used. And you can't catch an STI by being bitten by a mosquito, or from a toilet seat, no matter what people may tell you.

The most common STIs

There are many STIs, but the most common ones are:

- *Parasitic infections*: pubic lice, scabies.
- *Bacterial infections*: chlamydia, gonorrhoea, syphilis.
- *Viral infections*: genital warts, herpes, hepatitis B, hepatitis C, HIV/AIDS.

People can have more than one STI at one time, and, in fact, the presence of one can make it easier to become infected with another one.

You don't need to know about every STI in detail in order to protect yourself and stay healthy. If you are interested, you can read about each of the STIs on the many informative sites on the internet (see the **Useful Websites** at the back of this book). It is useful, though, to know what the usual symptoms may be, and also to understand that *very often there are* *no symptoms* (even though the infection may be doing damage in the person's body).

The most likely symptoms of an STI are:

- unusual vaginal discharge (unusual colour (e.g. greenish, greyish, yellowish); strong, unpleasant fishy odour)

- prolonged itchiness or general irritation around the genitals

- a white or yellow discharge from the penis

- pain or discomfort when passing urine

- a sore, a wart or a blister on or around the genitals or anus

- pain during sexual intercourse

- pain in the lower abdomen.

It is very important that when a person has any of the above symptoms, they should refrain from sex, and go for a check-up at the doctors or the sexual health clinic as soon as possible. Many of these symptoms don't necessarily mean that the person has an STI, but it is still important to find out what is wrong, and treat the problem.

Check-ups and treatment
WHEN THERE ARE NO SYMPTOMS

Why would someone even think about going for a check-up if they have no symptoms? The fact is, if a person has had unprotected sex with someone whose sexual history they don't know – someone who could easily have an STI – then they could well have caught an infection, so it is advisable to go for a check-up.

Some couples choose to go to the clinic together and both get checked before they start to have sex. This is a very sensible thing to do, and very reassuring for each other. If neither one of them has an STI, and if they remain faithful to each other, only ever having sex with each other (this is known as *monogamy*), then there is no likelihood of them getting an STI.

GOING FOR A CHECK-UP

Sometimes people put off going for a check-up because they are afraid of being told they have an STI. But they shouldn't be scared – there is treatment for all the STIs. Many of the infections can be completely cured, especially if they are treated early enough. Others can be managed and the symptoms treated so that the person feels okay, and any long-term harm can be minimized.

The other reason people are afraid to go for a check-up is that they may feel dirty or ashamed about getting an STI. They worry that they might be judged or made to feel bad by the medical staff. Of course this doesn't happen. An STI is an infection just like any other infection, except that it happens to be passed on through sexual contact. Nurses and doctors are helpful and professional, and go about treating an STI as they would any other infection.

First the doctor or nurse will take a close look at the infected area. They may need to take a swab of the secretions from the vagina or penis, or the discharge from a sore. Even STIs that aren't showing any symptoms yet may be diagnosed by a blood test or urine sample. Any samples are then sent away to the laboratory for analysis. Medical staff will explain the treatment that will be needed. They will also talk about the importance of passing on the information about the STI to all of the person's sexual partners, so that they can be treated too.

Ways to avoid STIs

- Don't have any sexual contact! This is the only 100 per cent certain way of not coming into contact with an STI.

- Avoid making any sexual decisions if you are under the influence of alcohol or drugs.

- If you do choose to have a sexual relationship, enjoy 'safer sex' activities. Safer sex activities are those that don't involve the exchange of body fluids, and include such things as massage, hugging, kissing, touching, masturbation and fantasy.

- If you do choose to have sexual intercourse, use condoms every time.

- Enjoy a monogamous relationship; that is, one where you and your partner are faithful to each other. If either of you have been in sexual relationships before, especially any where you may have had unprotected sex, or come into contact with an STI, get tested before you start having sex.

- Have fewer sexual partners. The more people you have sex with, the greater the risk that you will encounter someone with an STI.

- A person who has had an STI should wait to have sex again until they have had the 'all clear' from the doctor.

And one more thing...

THRUSH

Thrush (otherwise known as Monilia or Candida) is not an STI, though it has symptoms that are very similar to those of STIs. It is very common and occurs for many reasons, not usually to do with sex. However, it can be passed from the female to the male during sex.

Thrush is caused by a change in the delicate balance of the normal bacteria and micro-organisms that live in the vagina, and is known as a *yeast* or *fungal* infection. There is an overgrowth of the normal vaginal yeast, which can be caused by a number of things, including heat, moisture, diabetes, antibiotics, the contraceptive pill, pregnancy, a poor immune system or poor hygiene.

The symptoms of thrush usually include a whitish or yellowish, lumpy discharge and slight swelling, irritation and itching of the vulva. Sometimes it can be painful to pass urine. These symptoms can range from very mild (almost unnoticeable) to severe. It is always a good idea to go to the doctor for a check-up before starting any treatment, just in case it is an STI, but also to discuss what the cause might be, and what can be done to prevent it recurring.

The treatment for thrush is available from the pharmacy, and usually comes in the form of an anti-fungal tablet, or a cream that can be applied directly to the vagina. As well as treatment, though, there are several measures that can be taken to prevent thrush recurring:

- the vulval area should be carefully washed and dried every day

- minimal soap should be used – a non-soap product is usually better

- the use of 'feminine hygiene' products should be avoided, and perfume should not be sprayed on the vulva

- the woman should wipe herself from front to back after she has used the toilet, to reduce the risk of introducing micro-organisms from the bowel into the vagina
- underwear should be cotton – or at least have a cotton gusset – and shouldn't be too tight
- nylon pantyhose and tight trousers should be avoided, or certainly not worn for too long at a time
- scented or chemically treated toilet paper and sanitary napkins should be avoided
- if the infection appears to be related to the use of a particular contraceptive pill or antibiotic, it may be necessary to change brands
- it helps to have a generally healthy lifestyle, to increase natural immunity.

10

Fertilization, Pregnancy and Birth

As you go through puberty, your body is developing so that you will become capable one day of reproduction – that is, having or creating a baby – if you choose to, and if the situation is right.

Although not everyone wants to have children, and some people can't for various reasons, pregnancy and childbirth are events that affect us all at one time or another. You may already have been closely involved in the birth of a younger brother or sister, or have had a friend or a relative who has gone through a pregnancy. The chances are that, if you do know someone who has had a baby, you have been kept well-informed about what was happening. Pregnancy and childbirth used to be very private events, but these days people are much more open, happy to answer questions, describe how they are feeling, and even have several people present at the birth of their baby.

But perhaps you don't know very much about pregnancy and childbirth; and even if you do know someone who has had a baby, there may be some things that weren't explained. This chapter aims to fill in some of those gaps in your knowledge. As well as looking in some detail at the topics of fertilization, pregnancy and birth, including ways that a woman can be as healthy as possible during her pregnancy, and some of the alternative ways that babies can be helped into the world, we will also look briefly at reproductive technology ('test-tube babies') and genetics.

First, let's look at what happens right at the beginning – the process of fertilization.

Fertilization

The beginning of new human life happens when a male sex cell (a *sperm*) and a female sex cell (an *ovum*) join in a process called *fertilization*.

Usually this happens when a man and a woman have sexual intercourse. However, this isn't always the case. It is possible for a sperm to fertilize an ovum outside the body, in a laboratory situation. You can read more about reproductive technology in a later section.

During sex, the man may ejaculate semen, containing hundreds of thousands of sperm, into the vagina of his female partner. As you read in Chapter 1, **Your Body**, the sperm are specialized cells that are able to propel themselves by beating their tails. Thousands of them swim up through the narrow opening, the cervix, at the base of the uterus. During the first part of their journey, the sperm are nourished and helped along by the semen. Now, as they enter the female reproductive tract, they are nourished by the secretions in the cervix and the uterus. Hundreds of sperm swim up through the uterus to the Fallopian tubes, and then along each tube. If the woman has recently ovulated (see Chapter 2, **Puberty**), there may be a mature ovum at the end of one of the tubes.

Fertilization

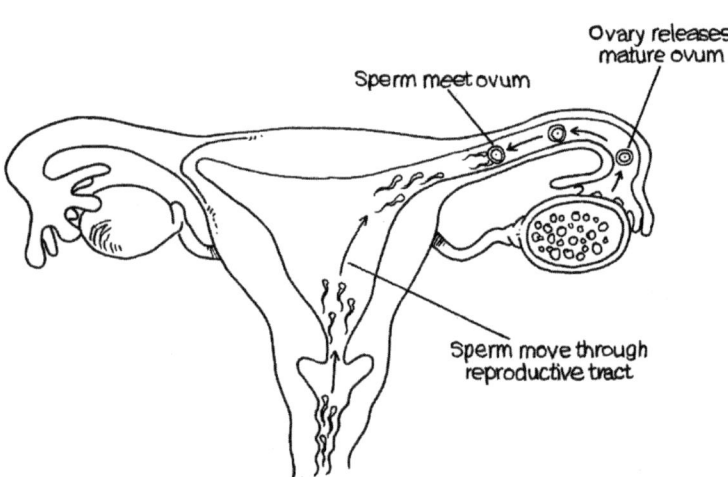

Ovary releases mature ovum

Sperm meet ovum

Sperm move through reproductive tract

By this stage, a few hundred sperm remain, and they cluster around the ovum – but only one can penetrate. As soon as it does, a particular chemical reaction occurs, preventing penetration by any more sperm.

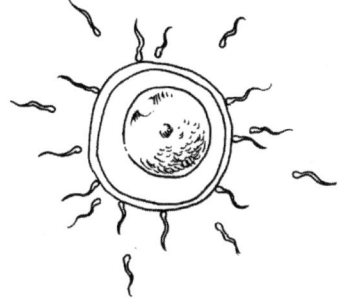

Sperm cluster around ovum

If the man and woman have intercourse just a few days before ovulation occurs, it is still possible for pregnancy to happen. This is because sperm are able to survive for about three or four days in the Fallopian tubes. When the ovum is released, it is possible for it to become fertilized by one of the surviving sperm.

However, if an ovum isn't already present in the tube, or the woman does not ovulate soon after sexual intercourse, then pregnancy can't happen. Equally, if a woman ovulates but doesn't have sexual intercourse, then she can't get pregnant. Pregnancy can only happen when there is both an ovum and a sperm present at the same time.

The ovum and the sperm unite to become one cell, called a *zygote*. This is the very beginning of a baby. Almost immediately, the zygote starts to divide and multiply.

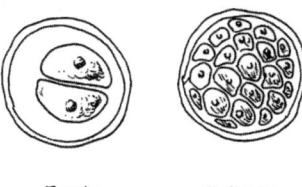

Zygote   Cell division

This continually dividing 'ball' of cells is moved along the fallopian tube by the waving motion of tiny hairs, known as *cilia* (see Chapter 1, **Your Body**), towards the uterus. Once it reaches the uterus, about a week after fertilization, the zygote embeds itself into the nourishing lining, which is well-supplied with blood, and continues to divide. The woman is now said to be *pregnant*.

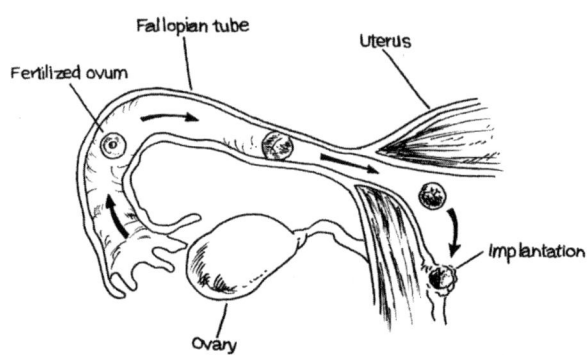

How are twins and triplets formed?

Sometimes two *ova* (eggs) are released at ovulation. If both of these are fertilized, they can both begin the process of cell division and move along to the uterus. If they implant successfully in the uterus, then twins can develop.

Another way for twins to develop is for one fertilized ovum to split soon after fertilization. This divided ovum becomes two separate but identical cells. This is how identical (*monozygotic*) twins are formed. Twins that develop from two fertilized ova are non-identical (*dizygotic*). Whereas identical twins are always the same sex, non-identical twins can be the same or different sexes.

Triplets can happen three different ways: three separate ova are fertilized; two ova are fertilized, but one splits, as it does with identical twins; or one fertilized ovum splits three ways. However they happen, triplets are much more rare than twins.

Trying to get pregnant

Some people become pregnant the very first time they have sex. Others may have to try many times before they achieve a pregnancy. Generally, it is considered normal for a couple to take anything up to 12 months to become pregnant. If it is taking longer than this, it is possible that they have a problem, and they should seek medical help.

There are various reasons why people may be unable to become pregnant, and the problem can be with the woman, the man, or with both. For example, some women don't release ova frequently enough, or their Fallopian tubes might be blocked or damaged due to infection. Some men may not produce enough sperm, or the ones they do produce aren't healthy. These are just a few examples of many possibilities. Sometimes no cause can be found.

In the past, many couples had to accept that they couldn't have children of their own. Some would go on to adopt children, while others remained childless, but found many other worthwhile and enjoyable things to do in their lives, and perhaps enjoyed other people's children.

HOW TECHNOLOGY CAN HELP

In recent years, scientists have found several ways to help infertile couples have their own babies – this is known as *reproductive technology*. It involves first of all having the problem diagnosed by a specialist, and then many trips to the clinic, sometimes over many months, while a variety of procedures are carried out.

One method, for example, is to carefully remove a ripe ovum from one of the woman's Fallopian tubes in a small operation. It is placed in a dish in the laboratory with sperm from her partner, in the hope that fertilization may occur. When the ovum is fertilized, it can be returned to the woman's uterus, again during a small operation. If the procedure is successful, the fertilized ovum will go through the usual process of implantation and cell division, and a normal pregnancy may follow. Sometimes, to increase the chances of success, the woman is given drugs to stimulate her ovaries to produce several ripe ova. These may all be fertilized in the laboratory, and two or more put into her uterus in the hope of at least one of them implanting successfully. When several do implant and develop, a *multiple pregnancy* may follow – that is, twins, triplets and so on. In fact, multiple pregnancies are more common nowadays than they were in the past, and this may be due partly to reproductive technology.

The particular method of reproductive technology described above is known as *in vitro fertilization* (IVF). There are several other methods, including the ova and sperm being introduced surgically into the Fallopian tube rather than the uterus. Sometimes this is done after fertilization has happened in the laboratory, and sometimes before, so that it can happen naturally in the tube. Sometimes ova or sperm can be donated by someone else in cases where either the male or the female are unable to produce sex cells of their own.

Reproductive technology is becoming increasingly successful, and many thousands of babies are conceived this way every year. However, it is expensive, and not all couples can afford it. It isn't always successful, either, and while some couples may go on to explore the possibility of adopting a baby, many others accept the reality of being childless.

'You've got your father's eyes!' (a brief look at genetics)

Young children have been known to get quite upset when someone says this to them, replying 'No, I haven't – they're mine!' Of course, this statement isn't meant to be taken literally, and it simply means that the child's eyes are very like his or her father's. But why is this? Why are so many of our features and characteristics – even our personalities, some-times – so similar to one or other, or both, of our parents?

Genes and chromosomes

At least part of the answer is 'genes'. Every single cell in your body, no matter whether it is a skin cell, a brain cell, a blood cell or any other of the billions of cells that make up your body, contains information about you. This information is held on thread-like structures called *chromosomes*, of which there are 46 in every cell. Lined up along every chromosome are hundreds, sometimes thousands, of *genes*, whose job is to produce protein. Proteins are the building blocks for everything in your body, including the physical features and organs, and the way they grow, work properly and stay healthy. It is the specific way that the genes are lined up, and thus the specific protein they make, that determines the exact function of each cell (a heart muscle cell functions very differently from a hair cell, for example). These 30,000 to 40,000 genes are uniquely combined to make you the individual you are, with all your individual *traits* (characteristics).

Whilst *almost* every cell in the body has 46 chromosomes (in 23 matching pairs), ova and sperm are slightly different. They have only 23 chromosomes each. When they unite at the time of fertilization, they become one cell with the full complement of 46 chromosomes. Thus half of the chromosomes in the zygote have come from the mother and half from the father.

Chromosomes and genes are made of a special chemical called deoxyribonucleic acid (DNA). DNA has the amazing capacity to make perfect copies of itself, and holds all the instructions to make an individual person. Thus, during the process of foetal growth and development, this newly formed combination of chromosomes copies itself again and again so that identical genetic information is passed on to every cell in the foetus's body.

A boy or a girl?

There isn't much difference between boys and girls in terms of their DNA and genetics. The real difference is in one of their chromosomes. Although 22 of the 23 pairs of chromosomes in each cell have nothing to do with sex, chromosomes 45 and 46 (the 23rd pair) are the *sex chromosomes*, and are the ones that determine whether the person is male or female. Because of their shape under the microscope, they are known as *X* and *Y*. An ovum only has the *X* chromosome, but sperm carry either *X* or *Y*. If a sperm carrying an *X* chromosome unites with the ovum, the resulting sex chromosome will be *XX*, and the baby will be a girl. If,

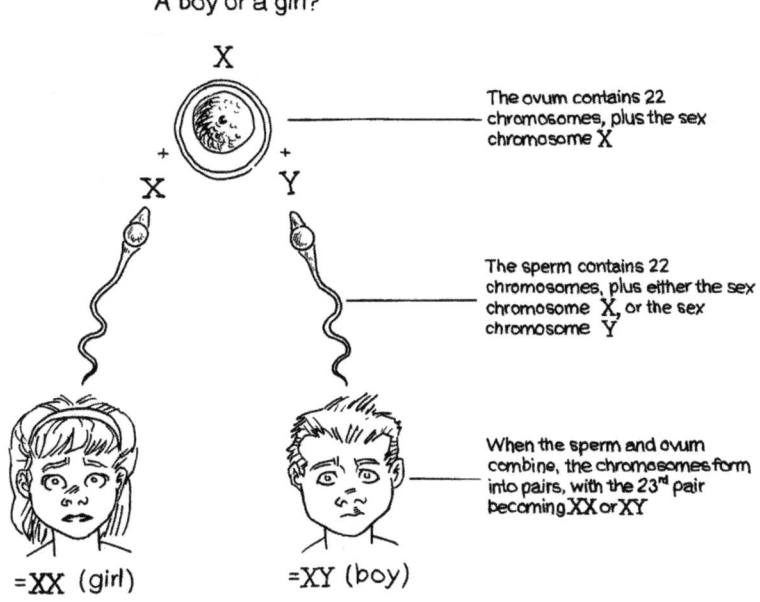

A boy or a girl?

The ovum contains 22 chromosomes, plus the sex chromosome X

The sperm contains 22 chromosomes, plus either the sex chromosome X, or the sex chromosome Y

When the sperm and ovum combine, the chromosomes form into pairs, with the 23rd pair becoming XX or XY

=**XX** (girl)   =**XY** (boy)

however, the sperm that fertilizes the ovum carries a *Y* chromosome, the zygote will contain one *X* and one *Y* chromosome (*XY*), and the baby will be a boy.

Inherited characteristics

The reason that some of your characteristics may be so similar to your parents' features is that you have inherited half of your chromosomes and genes from your mother and half from your father. The thousands of genes that lie along each of the chromosomes are responsible for every single feature of your body, from your hair and eye colour to your shape, the way you talk and the way you walk.

Sometimes, characteristics can skip generations, so that you may inherit a feature that someone in a previous generation had, but that didn't show up in your parent (even though they carried the gene for it).

Sometimes a gene can be defective, and may carry information that results in a disability or abnormality. Examples of such genetic disorders are Down's syndrome, cystic fibrosis and Huntington's chorea. Some genetic diseases can be inherited from just one parent, while others can only occur if both parents pass on the gene. Some genetic disorders, such as Down's syndrome, are not inherited, but instead result from a mutation of the gene that occurs during the development of the foetus.

But genes aren't the whole story...

Many other factors, such as the way you are brought up, the food you eat, the air you breathe, the amount of exercise you get and general life experiences you encounter all have a part to play in determining who you are. The degree to which your genetics or the environment influence certain traits is sometimes difficult to determine, and is often referred to as the *'nature versus nurture'* debate. For example, how much of your personality is due to your genetics, and how much is due to the way you have been brought up? Do people become criminals because of their genetic make-up, or because of negative experiences in their lives? These are not easy questions to answer, but it's quite likely that there is a significant mixing of nature and nurture in both these examples. Perhaps, for example, environmental factors 'trigger' a genetic predisposition to a particular trait.

One thing is certain, though – your unique combination of genes and experience make you the special, one-off individual that you are.

Pregnancy

Growing in the stomach...a myth

You have probably heard people say that a woman has a baby 'in her stomach'. Obviously, this is not true! The stomach, where food is digested, is high up in the abdominal cavity, just beneath the level of the breastbone. The *uterus* (sometimes called the *womb*) is much lower down, within the pelvic cavity. As the foetus develops, the uterus grows and eventually, towards the end of the pregnancy, extends up as high as the stomach.

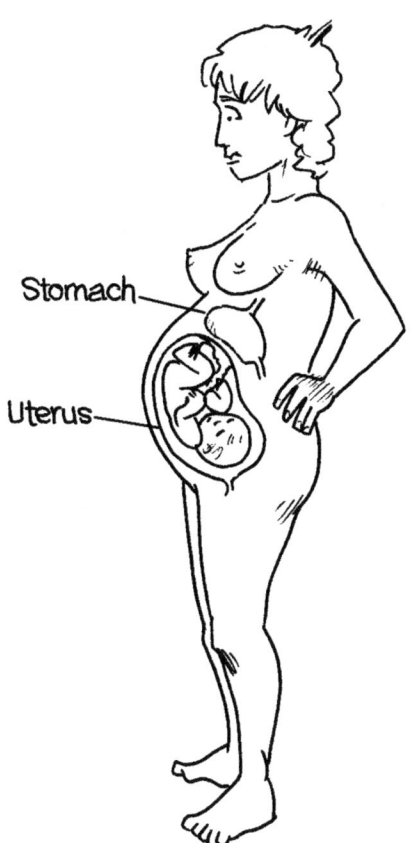

Stomach

Uterus

How long is a pregnancy?

This is calculated from the first day of the last period that the woman had before she became pregnant. Once she is pregnant, her periods stop and don't start again until about six weeks after the birth, or even longer if she chooses to breast-feed her baby.

Fertilization happens at the time of ovulation, which in most women is *approximately* two weeks after the first day of her period – a little sooner than this if she has a short menstrual cycle, and a little later if she has a longer cycle.

For many women, the first indication they may have that they are pregnant is at around four weeks, when they don't get their next period. It is at about this time that they are able to do a urine test to confirm the pregnancy. Pregnancy tests can be done at the clinic or at home, but only once the fertilized ovum has implanted in the uterus, because this is when pregnancy hormone can be detected in the urine.

The approximate time that the baby grows in the uterus is 38 weeks, but because the time is calculated from the first day of the last period, an extra two weeks is added to that; so a full-term pregnancy is said to be 40 weeks, which is about nine calendar months, plus one week.

Once the woman has visited her doctor or the clinic for the first time, she will be given an 'expected date of delivery' – though this is, of course, only approximate. A pregnancy that lasts anything between about 37 and 42 weeks is perfectly normal.

The development of the baby

As soon as the ovum has been fertilized by the sperm, it begins the process of division, over and over again, forming a cluster of cells. By the time this ever-growing cluster reaches the uterus, about one week after fertilization, it has divided many times, and consists of well over 100 cells. It embeds itself into the lining of the uterus; this is called *implantation.*

Soon, the cells begin a process known as *differentiation*, where they separate out into different types. The inner layer of cells will eventually form the skin, nervous system, skeleton and organs, while the outer layer attaches to the wall of the uterus and starts to establish blood vessels. This part becomes the baby's 'life support' – the *placenta, umbilical cord* and *amniotic sac.*

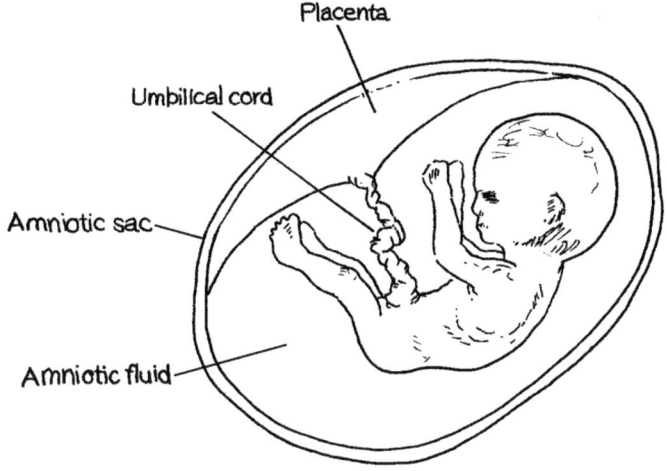

THE PLACENTA

The placenta is a network of blood vessels from both the mother and baby. It is attached to the wall of the uterus, and acts as a 'filter' to allow the diffusion of nutrients and oxygen from the mother's blood to the blood of the baby. Waste products and carbon dioxide are removed via the mother's blood.

THE UMBILICAL CORD

The umbilical cord is a soft, flexible cord containing blood vessels through which nutrients and waste pass to and from the baby. The cord is joined to the placenta at one end and to the baby's abdomen at the other.

THE AMNIOTIC SAC

The growing baby is protected inside the uterus by the liquid-filled *amniotic sac*. As well as protecting it from knocks and bumps, the *amniotic fluid* keeps the baby at a regular, even temperature, and allows it to move freely within the uterus. Amniotic fluid is produced by the placenta for the first few months of the pregnancy. After that, the baby's own kidneys continue the production. The fluid is constantly recirculated – the baby 'breathes' it in, which helps the lungs to develop, and also swallows and excretes it as 'urine', which helps the development of the digestive system and urinary tract. The amount of amniotic fluid varies from one woman to another, but, on average, there is about 1000 ml (one quart) of fluid towards the end of the pregnancy.

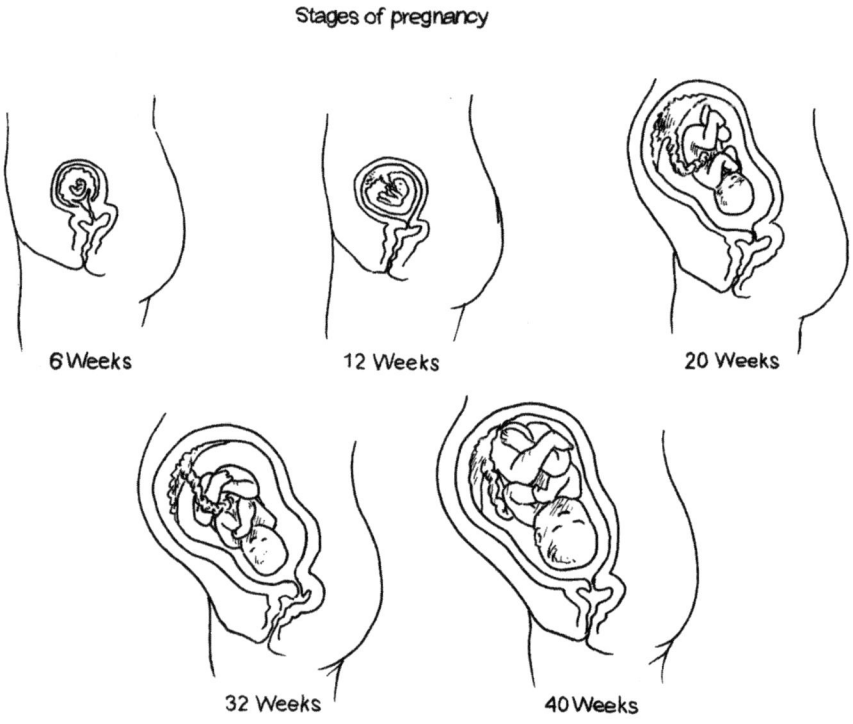

Stages of pregnancy

6 Weeks 12 Weeks 20 Weeks

32 Weeks 40 Weeks

From two weeks after fertilization until around eight weeks, the ball of cells is known as an *embryo*. The different layers of cells develop into the different organs and body parts, so that by six weeks the embryo is about 1.5 cm ($\frac{1}{2}$ in.) long, with the beginning of a backbone and a heart that has started beating.

From eight or nine weeks, the growing baby is known as a *foetus*. By 12 weeks, the foetus has grown to around 9 cm ($3\frac{1}{2}$ in.) long. All the organs are formed, and the foetus is beginning to look recognizably human.

At 20 weeks (five months), the pregnancy is half way through. The foetus, which is about 25 cm ($9\frac{3}{4}$ in.) long, is thin, with wrinkly, transparent skin. It has a covering of fine, downy hair over its whole body, and is beginning to develop hair on its head. The woman can feel the movements of the foetus inside her by this stage.

At 32 weeks (7½ months), the foetus is about 40 cm (16 in.) long. It is beginning to put on some body fat, and its lungs are starting to mature, ready for birth. If it is born at this stage it can survive, but will need to spend some time in an incubator to help it to breathe and feed.

The pregnancy is said to be 'full-term' at 40 weeks. Sometime after 36 weeks, the baby may settle further down into the pelvis, ready for birth. When it is born, the baby will be approximately 50 cm (20 in.) long.

A healthy pregnancy
THE RIGHT AGE TO BE PREGNANT

There is no 'right age' for a woman to be pregnant, although there are some physical factors involved. For example, as a woman ages she becomes less fertile, but this doesn't make pregnancy impossible, even right up until the age of menopause – just a little less likely. There are often more physical complications, such as high blood pressure, when a woman is older.

Every young woman needs to be aware that she is fertile as soon as she has started her periods, so this can be from as young as 10 or 11 years old.

No matter what her age, a woman needs to consider some important factors before she chooses to become pregnant, such as the following:

- Does she feel ready to look after a baby? Babies are vulnerable and hard work, since they need 24-hour care. Looking after a baby is a huge responsibility.

- Does she have emotional and financial security and support? Not only are babies expensive, they are mentally and physically exhausting a lot of the time.

- Has she finished her education? Having a baby can complicate things such as going to school or college.

- Some people believe you should be married when you have a baby. Although this is not a law, it can be a very strong personal belief for some people, and may affect their decision-making.

TO ENSURE A HEALTHY PREGNANCY

Ideally, a couple should plan their pregnancy so that they can both aim to improve their health before they conceive the baby. They should both give up smoking and drugs, and cut back on alcohol for a few months before the woman becomes pregnant. The woman should try to have a healthy, balanced diet, and should consult her doctor to check whether she needs to supplement any vitamins or minerals.

Obviously, it isn't always possible to plan so carefully, and pregnancy can happen unexpectedly. If this is the case, then the woman should embark on a healthy diet, with no drugs, cigarettes or alcohol just as soon as she finds out she is pregnant.

WEIGHT GAIN

Every woman gains quite a lot of weight during pregnancy – between about 9 kg (20 lb) and 13 kg (29 lb). But this is certainly not all fat. The growing baby accounts for quite a lot of it, along with extra blood to all her organs and to the baby. The placenta, uterus and amniotic fluid also weigh quite a lot – and even her breasts weigh more as they grow in preparation for breast-feeding.

EXERCISE AND ACTIVITY

A woman can usually continue with most exercise that she is used to, though obviously activities that require agility and balance, such as rock climbing, would be impossible as the pregnancy progresses. The woman should check with her doctor about what is and isn't suitable exercise. She must be careful not to strain her muscles with everyday activities, and pay particular attention to keeping her back straight.

Swimming is a great activity for a pregnant woman, as she can move freely in the water, and there is no pressure on her abdomen.

She should also get plenty of rest. At the beginning of the pregnancy, many women feel very tired, and sometimes sick or unwell (you have probably heard of 'morning sickness' – though it is not restricted to mornings, and can happen any time of day), due to the changing levels of hormones, so it is important to take it easy at this time. Towards the end of the pregnancy, the size of her abdomen and the extra weight she is carrying can make a woman very tired, and she will need to get plenty of rest at this time, too.

EATING

The old saying 'eating for two' isn't really true, although the woman may want to eat a little more than usual – sometimes in smaller portions, particularly towards the end of the pregnancy. She needs a nutritious diet to make sure she meets both her own needs and the needs of her baby. If she doesn't have a good diet, the baby will take what it needs, leaving the woman without the nourishment she requires for good health.

THINGS TO AVOID

Substances such as drugs, nicotine and alcohol are all able to cross the placenta, and can be harmful to the baby. The woman should always check with her doctor before she takes any medication, and she shouldn't take any illegal drugs at all. Nicotine in cigarettes reduces the amount of oxygen and nutrients getting through to the foetus, ultimately having an effect on its growth and development.

Certain infections can be very harmful to the foetus, especially in the first three months. One of the most common and damaging infections is *rubella* (German measles), which can result in the baby having serious physical and intellectual disabilities. Consequently, in most countries, young girls are immunized against rubella to ensure that they won't catch the infection during their pregnancy.

Some foods, including certain fish, soft cheeses, meat patés and caffeine, are potentially harmful to the foetus, and should be avoided. The woman should check with her doctor exactly which foods pose a risk, and also learn about healthy food preparation to avoid any problems.

PREPARATION FOR BIRTH

Women can attend 'ante-natal' (meaning 'before birth') classes, with their partner if they choose, to learn about the pregnancy, the process of the birth and parenting. They will also learn relaxation techniques to help them during the birth.

MEDICAL CHECK-UPS

Throughout the pregnancy, the woman should have regular check-ups with her doctor or *midwife* (a midwife is a nurse – male or female – who is specially trained in the area of pregnancy and childbirth). A check is kept on the woman's health and on the growth of the baby. She may have two or more *ultrasound scans* in the course of the pregnancy. During an ultrasound scan, sound waves are bounced off the foetus, producing a 'picture' of it in the uterus. This provides an accurate assessment of the size and rate of growth of the foetus, and occasionally it is possible to tell the sex of the baby by ultrasound scan.

Birth

Childbirth is a natural event, and can often be managed without much intervention by doctors, technology or painkilling drugs. However, our knowledge and medical facilities these days mean that not only can women give birth virtually pain-free if they choose, they also have access to expert help should difficulties arise. In the developed world, it is very rare for a woman or her baby to die during childbirth any more.

The process of giving birth is known as *labour*, for the very good reason that it is hard work. The length of labour varies between different women, and even in the same woman with each new baby, though it does tend to become shorter with each birth. It is usually quite a few hours (the average time for a first labour, for example, is around 12–13 hours).

Labour occurs in three stages: during the first stage, which is the longest, the cervix opens up to allow the baby to come through; the second stage is when the woman pushes the baby out through the birth canal; and the third stage is the delivery of the placenta, and amniotic sac.

The beginning of labour

Throughout the last few weeks of her pregnancy, the woman experiences occasional, but quite strong, *contractions* of her uterus. The uterus is a muscular organ, and a contraction is a tightening of this muscle. However, these are only practice contractions at this stage, preparing her uterus for the birth. Women may confuse these with the real thing (sometimes going to the hospital, only to be told to go home again). Once labour begins properly, the contractions are regular and very strong – their purpose is to open up the cervix and help push the baby out through the vagina.

Sometimes, just before labour begins properly, the amniotic sac can rupture – this is known as the '*waters breaking*', and can be anything from a slight trickle to a gush of fluid. However it happens, it indicates that the woman will need to get to the hospital or wherever she has arranged to have the baby. Mostly, however, the amniotic sac ruptures during labour, and quite often needs to be broken by the midwife immediately before the birth so that the baby can come through.

First stage

The contractions of the uterus are strong, and come at regular intervals. They begin by being many minutes apart, but gradually become more frequent, and much stronger, as labour progresses. During this first stage, the purpose of the contractions is to gradually open up the cervix at the base of the uterus. Normally the cervix is a very tiny opening, just big enough to allow through sperm or menstrual blood. During the process of labour, it has to open to a diameter of about ten centimetres (four inches) before the baby can come through. This can take many hours, and during this time, particularly at the beginning when the contractions are spaced well apart, the woman can move around and get on with things such as last-minute preparations if she wants to. As the contractions get closer and closer together, they are much harder work, and she will probably need to try to relax. She may enjoy a soothing warm bath or shower, and might appreciate a back massage from her partner. She might have learnt special breathing techniques at her ante-natal classes to help her deal with the strong sensations. If she is finding the contractions very painful, there are various methods of pain relief she can have (see later section).

Second stage

This stage begins once the cervix is fully dilated. The woman gets the urge to push down with each contraction, which helps to squeeze the baby out through the vagina.

The second stage can take anything from about five minutes to one or two hours, and is very hard work. The baby usually comes head-first through the vagina. The vaginal walls, which are stretchy and convoluted, are able to stretch enough to allow the baby through. Once the head is through, the rest of the body slips out quite quickly and easily.

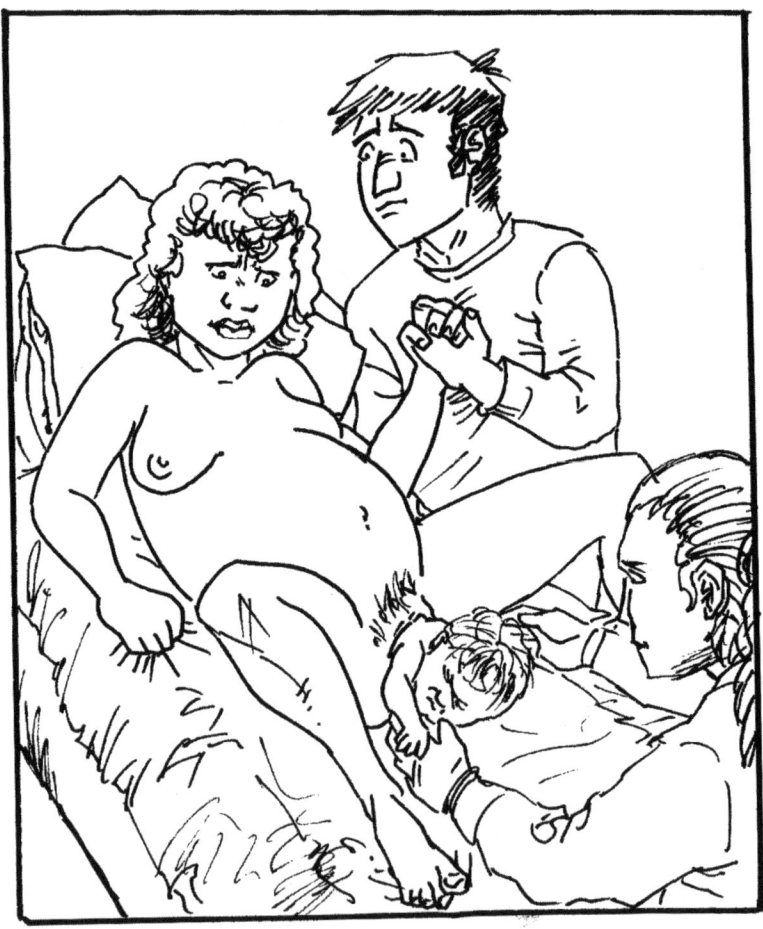

If the vaginal opening won't stretch quite enough, the doctor or midwife can make a tiny cut in the skin to make more room for the baby to come through. This is stitched up afterwards, and although it can be uncomfortable for the mother for a few days, it heals up well.

A woman can give birth in a variety of positions, and certainly doesn't need to be lying on her back. In fact, if she squats, or is helped to stand up by her birthing companions, gravity can help the baby to come out more quickly. Some women choose to be on all fours, or leaning forward over a stool. Some even give birth in water in a special birthing pool. The important thing is that there is someone there to gently ease the baby out, so that it doesn't come to any harm.

Third stage

When the baby is born, it has the umbilical cord attached to its abdomen. The other end of the cord is connected to the placenta, which is still attached to the wall of the uterus. Soon after birth, the umbilical cord is cut, as the baby can now breath, and will soon feed, by itself. The end of the cord closest to the baby is clamped, leaving a small segment that shrivels up and falls off in a few days (and the baby is left with its belly button).

With the last few contractions, the placenta detaches itself from the wall of the uterus. Together with the remainder of the umbilical cord and the amniotic sac, it comes out through the vagina. This is known as the *afterbirth*. This is a very quick process, and very few women are aware of it happening. It is, however, an important part of birth, and the midwife or doctor checks that the complete afterbirth has been passed. Sometimes the umbilical cord is saved, as the blood it contains can be used in research, or to help in the treatment of illnesses such as leukaemia.

The pain of childbirth

Without a doubt, for most women childbirth is a huge experience! Everyone experiences it slightly differently, though, and everyone has a different '*pain threshold*'. The experience of pain can be worse when a person is anxious or frightened, which is why ante-natal classes are so important. The better-informed a woman is, the more positive her experience of childbirth will be. It is possible to go through childbirth without needing any pain relief at all, and to consider the whole thing a wonderful experience! However, a lot of women do need some help to deal with the pain, and this can be in various forms. One of these is 'gas and air', which is nitrous oxide and oxygen delivered through a mask and breathed in with each contraction. Alternatively, she might choose to have an injection of a strong painkiller, or a 'spinal block' (*epidural*), which is a method of numbing the lower half of her body. With plenty of information and advice, the woman will be able to make the choice that is right for her. The interesting thing is that, soon after childbirth, a lot of the pain is forgotten – and, as you know, many women go through the experience again and again.

When help is required

Birth is a natural process, and often no intervention is needed at all. If there are complications, though, the knowledge and facilities that are available now mean that very few women or babies die these days during childbirth. Sadly, in the past this was a common outcome.

CAESAREAN BIRTH

A *Caesarean section* is a surgical procedure where the baby is delivered via a cut made through the abdominal wall into the uterus. The baby and the placenta are then lifted out. This can be done under a general anaesthetic, with the woman asleep, though these days it is more usual for her to have an epidural (see the previous section) so that she stays awake and can greet her baby as soon as it is born.

Caesareans are done for a variety of reasons. For example, there are cases where the baby needs to be born quickly to save its or its mother's life. Sometimes the pelvis is too small for the baby to come through, or perhaps the placenta has attached itself to the area of the uterus just above the cervix, thus blocking the cervix and preventing dilation.

FORCEPS

Sometimes the birth is taking too long and the baby is becoming deprived of oxygen. To speed things up, the doctor can use forceps to help the baby through the vagina. Forceps are surgical instruments, similar to tongs. They are fitted gently around the baby's head and help to hold the baby in place after each contraction, gradually easing it out through the vagina.

BREECH BIRTH

Usually babies turn into a 'head-down' position some weeks before the birth, but sometimes they don't, and at the time of the birth are still in a 'bottom-first' position, which is known as *breech*. This type of birth takes longer and is more difficult. It may require the use of forceps, or a Caesarean section.

PREMATURITY AND POST-MATURITY

Babies who are born before 37 weeks are said to be *premature*, and those born after 42 weeks are *post-mature* (or *post-term*).

Prematurity can happen for a number of reasons, such as the woman not having good ante-natal care or good nutrition, or the fact that she might have certain medical conditions such as high blood pressure or diabetes. It is also likely when there is more than one baby in the uterus. There are several problems for a premature baby, and these are worse the more premature the baby is. It will have immature organs that aren't ready to function properly, so will have problems breathing and be unable to digest food. It will also have difficulty co-ordinating swallowing and sucking, so will be unable to feed. For all these reasons, premature babies usually need to go into special care (see later section) until they are big enough to survive without help.

Post-maturity can also be a problem, mainly because the placenta ceases to function, and the baby becomes deprived of nutrients and, eventually, oxygen. A baby that is post-mature will often have dry, peeling skin, fingernails and toenails that are too long, and be very thin, with loose skin. This is because it has been surviving off its own fat supplies. The risk to such a baby is for brain damage caused by lack of oxygen and low blood sugar.

The decision that the doctor has to make is whether or not to start off the labour with drugs, or to wait for it to happen naturally. A close check is kept on the baby's heartbeat and movement to ensure it is still healthy. If there is any problem, labour may be *induced* (i.e. started off medically) or a Caesarean section may be done.

MULTIPLE BIRTHS

When there are two or more babies developing in the uterus, there is a much higher likelihood of them being born prematurely, and the more babies there are, the earlier they will be. There is also a greater risk of complications for the mother, such as high blood pressure. For this reason, women who are having multiple births are monitored very closely. If a woman's health, or the health of her babies, is at risk, a

Caesarean section may be done. After birth, the babies will often need to go into special care until they are big enough to breathe and feed independently.

MISCARRIAGE AND STILLBIRTH

For various reasons, the development of the baby can go wrong – perhaps due to a genetic or chromosomal abnormality, a serious infection, or very high blood pressure in the mother among many other possibilities – and when this happens, the baby can die in the uterus. If the delivery of such a baby happens before 20 weeks, it is known as a *miscarriage*. Miscarriages happen more often in the first few weeks of pregnancy, and often indicate that there was something wrong with the embryo or foetus. Even though the baby is very small when most miscarriages occur, it is still a very sad event for the parents.

If a baby dies and is delivered after 20 weeks, it is called a *stillbirth*. The event is even more traumatic for the parents, as they were well into the pregnancy, making plans and preparing for the birth. Fortunately, although they can't always be avoided, stillbirths are not common, particularly with the good ante-natal care that women receive these days.

Welcoming the baby into the world

A baby takes its first breath as soon as it is born, filling its lungs with air for the first time.

The umbilical cord is cut and clamped close to the baby's abdomen. The parents are able to hold the baby immediately – for most people a very exciting and special moment. Sometimes the baby is put to the mother's breast, and knows instinctively how to suck. Although it doesn't need nutrition straight away, as it is still very well nourished from the nutrients that have been supplied through the umbilical cord, the close cuddling and breast-feeding help the mother and baby to 'bond'.

The baby will be born with traces of *vernix* on its body. Vernix is a waxy, creamy coating on the skin to protect it during all those months in a watery environment. The baby will probably also have some blood on it from the small tears that happen as the vagina stretches. It can look quite gooey and messy, in fact, but in the eyes of its parents it is perfect and quite beautiful!

Eventually, the baby will be weighed and measured, given a bath and dressed in a nappy (diaper) and gown.

SPECIAL CARE

When a baby is very tiny, or has difficulty breathing (e.g. in the case of multiple births or prematurity), it may need help to survive during the first few weeks of life. It may be taken to the special care baby unit, and kept in an incubator for a few weeks. In this way it can be kept at a regular, warm temperature and be closely monitored around the clock by nurses and doctors. Its oxygen and nutrients are administered through tubes. After a few days or weeks it will have matured sufficiently to be able to breathe and suck independently, so it can go home and continue developing as a perfectly normal baby.

THE DECISION TO BREAST-FEED

Breast milk is the perfect food, as it contains all the ingredients the baby needs, at exactly the right temperature. Not only does it contain antibodies that help protect the baby from infection in the first few weeks of life, but also it is free, and there is no preparation involved. However, for various reasons, some women choose not to, or are unable to, breast-feed. If this is the case, the baby will be fed specially prepared *infant formula* from a bottle, which is a very good substitute for mother's milk. Whether a baby is breast-fed or bottle-fed, the process of feeding can be a time for close, loving contact, when the baby and its mother or carers can spend time getting to know each other.

11

Sexual Language

Sexual language should be straightforward, shouldn't it? A penis is a penis, sexual intercourse is sexual intercourse – or so you would think. But penises are sometimes known as 'dicks', 'cocks', 'willies' or 'doodles', and sexual intercourse may be referred to as 'shagging', 'doing it' or 'making love' – and these are just a few of the many words you may have heard for both these terms. In fact, you have probably noticed that when it comes to sex and private body parts, there is any number of different terms for the same thing. Some of these terms are sensible and scientific, some are childish or funny, and some are downright rude! While there aren't many alternative words for other body parts, there are dozens of words for breasts, several for vulva or vagina, lots for masturbation – and it is said there are around two thousand words for penis!

One possible reason that there are so many alternative words for sexual terms is that sex is viewed by many people as a slightly 'taboo' subject. This can make them feel uncomfortable when they try to talk about it, so they cover up their embarrassment by being indirect and using childish terms (*euphemisms*), or perhaps treating it as a joke, and using funny or rude words (*slang*). And many people simply don't know the correct terms for the sexual words, due to ignorance or lack of education.

We discussed at the beginning of Chapter 7, **Sex**, the importance of being able to talk openly, appropriately and without embarrassment about sexuality. This is very helpful if you ever need to see a health professional if something is wrong, or if you need to organize contraception or have a sexual health check (see Chapter 9, **Looking After Your Sexual Health**). It's also really reassuring to be able to talk about sex with someone you trust, particularly if you have any questions or concerns, and, of course, being able to discuss sex confidently is very valuable if and when you start having a sexual relationship with someone.

Whatever the situation, when you talk about sex, or issues related to sex (private body parts, sexual activities or sexual health), it's important that you know the right words in order that the person you are talking to can understand you. If the only words you know are childish or rude, it can make you look silly or ignorant, and end up causing confusion or embarrassment. But there are times when the slang terms are appropriate, too. If you are talking casually or making jokes with a group of friends, the correct terminology can sometimes sound a bit *too* formal. The trick is to know just what type of language to use in a given situation, so that your message is clear and appropriate, and nobody (including you) is made to look or feel foolish.

Categories of sexual language

Sexual words can be divided into four main 'levels' or categories:

- scientific or medical

- correct, commonly used terms

- slang or street language

- euphemisms or 'baby talk' (a euphemism is where a word that is considered to be offensive is replaced by one that is milder but often less accurate).

Most of the sexual words have alternatives that fit into each of these categories. Let's take the example of 'sexual intercourse', a term that you are familiar with, and have come across frequently in this book:

- *Scientific*: coitus

- *Common terminology*: sexual intercourse, having sex

- *Slang*: fucking, screwing

- *Euphemism / baby talk*: making love, sleeping with, nookie.

Each of these words can be appropriate or inappropriate, depending on the situation.

Using sexual language appropriately

SCIENTIFIC TERMS

You can see from the example above that the scientific term is one that you would hardly ever hear. *Coitus* is a Latin word, and might be used in academic papers and medical books. You may occasionally come across the term 'coitus interruptus', which means literally 'interrupted sex'. It is the scientific term for the withdrawal method of contraception, when the penis is withdrawn from the vagina before ejaculation (see Chapter 9, **Looking After Your Sexual Health**). In many instances, the most commonly used, correct term *is* the scientific term (e.g. penis, vulva, ejaculation and so on.) Where a scientific term differs from the commonly used, correct term you probably won't come across it very often, and unless you happen to be writing an academic paper you almost certainly won't need to use such formal terminology.

COMMON TERMINOLOGY

The common terms ('sexual intercourse', 'having sex') are universally understood. The same goes for the commonly used, correct terms for all the sexual words. They are the ones that have been used throughout this book. The value of this type of language is that it is clear and straightforward. You can talk to the doctor, ask questions in class or be heard in public using these common terms, and shouldn't offend anyone.

The only time it can sound slightly wrong to use the correct terminology is when you are messing around with a group of teenage friends, telling jokes and so on. If their usual language is slang (see next section), you can sound too formal or a bit of a know-all if you use the correct term, and you might be laughed at or teased. But you can also be laughed at if you get the slang word wrong, so if you're not sure of the *exact* words they usually use, it's always safer to use the correct terms. You might sound a bit prim and proper, but at least everyone will know what you are talking about.

SLANG OR STREET LANGUAGE

There are dozens of slang terms for sexual intercourse, and for most of the other sexual words, too – you probably know quite a few. Although many of these words can be quite funny, they are often disrespectful and usually offensive. Many of them are used as swear words, as you are no doubt aware. Don't *ever* use this type of language in formal situations (e.g. at the doctor's surgery or health clinic, giving a talk or asking questions in class), in polite company (e.g. in front of adults, at the family dinner table) or in public. The trouble is, the more often you hear or use a particular word, the more familiar you become with it, so that sometimes you simply don't recognize that it may be offending other people. Don't forget, even people your own age can be offended by some of these slang words, so it's important to respect others' feelings, and only use this sort of language if you are *sure* that the person or people you are with are okay with it (perhaps, for example, you have heard them use this language themselves). And, of course, if you do choose to use a slang expression, make sure it's the one that your friends use, if you want to avoid being teased (see previous section).

EUPHEMISMS AND BABY TALK

Euphemisms are used by people who want to 'soften' a word that they feel is too harsh. 'Making love' is a commonly used euphemism for sexual intercourse, and as such is widely understood. People like it because it sounds respectful and gentle. Other euphemisms, however, such as 'sleeping together' or 'doing it', are much less clear, and it would be very easy to misunderstand them. Imagine, for example, if you were told that you could get pregnant, or cause a pregnancy, by 'sleeping with someone'. If you didn't know this term for sexual intercourse, this might make you very nervous about going on school camp and sharing a dormitory with other people, mightn't it! But worse, you could easily believe that it would be okay to have sexual intercourse with someone just so long as you didn't fall asleep together. As you can see, euphemisms are too indirect, and for this reason can cause confusion and be very misleading. Only use this sort of language if you know that the person you are talking to does understand you. If someone uses a euphemism that you don't understand, be sure to ask them what they mean, rather than trying to guess.

Baby talk, such as 'nookie' in the above example, or 'wee wee' for vulva (see Table 11.1 below) may be okay for small children, but is not really appropriate for anyone else. Even young children need to learn the proper terms eventually, if they are going to be able to communicate effectively. The trouble with baby talk is that each family tends to have its own words, and anyone who isn't part of the family may not know what they mean. As with euphemisms, baby talk can be confusing, and usually sounds silly, especially if you are more than about eight years old!

Sexual words

In the table of sexual words that follows (Table 11.1), you will see that some of the words don't have an entry in every category (e.g. there are no medical or scientific terms for 'going out with someone' or 'flirting', and no baby talk for 'orgasm'). You will also see that, while there *are* dozens of slang terms for many of the words, only a few are listed here. These are the most commonly used terms by people of your age. However, when it comes to slang, words do tend to go in and out of fashion, and terminology can vary widely from region to region and between families and groups of friends. If the words that you are familiar with don't appear in the list, check with a good friend or your social mentor what the most frequently used expressions are among the people you know, so that you do get it right if you need to.

In conclusion...

Learning to talk about sex with confidence is a skill, and one that comes with practice. You may choose to use slang terms to fit in with your friends or when you are telling jokes, and this can be okay in the right situation (that is, out of earshot of adults or members of the public). Just remember, though, that not everyone uses slang, even other people your own age, and you certainly don't have to if you don't want to. Equally, you might use childish or euphemistic expressions around your family if this is the language you have always used, but you need to be aware that people outside your family may not know what you are talking about, and you run the risk of sounding silly and inappropriate.

If you want answers to questions, or need to discuss sexual issues that concern you, the best way to do this is to become familiar with the acceptable sexual terms, such as the ones that are used throughout this book. This helps to avoid confusion and embarrassment, shows respect for the person you are talking to, and, best of all, goes a long way towards ensuring that your communication is successful.

Table 11.1 Sexual words

Common, correct terminology	Scientific or medical terms	Slang or street language	Euphemisms and baby talk
Breasts	Mammary glands	Boobs, tits, knockers, jugs	Boobies, titties
Bottom, buttocks	Buttocks	Butt, bum, ass (arse), fanny (USA), cheeks	Behind, rear
Vulva	Vulva	Lips, flaps	Wee wee, front bottom, 'down there'
Vagina	Vagina	Pussy, fanny, muff, vag, cooch	Wee wee
Penis	Penis	Dick, cock, knob, schlong	Doodle, willy, old man
Testicles	Testes	Balls, nuts, nads, knackers	Crown jewels, family jewels
Scrotum	Scrotum	Sack, ball sack, scrote	
Pubic hair	Pubic hair	Pubes, muff (girl)	Short and curlies, bush
Erection	Erection	Stiffy, hard-on, boner	
Period	Menstruation	Rags (Australia) coming on	Monthly
Sanitary towels, pads			Things (plus raised eyebrows)

Common, correct terminology	Scientific or medical terms	Slang or street language	Euphemisms and baby talk
Condoms	Condoms	Rubbers, wrappers	
Heterosexual	Heterosexual	Straight, normal	
Homosexual (male)	Male homosexual	Gay, homo, poofter, queen, queer	
Homosexual (female), Lesbian	Female homosexual, Lesbian	Lez (lesbo, lezzie), dyke, gay	
Having a crush		Fancying someone, having the hots	'liking' someone
Flirting		Hitting on him/her, tuning, coming on to	
Kissing (passionate kissing, using tongues)	Osculation	Pashing, snogging, making out, hooking up, hooking in, frenching, French kissing	Tonsil hockey
Touching, caressing		Feeling each other up, fondling, groping, petting	Touching
Ejaculation, to ejaculate	Ejaculation	Spunk, cum, cumming, blowing your load	Spilling the seed
Orgasm	Orgasm	Cumming, coming, peaking, climaxing	

Table 11.1 Sexual words *continued*

Common, correct terminology	Scientific or medical terms	Slang or street language	Euphemisms and baby talk
Masturbation (male)	Auto stimulation, self-stimulation	Wanking, jacking off, jerking off, tossing off, hand job	Time well spent
Masturbation (female)	Auto stimulation, self-stimulation	Fingering (yourself), poking (yourself)	Touching yourself
Sexual intercourse, having sex	Coitus	Fucking, rooting, humping, shagging, screwing	Making love, doing it, sleeping with, nookie
Oral sex (on a man)	Fellatio	Blow job, giving head	
Oral sex (on a woman)	Cunnilingus	Licking out, muff dive, eating out	Going down, getting down
Mutual oral sex	Mutual orogenital stimulation	69 (69er)	
Anal sex	Anal intercourse	Anal, bumming, butt fucking	Back door

Recommended Reading

If you go onto the internet, you will find that there are dozens of books about puberty, sex and relationships, and plenty on the topics of friendships and bullying. The following list comprises books that I have enjoyed during my time as a sexuality educator, and a few that I have referred to and found very helpful during the writing of this book – they are all very good.

Puberty: boys and girls

Darvill, W. and Powell, K. (2007) *The Puberty Book*. Sydney: Hachette Livre Australia. (This is published in the USA as Darvill, W. and Powell, K. (2006) *In Your Jeans*. Berkley, CA: Ulysses Press.)

Harris, R. H. (2005) *Let's Talk About Sex*. London: Walker Books.

Meredith, S. and Gee, R. (2004) *Facts of Life*. London: Usborne Publishing.

Puberty: girls

Gravelle, K. (1997) *The Period Book*. New York, NY: Walker Publishing Company, Inc.

Puberty: boys

Gravelle, K. (1999) *What's Going On Down There?* New York, NY: Walker Publishing Company, Inc.

Fisher, N. (1994) *Living With a Willy*. London: Macmillan Children's Books.

Sexuality for older teens: boys and girls

Donaghy, B. (1999) *Unzipped: Everything Teenagers Want to Know About Love, Sex and Each Other*. Sydney: Harper Collins Publishers.

Stoppard, M. (2001) *Sex Ed: Growing Up, Relationships and Sex*. London: Dorling Kindersley.

Sexuality for older teens: boys

Whyman, M. (2007) *Unzipped: A Toolkit for Life*. London: Hodder Children's Books.

Friendships: young teens

Herron, R. and Peter, V. J. (1998) *A Good Friend: How to Make One, How to Be One*. Boys Town, NE: Boys Town Press.

Friendships: older teens or young adults

Canfield, J., Hansen, M. V. and Kirberger, K. (1998) *Chicken Soup for the Teenage Soul Journal*. Florida: Health Communications, Inc.

Gabor, D. (2001) *How to Start a Conversation and Make Friends*. New York, NY: Simon & Schuster.

Matthews, A. (2002) *Making Friends: A Guide to Getting Along with People*. Singapore: Media Masters.

Bullying

Macfarlane, A. and McPherson, A. (2004) *Bullying: The Truth*. Oxford: Oxford University Press.

Asperger's syndrome
Adolescent issues

Jackson, L. (2002) *Freaks, Geeks and Asperger Syndrome*. London: Jessica Kingsley Publishers.

Sex and relationships: young adults

Edmonds, G. and Worton, D. (2005) *The Asperger Love Guide*. London: Paul Chapman Publishing.

Edmonds, G. and Worton, D. (2006) *The Asperger Social Guide*. London: Paul Chapman Publishing.

Parents and carers

Dubin, N. (2007) *Asperger Syndrome and Bullying*. London: Jessica Kingsley Publishers.

Heinrichs, R. (2003) *Perfect Targets: Practical Solutions for Surviving the Social World*. Kansas: Autism Asperger Publishing Company.

Henault, I. (2006) *Asperger's Syndrome and Sexuality*. London: Jessica Kingsley Publishers.

Useful Websites

There are numerous websites covering the topics of puberty, sexual health and relationships, and some are better than others. This is a list of some of those I came across while researching this book, and found to be particularly well-written, reliable and, in many cases, good fun.

Puberty

- www.likeitis.org: produced by Marie Stopes International for young teenagers, it is lively and colourful and includes lots of up-to-date, straightforward information on sexuality and teenage issues.
- www.puberty101.com: for both young people and their parents. Includes good clear diagrams of the reproductive organs, and of body development at puberty. Also includes information on STIs, drugs and mental health.

Bodies and general health

- www.acne.org.au: excellent, sensible information about acne and skin care.
- www.cyh.com: excellent – one of the most comprehensive websites I came across. Separate sections for parents, young children, teens and young adults. Huge range of well-written, informative fact sheets on everything to do with health, sexuality and relationships.
- www.dermatology.svhm.org.au: click on 'clinical services', then 'information sheets', then 'secondary school – skin conditions'. Good information about acne.
- www.en.wikipedia.org: type into search box, 'female (or male) reproductive system'. Great diagrams and information.
- www.howstuffworks.com: click on 'health'. Detailed information on all sorts of things to do with the body, health and so on (not specifically sexuality).
- www.007b.com: all about breasts. This site aims to normalize breasts as a functional part of a woman's body. It provides reassurance for young women

who may feel their breasts aren't normal. Includes a huge 'gallery' of photos of breasts of all shapes and sizes.

Sexual health

- www.fpahealth.org.au: for mid- to late-teens. Plenty of sexuality and relationship information, including some excellent fact sheets and very good Frequently Asked Questions (click on 'sex matters').

- www.fpq.com.au: variety of well-written, informative fact sheets for parents and teenagers on wide range of issues to do with sexual health, children's sexuality and puberty.

- www.iwannaknow.org: straightforward, easy-to-read information on all aspects of sexuality – puberty, safer sex, STIs, sexual health, gay issues and so on. Lots of interesting and useful links.

- www.kidshealth.org: lively, up-to-date information on all aspects of health and growing up. Includes a very good explanation of fertilization.

- www.teenshealth.org: reliable, lively site providing wide variety of easy-to-read health and sexuality information for young teenagers.

- www.teenwire.com: clear, simple visual information, particularly good on management of periods. Includes very good animated instructions for inserting a tampon.

Young adults

- www.coolnurse.com: information for older teenagers and young adults about a wide range of health issues, including detailed sexual information.

- www.ruthinking.co.uk: good, simply explained information about safe sex, STIs, sexual health, relationships and so on.

- www.yoursexhealth.org: very clear, direct and reassuring information about sexual practices, sexual health and relationships.

Parents

- www.bsped.org.uk: click on 'patients', then on 'Nick's notes'. Accurate and interesting medical information on a range of issues, such as breast development in boys, growing pains and delayed puberty.

- www.canadianparents.ca: informative site for parents. Plenty of information on children's sexuality, puberty and so forth.

- www.cyh.com: separate parents' section. Includes great fact sheets on a wide range of social, health and sexuality issues.

- www.fpahealth.org.au: good fact sheet on answering children's questions about sexuality.

- www.fpq.com.au: good range of fact sheets on children's sexual development, and how to talk to your children about sexuality – includes one for parents of children with Asperger's syndrome.

Internet safety

- www.cyberquoll.com.au: excellent, good-fun, interactive site for younger teens. Very clear messages about safety on the internet.
- www.kidsmart.org.uk: practical internet safety program for schools, children and parents.
- www.netalert.net.au: fun, interactive, informative site encouraging safety on the internet.
- www.staysafe.org: addresses all aspects of internet safety, from PC security to guidelines for keeping yourself safe from online predators and cyber-bullies.
- www.stopcyberbullying.com: plenty of info about bullying online, including identifying whether you might have been guilty yourself. Can select relevant age group.
- www.thinkuknow.co.uk (also www.thinkuknow.com.au): interactive website, which helps you to stay safe yet still have fun on the internet, and also while blogging, gaming, using your mobile phone and so on.
- www.wiredkids.org: for parents, teachers and teenagers. Good, clear description of what cyber-bullying is. Multiple links to other sites, and to professional help.

Index